PICTURES WITH
IMPACT

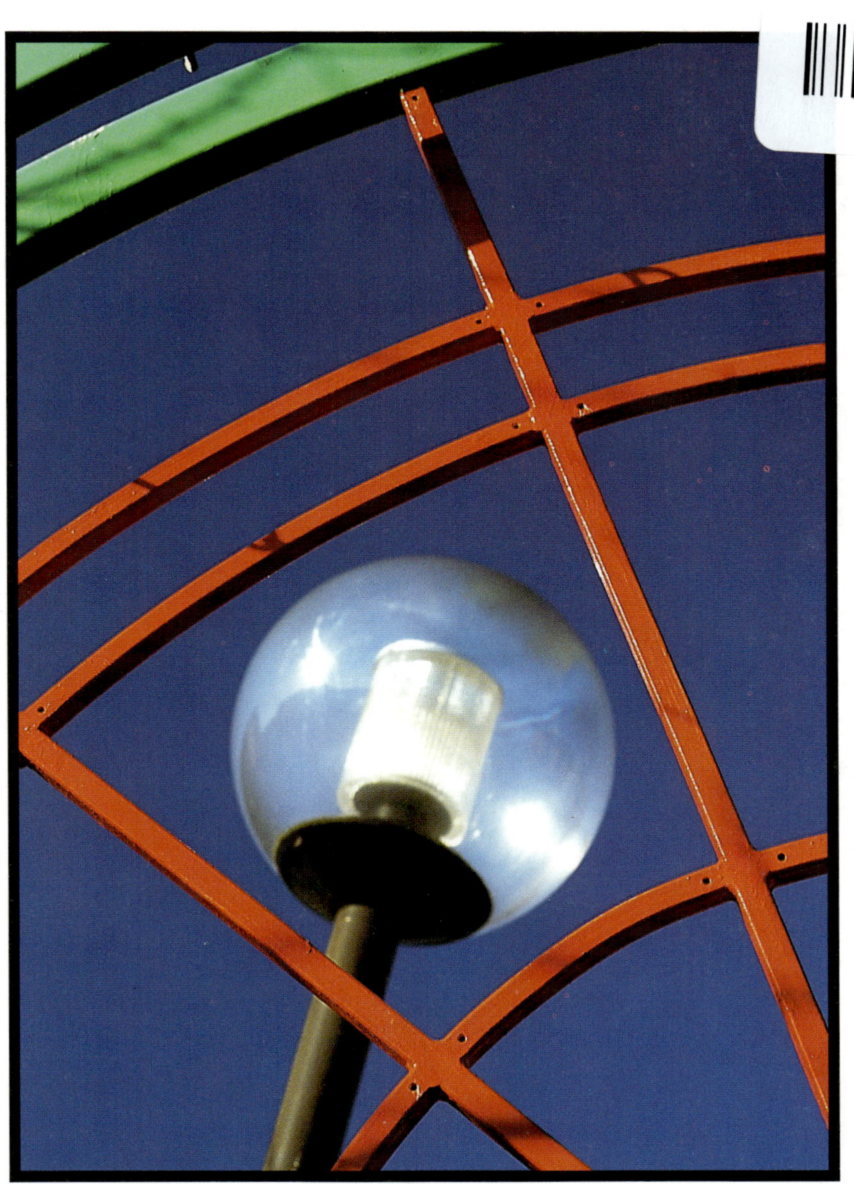

Secrets of effective composition

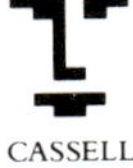

CASSELL

ACKNOWLEDGEMENTS

Front cover; (main) TIB, (top inset) TIB/A Rosario, (centre inset) TIB/John Kelley, (below inset) John Heseltine, 1 ICL, 2-3 ICL, 4 RHPL, 5 ICL, 6 ICL, 7 Zefa, 8-9 Richard Platt, 10(t) Michael Busselle/Eaglemoss, 10(b) TIB, 11 TPL, 12(t) Zefa, 12(c) Spectrum, 12(b) TSI, 13 Zefa, 14(l) Zefa, 14-15 TPL, 15 Allsport/Pascal Rondeau, 16 Zefa, 17 Michael Busselle, 18(t) Robin Bath, 18-19 TPL, 19(t) Michael Busselle, 19(b) Zefa, 20(t) Alastair Scott, 20(b) TSI, 21 Robert Eames, 22(t) Stuart Windsor, 22(b) Roger Howard, 23(t) Zefa, 23(b) Allsport/Mike Powell, 24(t) Roger Howard, 24(b) Stuart Windsor, 25 TPL, 26(t) Robin Bath, 26(b) Michael Freeman, 27(t) Zefa, 27(b) Michael Freeman, 28(t) Steve Mansfield, 28(b) Roger Howard, 29 RHPL, 30(t) TIB, 30-31 Zefa, 31 Robert Eames, 32(t) Michael Busselle, 32(b) TIB, 33 Tim Woodcock, 34(t) Michael Busselle, 34(b) TPL, 35(t) Robin Bath, 35(b) TIB, 36(t) Zefa, 36(b) TIB, 37 Adam Eastland, 38 Michael Busselle, 39(t) Jennifer Rigby, 39(b) TSI, 40(t) TSI, 40(b) Jennifer Rigby, 41 TSI, 42 Richard Platt, 43(t) Michael Busselle, 43(b) Roger Howard, 44 Zefa, 45 Derek Forss, 46 Jennifer Rigby, 47(t) Allsport/Vandystadt, 47(b) TSI, 48(tr,cr) Richard Platt, 48(bl) Jennifer Rigby, 49 Sylvia Cordaiy Picture Library/John Parker, 50(t) Richard Platt, 50(b) Robert Eames, 51 Mei Lim, 52(t) Vincent Oliver, 52(b) TIB, 53 TIB, 54 Robin Bath, 55(tl) Ed Buziak, 55(tr) Robert Eames, 55(b) Michael Busselle, 56(t) Allsport/Vandystadt, 56(b) Jonathan Vince, 57 Michael Busselle, 58(l) Allsport/Steve Powell, 58(r) Allsport/Bob Martin, 58(b) Jennifer Rigby, 59 Allsport/Chris Cole, 60 Michael Hoppen/Eaglemoss, 61 Michael Hoppen/Eaglemoss, 62(l) Eric Hayman, 62(r) TIB, 63 Zefa, 64(l) Planet Earth Pictures, 64(r) Jonathan Vince, 65 Robin Bath, 66(t) Eaglemoss, 66(b) Zefa, 67 TIB/Renzo Mancini, 68(t) Ed Buziak, 68(b) Michael Busselle, 69(l) Dev Raj Agarwal, 69(r) Chris Lees, 70(t) Robert Eames, 70(b) John Heseltine, 71(tr) Adam Eastland, 71(l) TIB, 72(t) TPL, 72(b) TIB, 73(tl) TIB, 73(tr) TPL, 73(b) John Heseltine, ctd/...74(t) Michael Busselle, 74(b) Stuart Windsor, 75 ICL, 76(t) Allsport/Steven Dunn, 76(b) Ed Buziak, 77(l) Zefa, 77(r) Ardea, 78(t) Stuart Windsor, 78(b) TIB, 79 ICL, 80(tr) TIB, 80(b) Modes et Travaux, 81(l) Neil Holmes, 81(r) NHPA/Stephen Krasemann, 82(t) TIB, 82(c) TSI, 82(b) Ed Buziak, 83(t) TIB, 83(bl) Allsport/Simon Bruty, 83(br) Ken Powell, 84 Allsport/Dan Smith, 85(l) Zefa, 85(r) TIB, 86 NHPA/Steven Dalton, 87 TIB, 88(b) Zefa, 88-89 TIB, 89(t) Michael Busselle/Eaglemoss, 89(b) Ffotograff/Patricia Aithie, 90 Professional Sport/Chris Cole, 91 Zefa, 92(t) ICL, 92(bl) TIB, 92-93 TSI, 93 Arcaid/Richard Bryant, 94(t) Robert Eames, 94(b) ICL, 95 Rex Features, 96(tl) Zefa, 96(tr) Hulton-Deutsch Collection, 96(b) TPL, Back cover Zefa.

Key: ICL - Images Colour Library; NHPA - Natural History Photographic Agency; RHPL - Robert Harding Picture Library; TIB - The Image Bank; TPL - The Photographers Library; TSI - Tony Stone Images

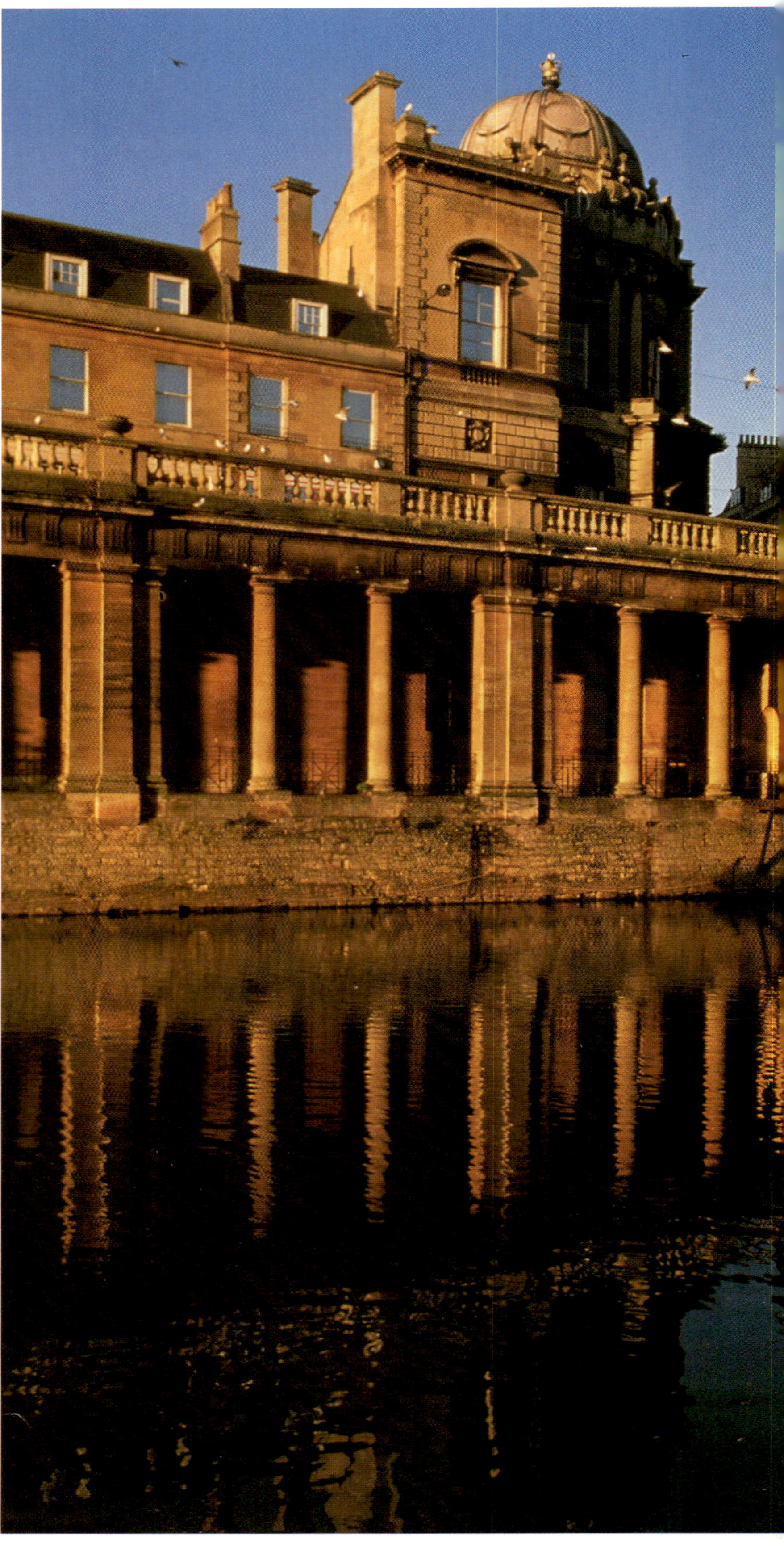

Consultant editor: Roger Hicks

First published 1993 by Cassell
Villiers House, 41/47 Strand, London WC2N 5JE

Distributed in Australia
by Capricorn Link (Australia) Pty Ltd
P. O. Box 665, Lane Cove, NSW 2066

British Library Cataloguing-in-Publication Data
A catalogue record for this book is available from the British Library

ISBN 0-304-34350-1

Printed in Spain by Cayfosa Industria Grafica

CONTENTS

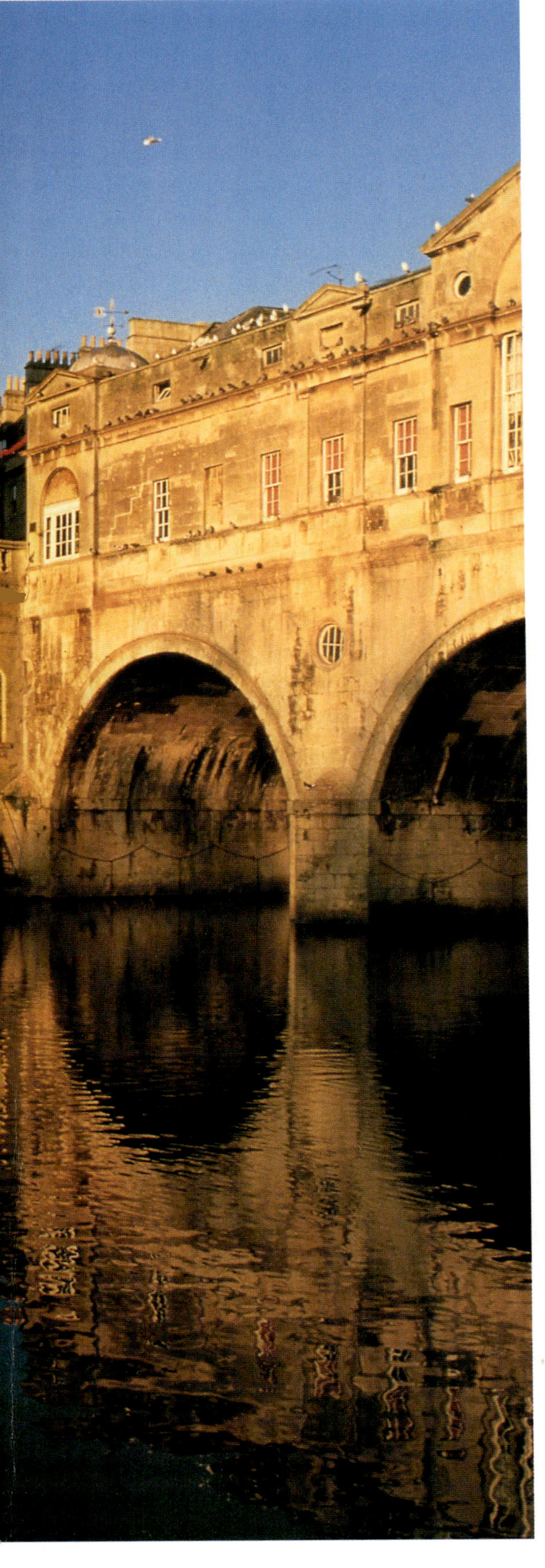

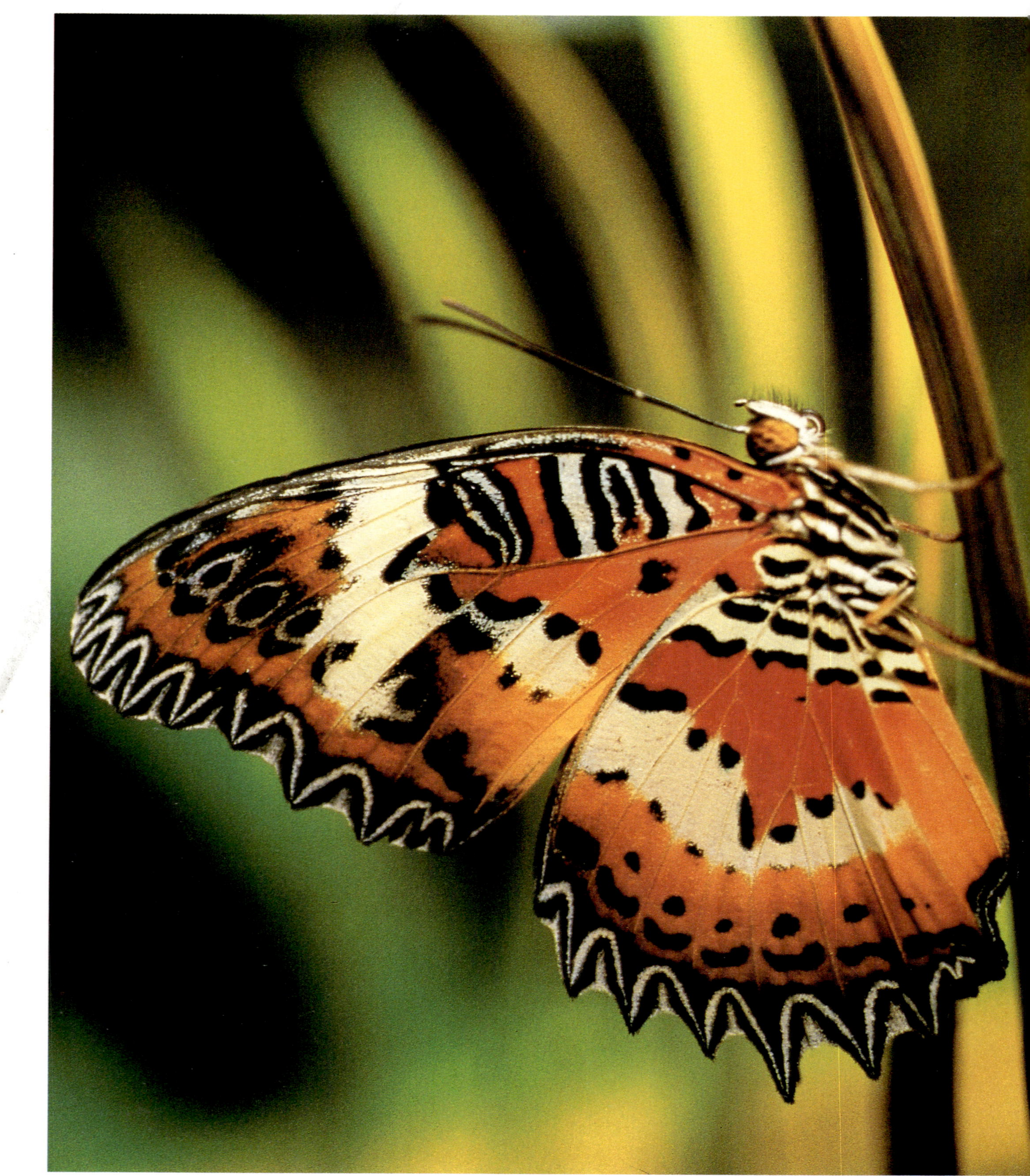

INTRODUCTION

THERE is a mysterious and seemingly indefinable quality which lifts some photographs out of the ordinary. Instead of just skimming past them, as we so often do, we pause to admire them. This book shows you how to put that extra "something", that extra dimension which we call "impact", into your photographs.

In reality, impact is easier to achieve than most people realize. The pages of this book are crammed with techniques which top professionals and successful amateurs apply almost without thinking. The terminology may seem offputting at first, but you'll soon become familiar with concepts such as the "rule of thirds" or "colour harmony", and decisions about where to put the subject in the frame, or whether to use a vertical or horizontal format, quickly become second nature.

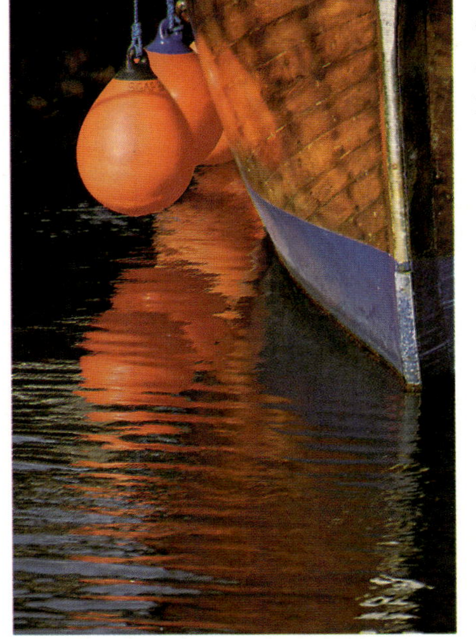

As you read, you will probably realize that your best pictures already demonstrate many or all of these techniques. The real key is using them systematically and reliably, instead of on a hit-or-miss basis.

Learning to do so isn't a dull grind, though. As you apply the lessons presented in this book, you will reap powerful rewards in the shape of better images: pictures that you are proud to show, and pictures that other people want to see.

In order to do this, of course, you need to take more pictures. Instead of a single photograph, take two or three shots of the same subject. Change the viewpoint, stand on a wall or crouch down low, come closer or walk further away, shoot one picture horizontally and another vertically. Shoot "around" the subject, too: show details, people's reactions, the same place at different times of day.

There is one professional secret that isn't covered on the pages which follow. The way to become known as a really good photographer is to edit your pictures ruthlessly. Throw the failures out or (if the subject matter is too precious) put them safely away in a family album where no-one else will see them. Show someone a few good pictures, and they will look forward to seeing your next shots; show them the whole roll, the good mixed with the bad, and the bad will overwhelm the good.

In addition, don't show too many similar pictures. If you have (say) half a dozen shots of a child's first steps, select just one or two which really convey that first tottering, wavering journey. Thin the pictures out, put them in order, and let them tell their own story.

Professionals sometimes shoot a whole roll in order to get just one or two good pictures. You need not go that far, but as a rule of thumb, at least one-third of the pictures you shoot should probably be edited out. Although your processing and film costs will rise, and some of your pictures will never be seen, the selection that you do show will build your reputation as a photographer.

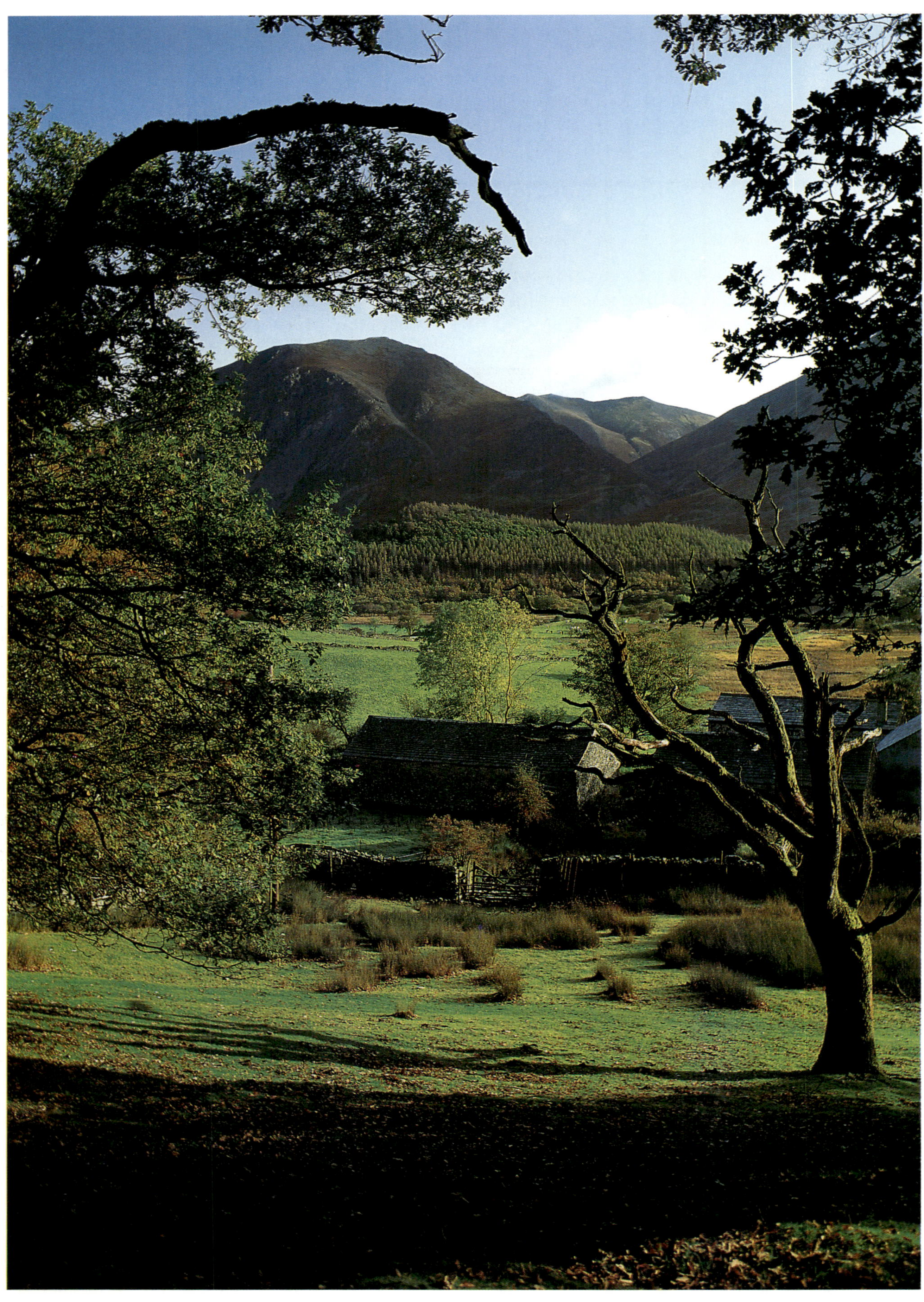

Composing better pictures

Much of the pleasure and challenge of photography lies in creating a strong composition. Setting technical expertise aside, taking good pictures comes from developing your skills of looking and seeing.

Accepting the challenge of photography means much more than achieving technical perfection. An advanced camera makes it easy to take technically perfect photographs – just as a computer lets you call up images. But a modern camera cannot supply creative vision, any more than software can help you create a masterpiece.

You can learn a lot from examples – by looking at other people's photographs and thinking about how they took the picture and why it was successful or not. But most of all you gain picture-making skills by combining looking and practice.

An essential ingredient of creating pictures with impact is composition, which means thinking about many aspects of the picture: the viewpoint, the foreground, the background, the shape of the picture and where to position the subject in the frame.

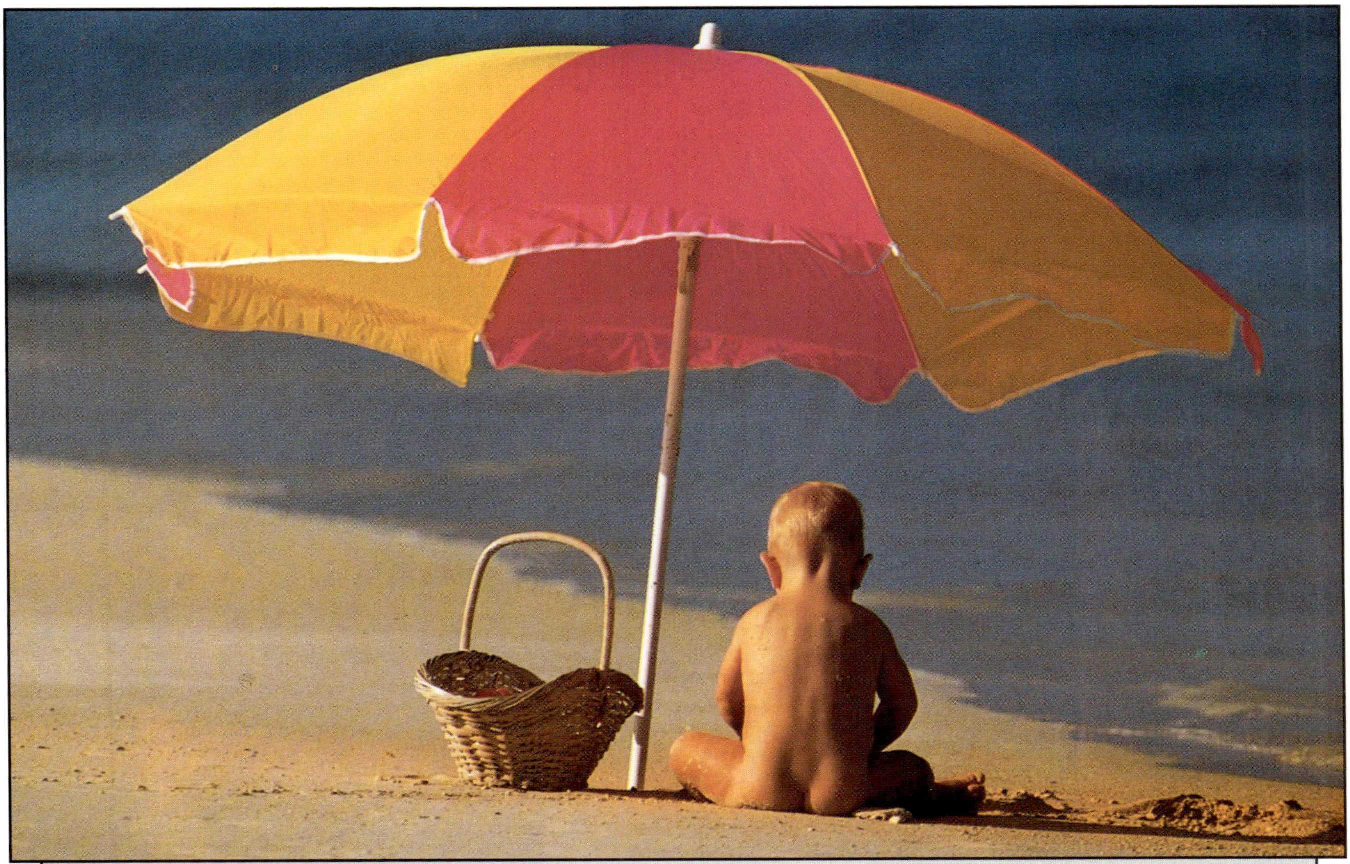

Elements in a strong picture

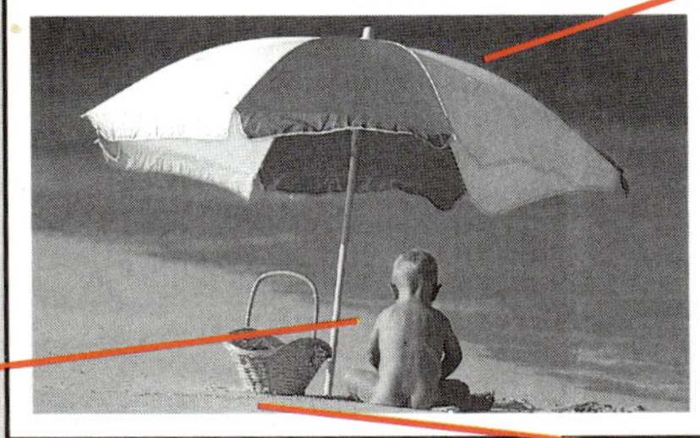

FORMAT
Your first choice is what shape to make the picture – horizontal or upright. Here, the horizontal format allows the umbrella to fill the frame generously.

THE SUBJECT
Every picture needs a subject – on pages 11-16 we discuss where in the frame to place it. With the child slightly off centre the image is more dynamic than if the composition were symmetrical.

VIEWPOINT
Whether you're looking up or down at your subject makes a big difference. On page 24, we look at the effects of camera position and vieiwpoint. In this example a fairly high viewpoint meant the photographer could miss out the horizon and simplify the background.

THE BACKGROUND
The background should be an acting part of every picture but not so strong that it detracts from the subject. Simplicity is the key to this photograph.

THE FOREGROUND
How to use the foreground in your pictures completes the first series on composition. Foregrounds can contribute strongly, or distract from the subject: here, the photographer left out nearly all of the foreground to keep the image simple.

Thinking about format

As a pair, human eyes tend to see the world as a horizontal oval with fuzzy edges. They also see a much wider span than the standard lens on a 35mm camera.

However, the human eye flits about a scene, focusing on different parts. This is why photos can be disappointing compared with the original subject – the camera 'sees' one scene in the shape of a hard rectangle, the human eye sees lots of softly outlined images.

Horizontal format

It's natural to look through the viewfinder so you see your image as a horizontal rectangle. The camera encourages you further – it's designed to make it easier to hold that way.

This is the classic picture shape for general views and landscapes and is often known as landscape format. Photographers tend to start out taking most of their pictures horizontally. It seems natural, it suits many views and it feels comfortable.

But there's no rule that you have to put landscapes in a landscape format. Always see what a landscape – or any other subject – looks like when you turn the camera round. You may decide against the first and simplest option – a horizontal photo.

While the horizon often looks comfortable in a landscape picture in the horizontal format, some landscapes are strengthened by a vertical shape. All you can do is try it and see.

Looking at landscape

The photographer was impressed by a grand, dramatic view – his eye darting from one part of the scene to another to form an overall impression. First he looked at the stately home in the distance, then his gaze took in the frozen lake before pausing on the trees silhouetted against a stormy sky.

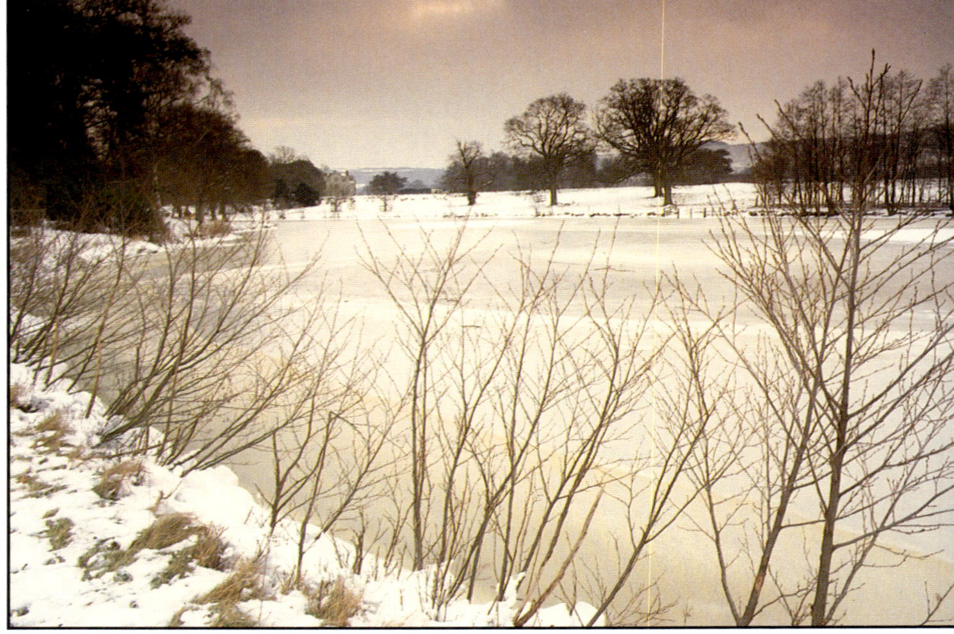

▲ CAMERA'S VIEW
What a disappointment! Through the viewfinder the camera sees a rather messy picture, with no real centre of interest. It's boring compared to the breathtaking view the photographer saw – the photo doesn't begin to reflect the beauty of the scene and the house is barely visible.

► CHANGING THE FORMAT
Turning the camera round to an upright format immediately makes a stronger picture. Some elements get lost, but one or two interesting things start to happen. The stronger diagonal line in the foreground leads the eye into the picture and gives more depth.

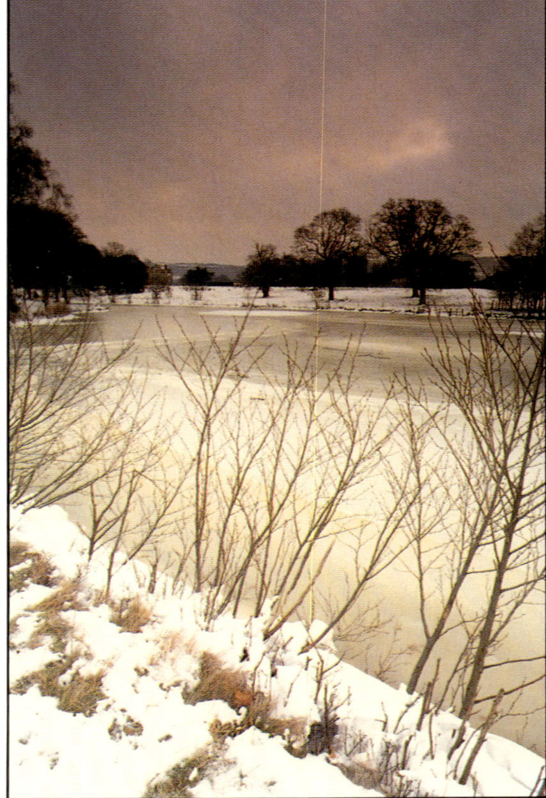

Hand framing

Even when you haven't a camera to hand, you can still keep looking at the picture-making potential of things around you. Just do what film directors do – imitate seeing through the viewfinder. Make a frame with your hands and look through that. Frame every scene in a vertical rectangle as well as a horizontal one.

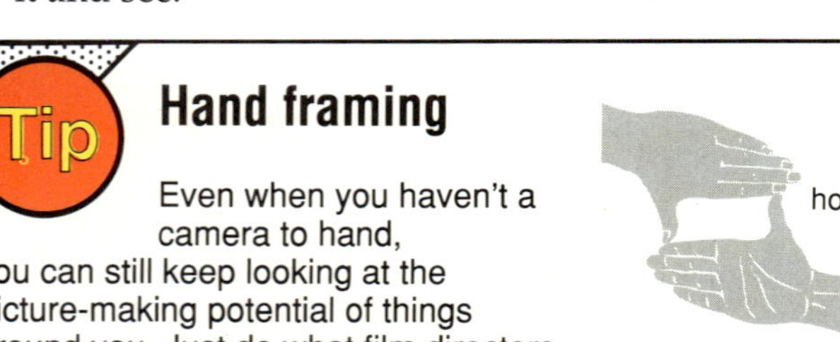

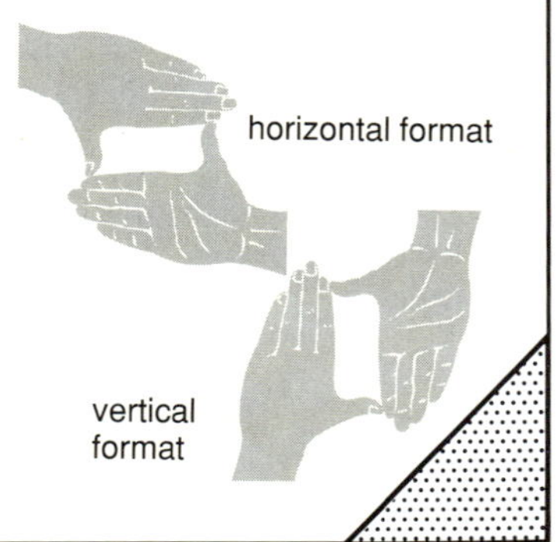

"

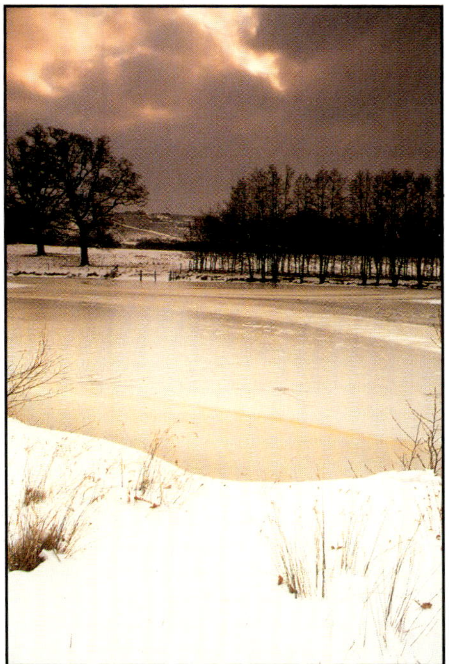

▲TRY ANOTHER VIEWPOINT
Moving a few steps gets rid of the scratchy branches and focuses the eye on the frozen lake. But the effect is weaker. Horizontal bands of snow, ice, trees and sky divide the picture into equal elements so there is no dominant point of interest.

▼ HORIZONTAL DETAIL
Moving in closer (or zooming in) often makes for a stronger picture. In the end, it may work better to tell part of the story well rather than trying to include everything. In this case, returning to the horizontal format captures perfectly the wide and lonely sweep of the view.

Format facts

Most SLR and compact cameras these days are designed to take 35mm film. The 35mm refers to the width of the film from one outside edge to the other.

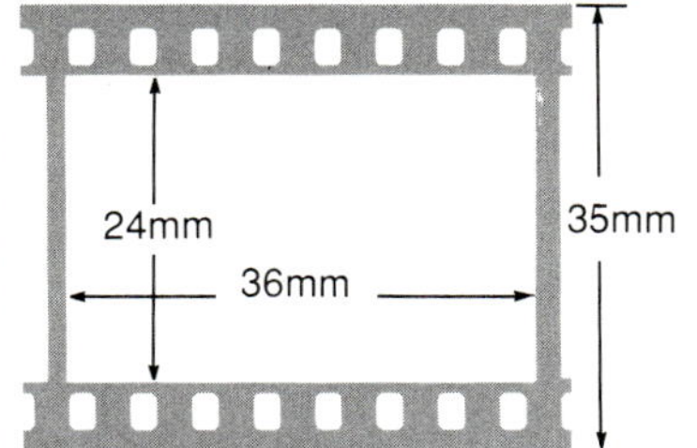

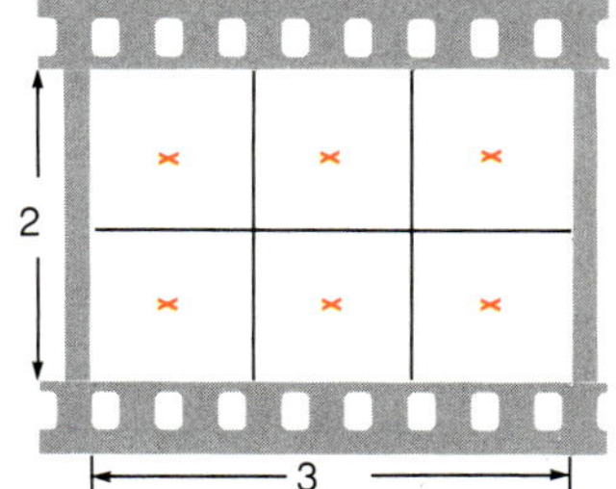

35mm film forms a rectangle with a ratio of 3:2. It's a classic, balanced proportion that pleases the eye more than a square. Think about maintaining interest in most of the six areas of the picture.

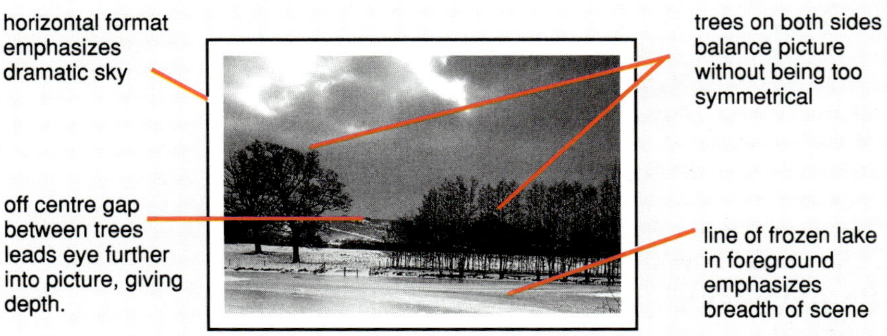

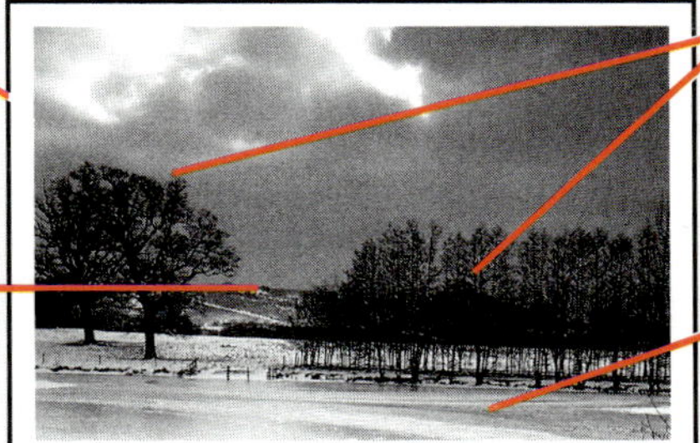

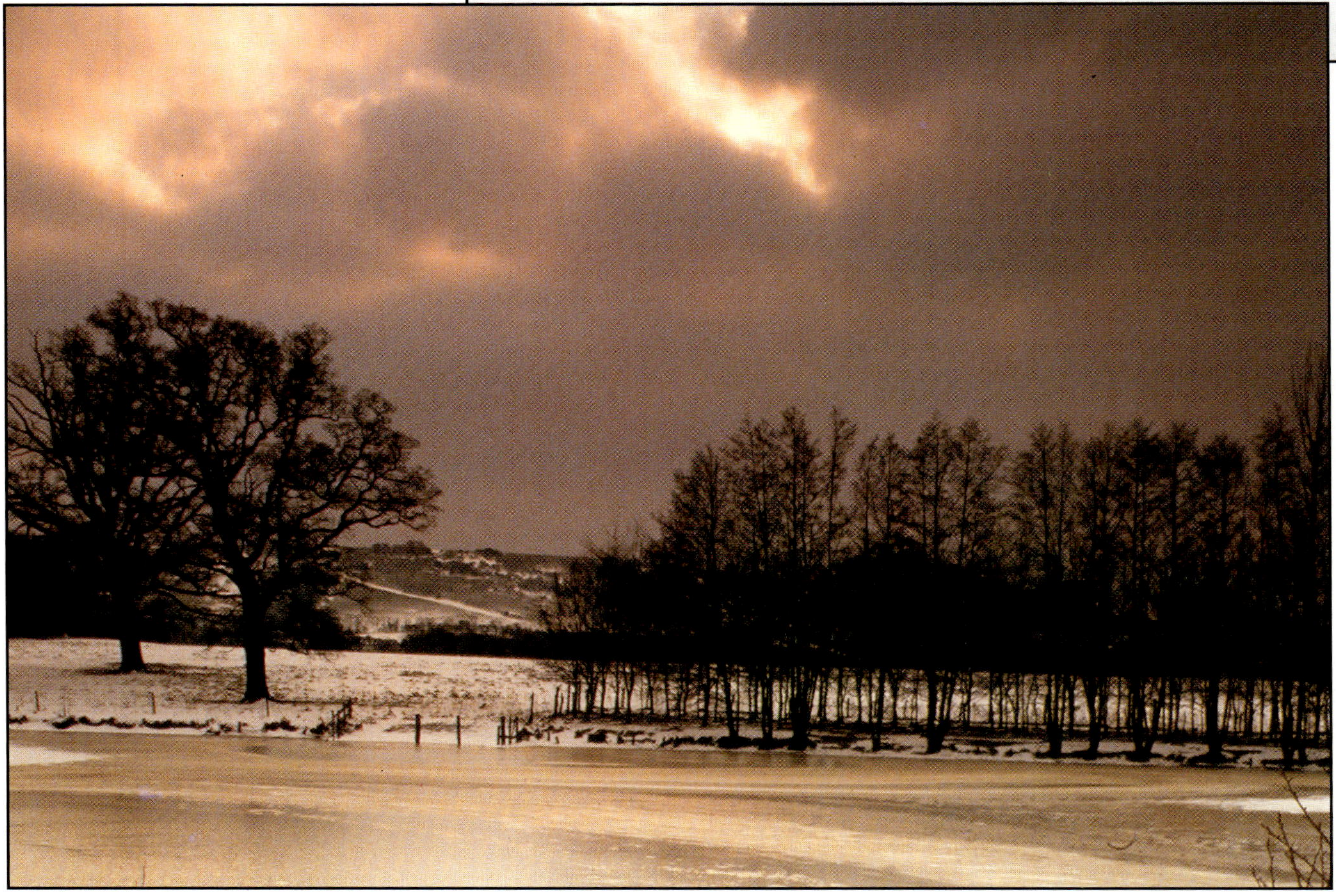

Formats for people

Vertical format When you see someone walking towards you, you automatically 'cut out' most of the surroundings and focus on that person. Photographically, you get the same effect by turning the camera round and using the vertical format.

Occasionally a horizontal portrait works really well but most are weakened by a landscape composition that leaves the naturally upright human figure flanked by empty spaces or cluttered background detail. And if you put a vertical subject in a horizontal format there's a danger of chopping bits off top and bottom, which looks awful.

You can fill the frame much more easily with a vertical rectangle and, because of this, it is often called the portrait format.

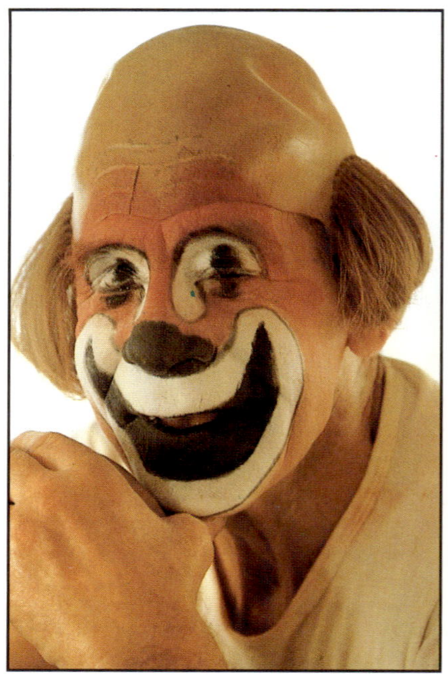

▲ FILLING THE FRAME
A head and shoulders portrait usually works best in a vertical format. It's much easier to fill the frame with the subject and leave out distracting background detail.

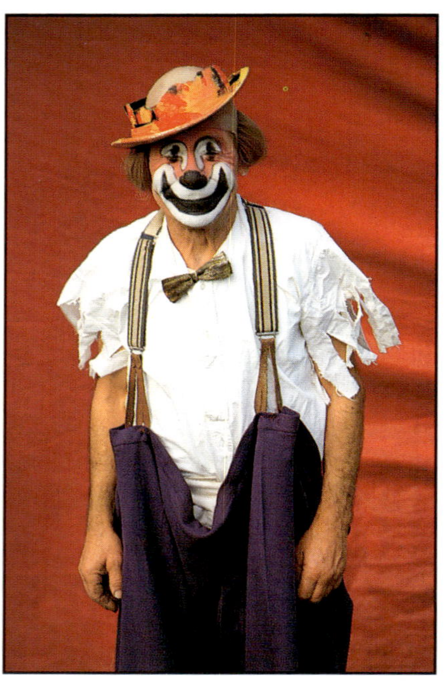

▲ FIGURE SHOTS
Like all upright subjects, the human figure is naturally suited to a vertical format. If you're not including the full figure, however, avoid using the knees or waist as cut-off points.

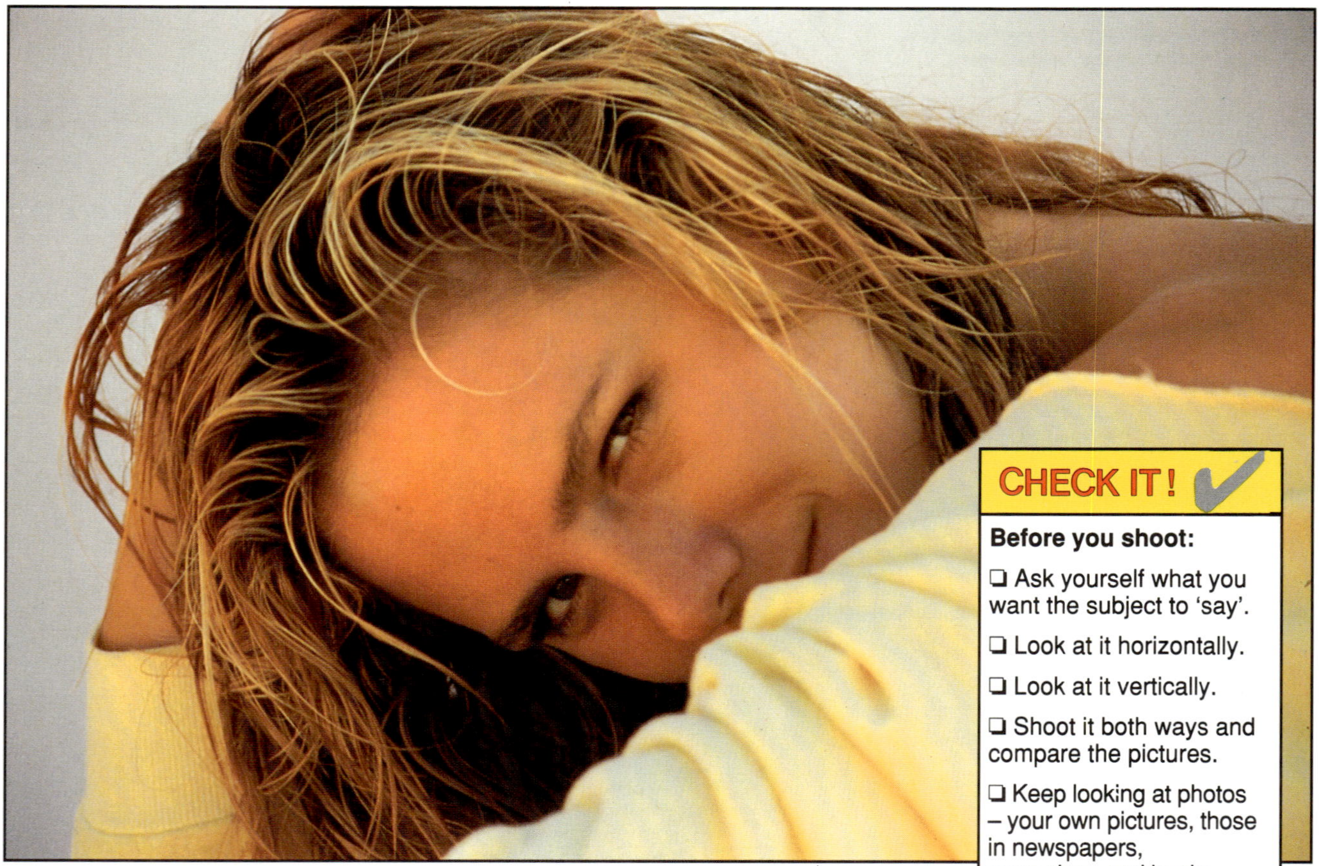

▲ CREATIVE COMPOSITION
Portraits in a horizontal format have the immediate impact of the unusual. For the unexpected to sing out it's especially important that you make strong use of the entire frame – with no unwanted expanses on either side!

Before you shoot:

❏ Ask yourself what you want the subject to 'say'.

❏ Look at it horizontally.

❏ Look at it vertically.

❏ Shoot it both ways and compare the pictures.

❏ Keep looking at photos – your own pictures, those in newspapers, magazines and books – and ask yourself if that's the format you would have chosen.

Where to put the subject

Put a few useful guidelines into practice and you'll soon develop a sixth sense on where the best place is for the subject. A central subject often makes a pleasing picture, but before you take a shot consider the options.

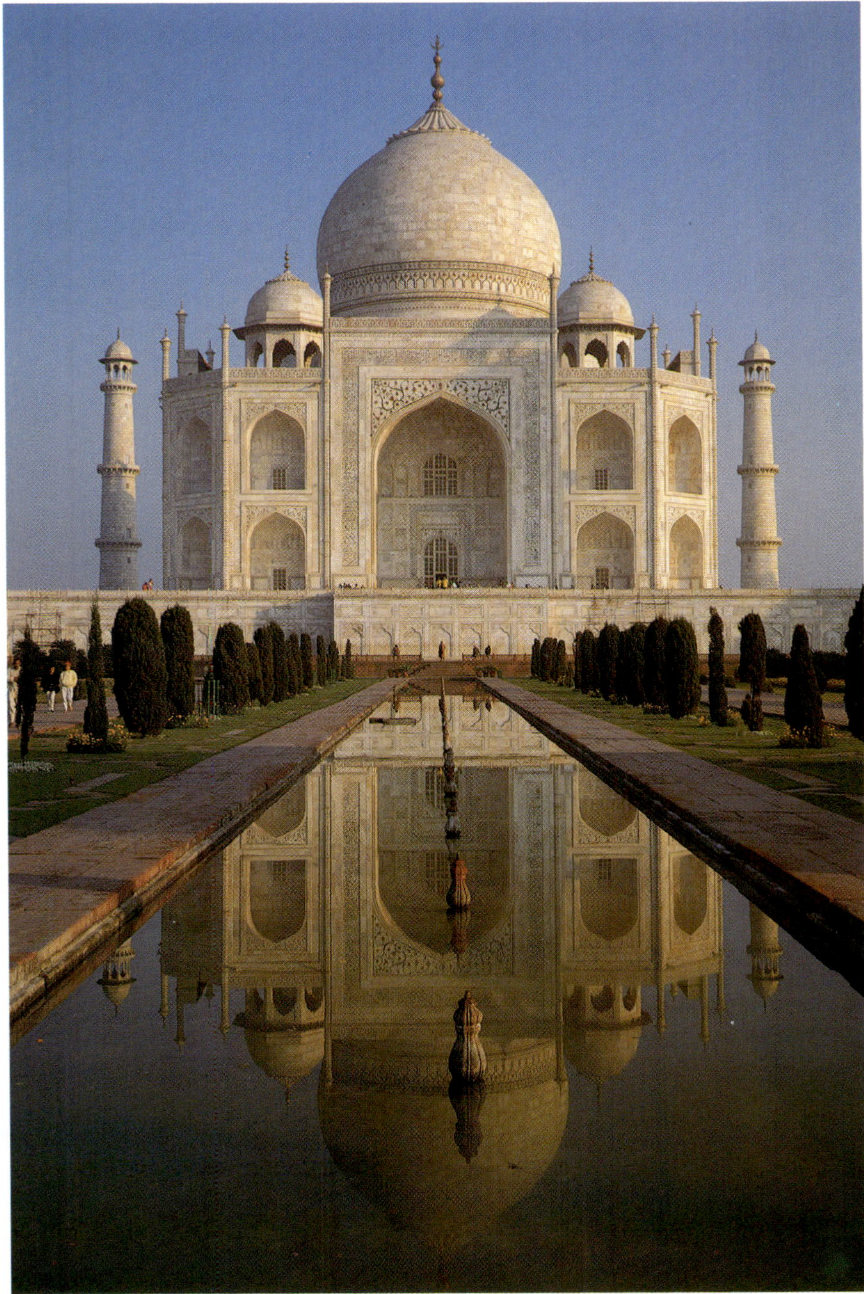

Every picture needs a subject, otherwise the eye wanders restlessly from one spot to the next without knowing where to linger. So before you compose a shot it's always a good idea to ask yourself why you're taking the picture.

What has made you respond to the image in front of you? Do you have a clear subject in mind? And what exactly is it you want to capture on film?

When you know the answers you can start thinking about composition – and about what happens when you put the subject in the centre and off centre.

Going for the centre

Many people put the subject in the middle of the frame most of the time. It's where the eye naturally looks first and so is the obvious spot for the important element of the picture. It also creates a restful, well balanced image.

Because of this, a central subject is particularly effective for something symmetrical such as a classical building or the front end of a car or aeroplane. But if it's going to work you must be exact in getting the subject spot on centre. A slight miss ruins the whole effect.

However, taking too many pictures with centrally placed subjects may start to look static and dull. Some photographs look stronger with the main interest to one side. This also ensures that you avoid repetition in your pictures.

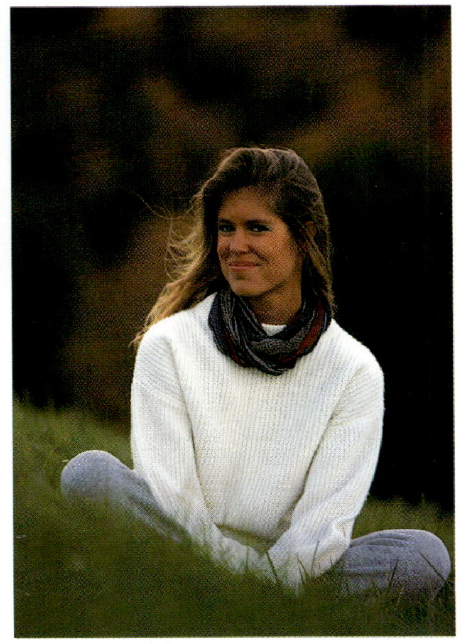

The rule of thirds

Photographers and painters share many of the same creative ideas, one of which is the rule of thirds.

A classic way of creating a satisfying composition is to divide an image into vertical thirds in your mind, and then position the subject roughly on one of the dividing lines.

A dynamic image

It works whether you use a horizontal or a vertical format – try it and see. Use it as a guide – the subject doesn't need to be *precisely* on one of the lines. In any case, there's no grid on the back of the camera so you'll have to do a bit of guesswork.

By placing the subject off centre you often create a more dynamic image than one with central emphasis. It's dynamic because it makes your eye move round the picture when you look at it.

Using the rule of thirds also lets you show a subject in context. A central subject usually needs to fill the frame to have any impact while an off centre one reveals the setting. Even when the subject is quite large its surroundings show.

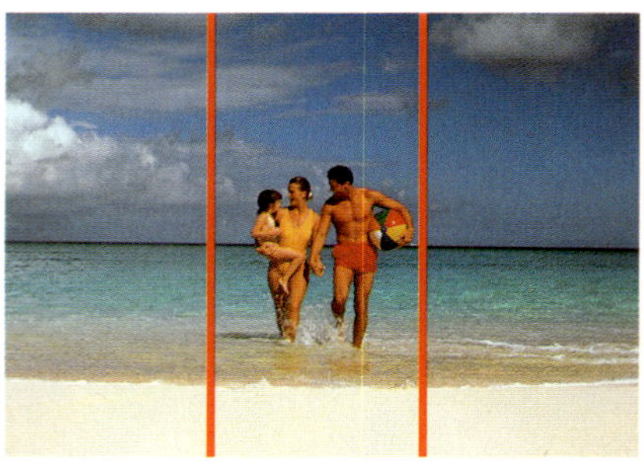

▲ **CENTRAL SUBJECT**
Placing figures in the middle is a perfectly valid, safe option. But interesting things start to happen when you move the subject towards one of the imaginary vertical lines.

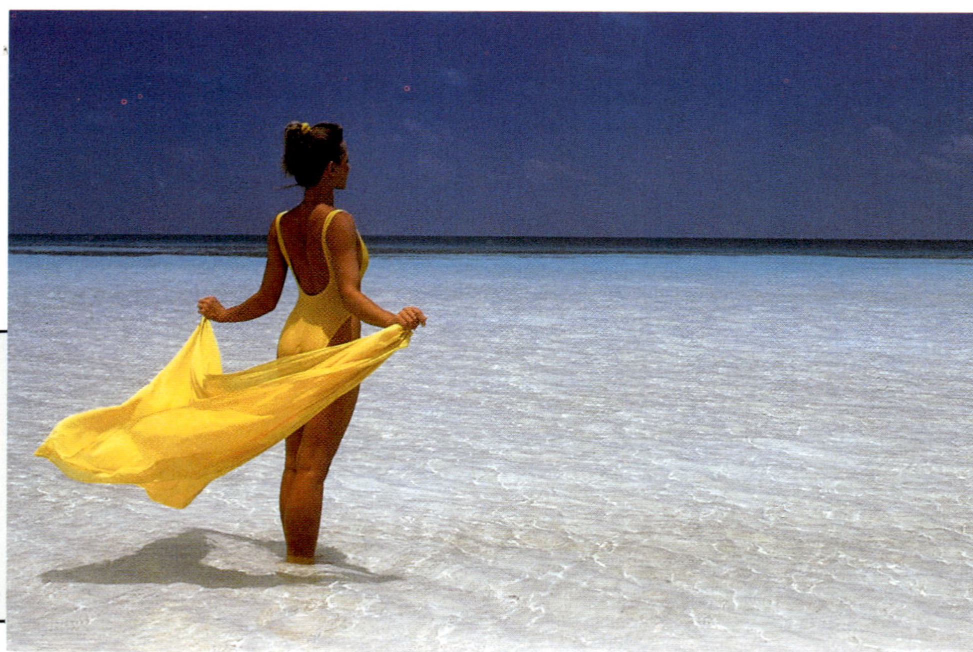

◀ **OFF CENTRE**
With the subject on a third your eye travels around the picture – to the figure and across the wide expanse of sea then back to the figure again – rather than resting in the centre.

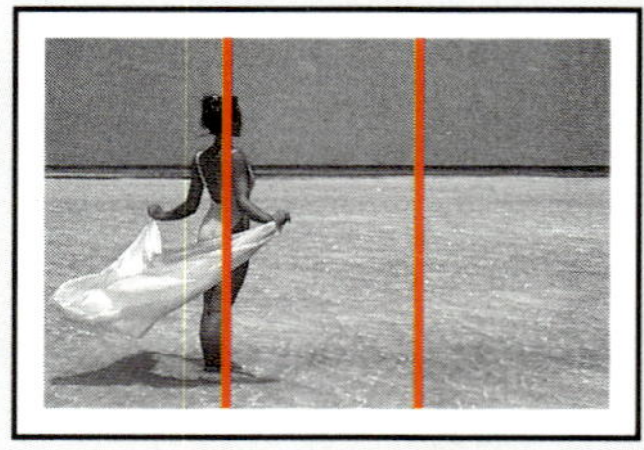

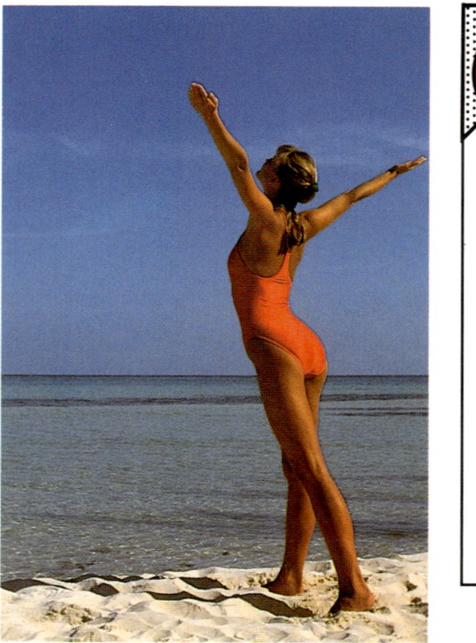

▶ **ALTER THE FORMAT**
Whichever format – vertical or horizontal – you choose, putting the rule of thirds into practice makes for a stimulating picture that's pleasing to the eye and shows the subject in a setting.

Using brackets

An ideal way to think about where best to put a given subject is to experiment with brackets.

Cut out two L-shaped pieces of card and place them over your photos or those in books and magazines. By moving the brackets to and fro you can see how the same picture looks with the subject in the centre and off centre.

The four key points

As well as vertical third lines, you can add two more lines going across to make an imaginary grid like a noughts and crosses board. Where the dividing lines meet they create four key points.

These four spots are ideal places for the subject or – because they're only pinpoints – the most eyecatching part of the subject.

If you want to balance the subject with a less important picture element an effective place is the diagonal key point. But make sure that it doesn't compete for attention with the subject.

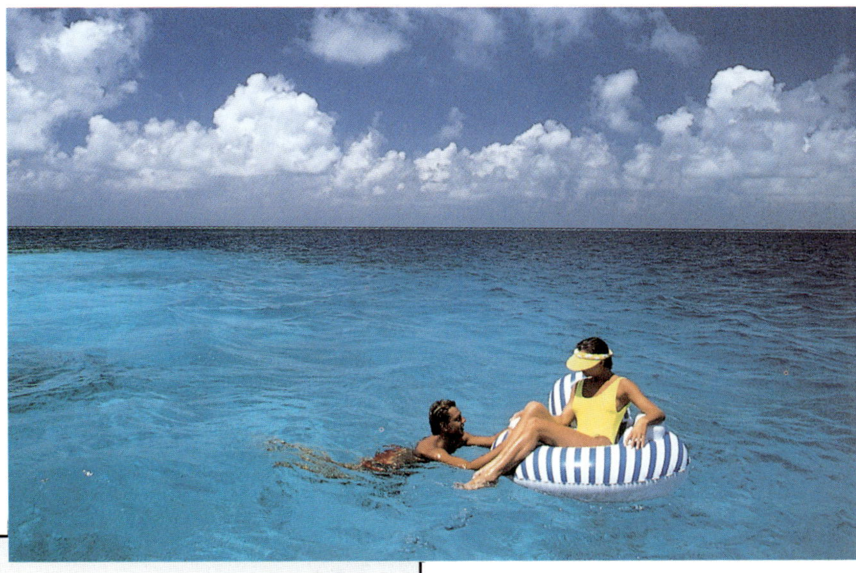

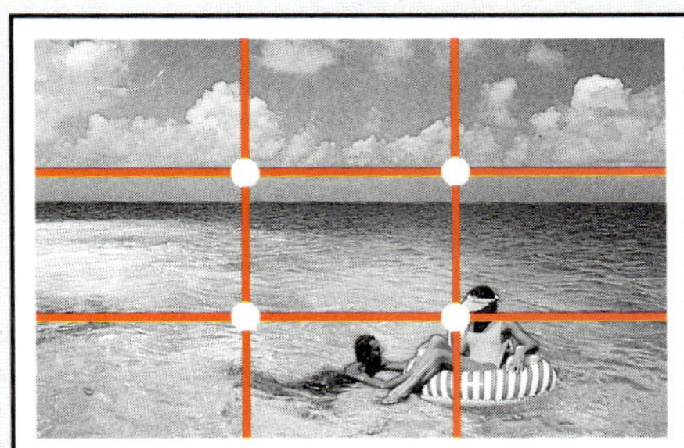

highlights and shadows on sea occupy the eye when it strays from the subject

yellow costume stands out brilliantly from blue sea

head leans towards key point

▲ KEY POINT
The four pinpoints are key parts of the grid. Putting the focal point of the subject on one of these makes it doubly effective. With a figure the focal point is usually the head, in particular the eyes.

▼ BALANCING ACT
Putting the subject on one key point balanced with something else diagonally opposite makes a strong composition. People always draw the eye so, even though the deckchairs are nearer, the figures are still the main subject.

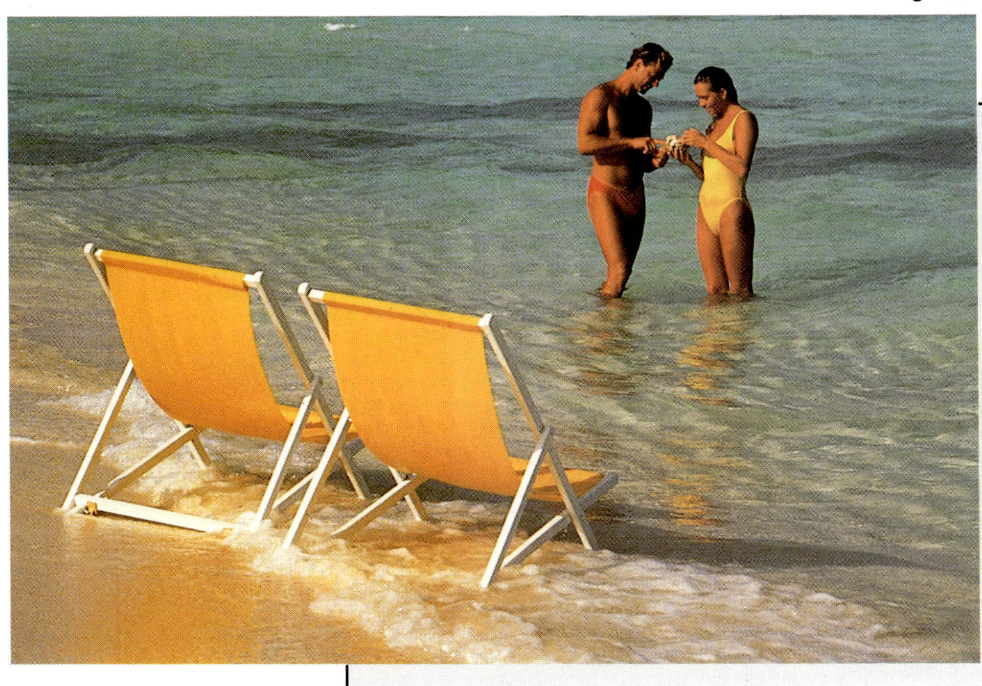

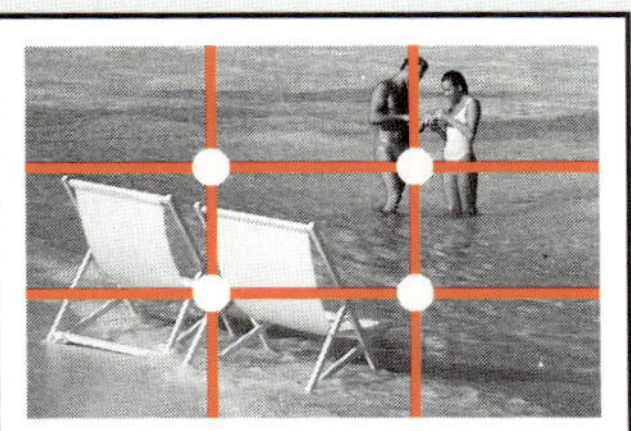

high viewpoint keeps horizon from crossing behind the figures

reflection continues down third line

matching deck chair and costume colour helps the eye jump back to main subject

Composing landscapes

The rule of thirds applies to all subjects, not just figures. When you look at a landscape it's worth trying the same procedure. Imagine a vertical third line and then add a horizontal one. Position a focal point in the landscape – say, a white gate or a bright red barn – on the spot where they cross for maximum effect.

In a landscape a focal point becomes all the more important if the eye is not to drift aimlessly around the picture. But bear in mind that you may have to move yourself – you can't really ask the subject to move!

dark tone of grass and foliage makes white house stand out

horizon roughly marks upper third line

shaft of light where clouds have parted spotlights house

▶ **FOCAL POINT**
It takes only a touch of brightness in a landscape to act like a magnet for the eye. By placing it on a key point, the house draws the eye even more intensely. Once enticed into the picture, your gaze roams across the hills before travelling back to the mountains and forward to the detail of the trees.

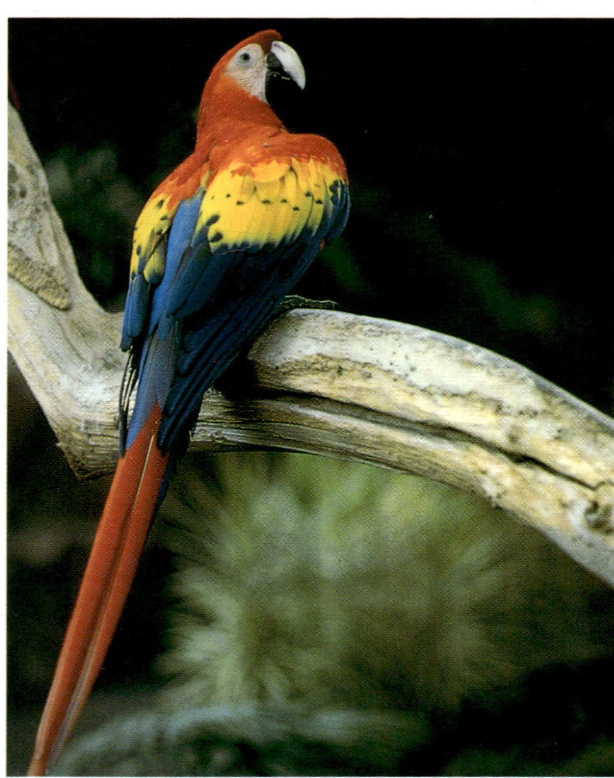

▲ **VERTICAL THIRDS**
Before you plump for putting any subject matter in the middle try it off centre. This often gives your subject space to 'breathe'.

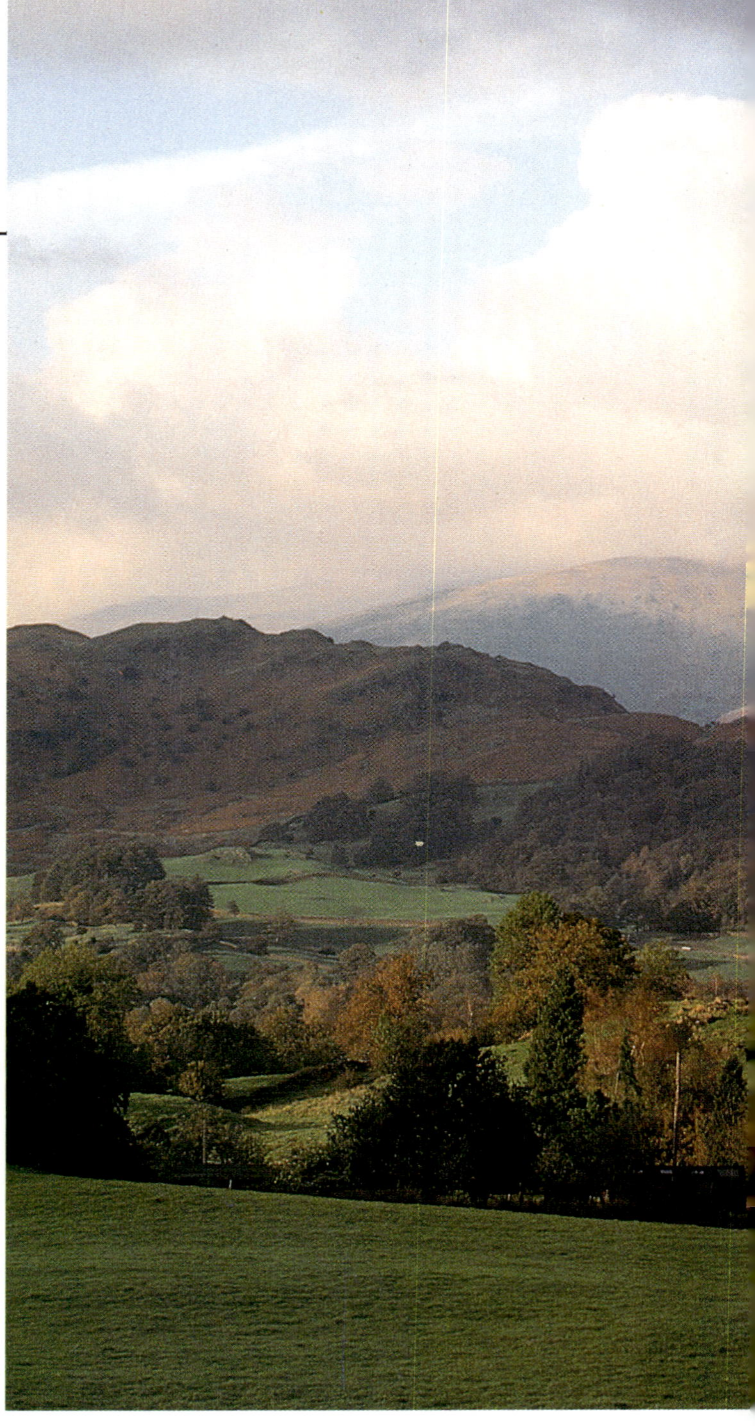

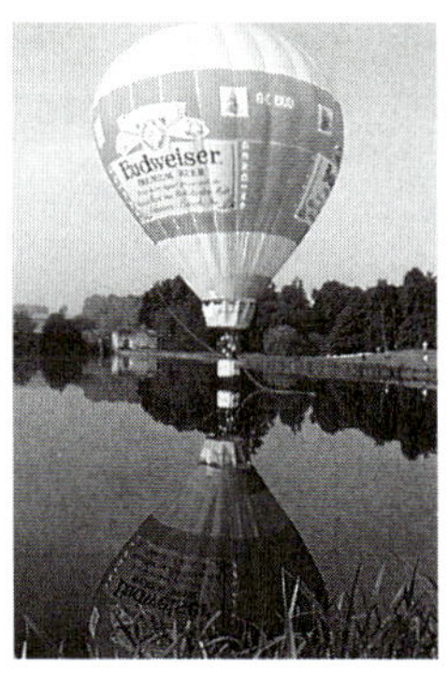

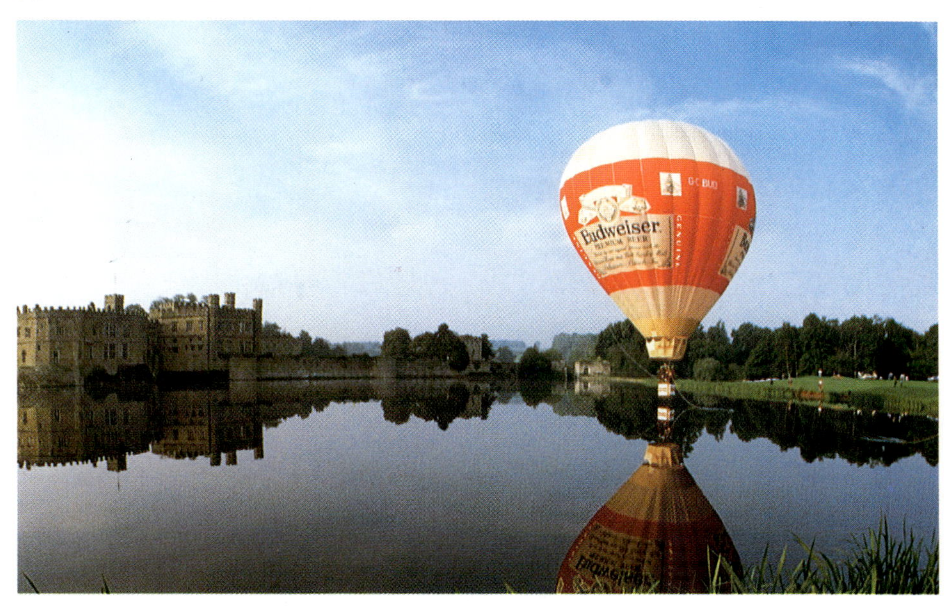

▶ BALANCE AND CONTEXT
Because they're both placed on a third line, the balloon and castle balance one another . The castle also puts the balloon in context. In contrast, the centred close-up looks static and uninteresting, and reveals nothing of the setting.

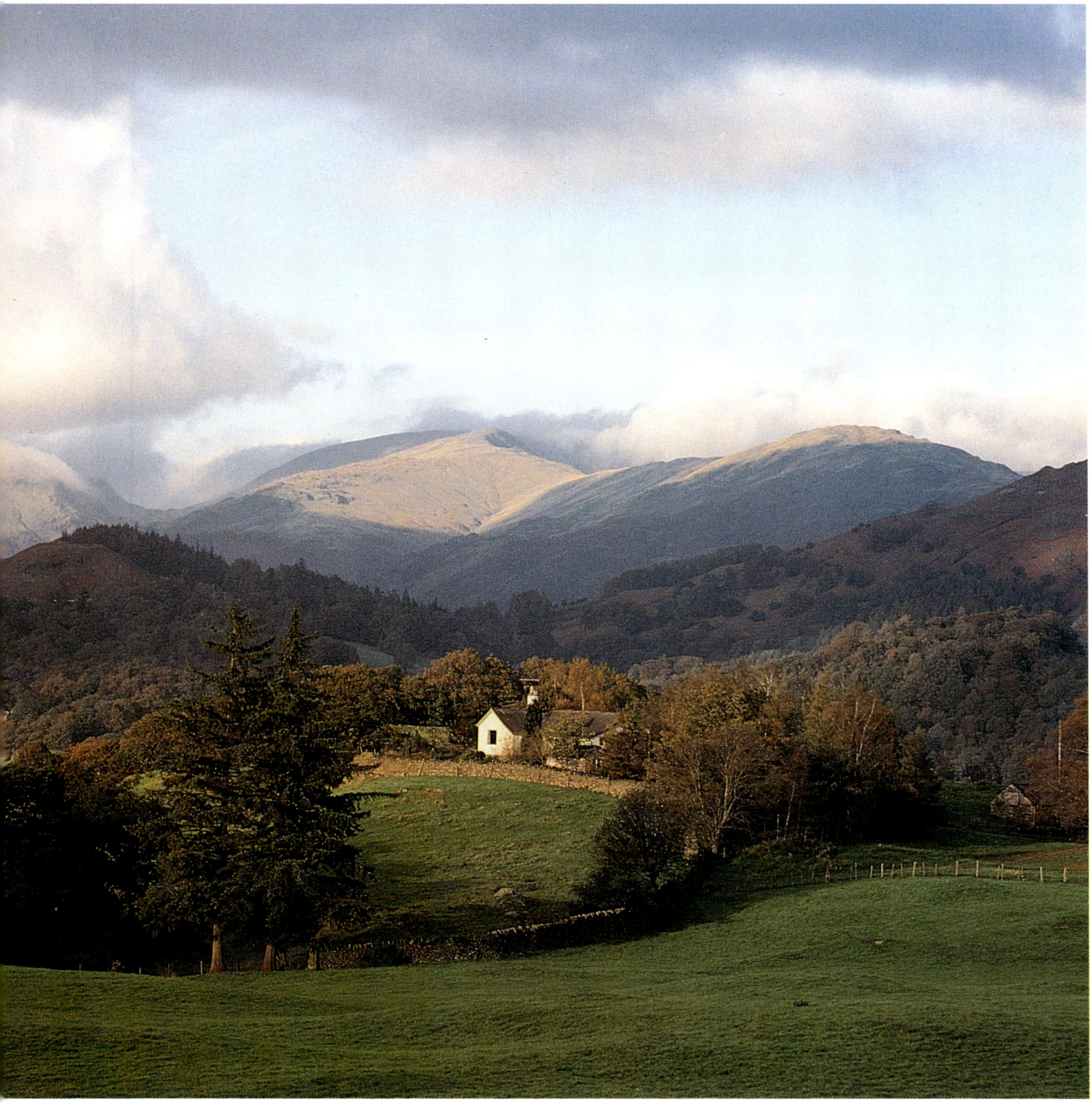

Moving subjects

Another reason for placing the subject off centre is that a moving subject seldom looks right when placed in the middle of the frame. It's not only a question of balance, but also that a moving subject needs space to 'move into'.

As well as involving the viewer, a subject with space in front of it suggests activity and direction.

This is why sports photographers often choose to place the subject off centre, leaving space on the side of the frame for the subject to move into. You needn't place the subject far off centre for this device to work, but always ensure that the subject is facing into the space created. Leaving the frame tells a different story.

When you position the subject

❏ See how it looks centrally placed.
❏ See if it looks more dynamic on a vertical third line.
❏ Think whether or not a balancing feature would help.
❏ Consider putting the focal point on a key point.
❏ Try it in vertical and horizontal format.

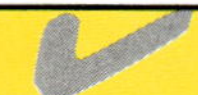

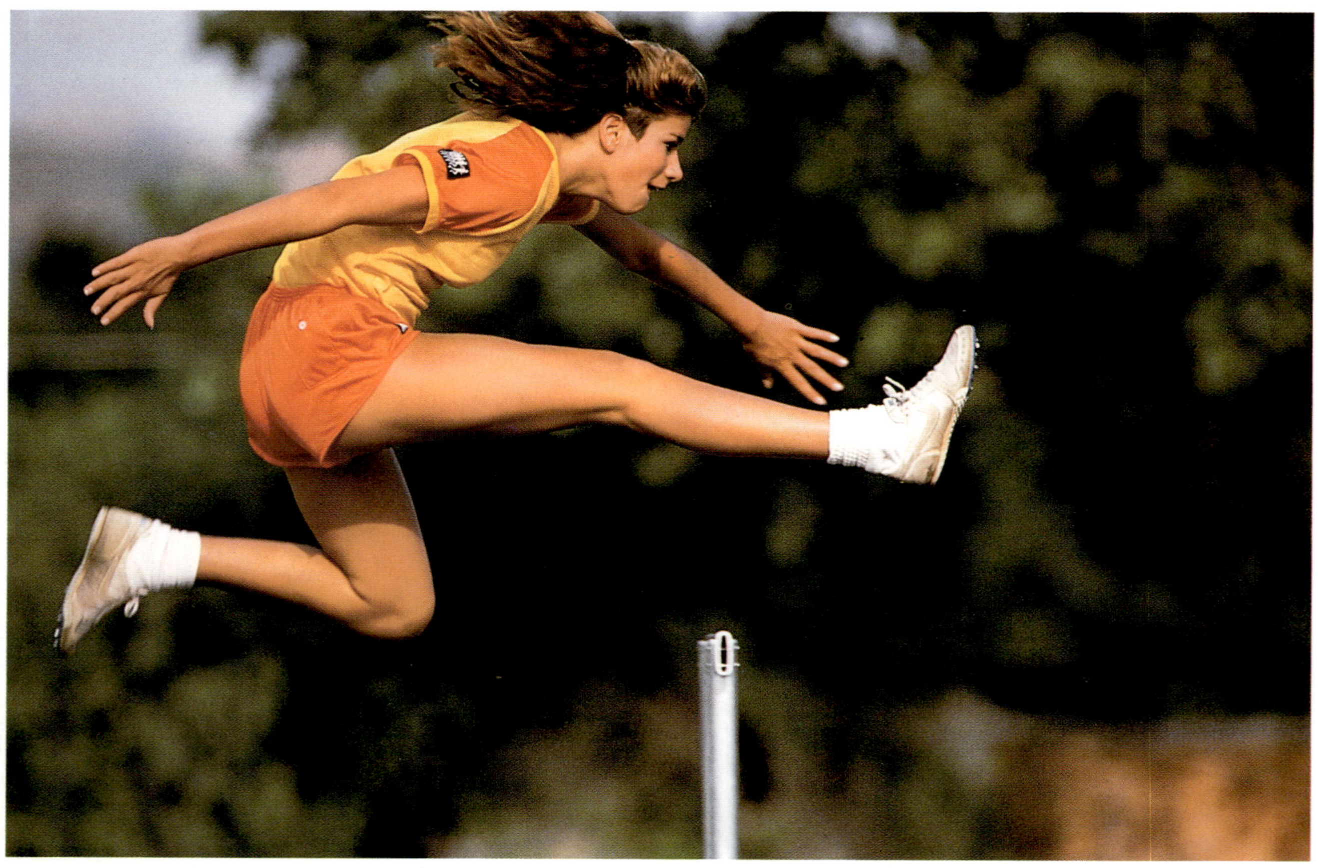

▲▶ OFF CENTRE FOR MOVEMENT
When your subject is moving, try to leave space in the picture for it to move into. If you go in too close (right) the subject looks cramped and you spoil the flow and direction of the image.

Notice how the athlete's centre of gravity lies on one of the third lines, and that some of her hair is out of frame – which stresses vibrant activity.

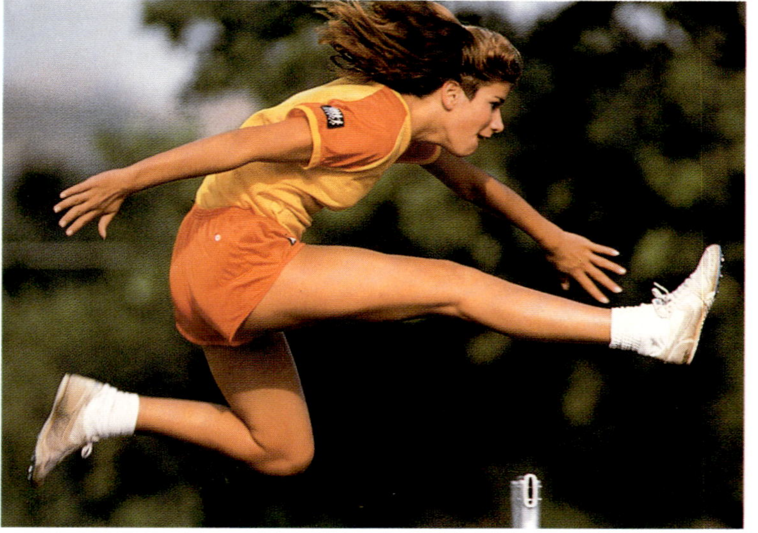

The focal point

All too often a photograph can be frustrating to look at because your eye isn't drawn to one particular element in the scene. But by including or emphasizing a focal point in an image you immediately direct the viewer's attention.

When a scene has no obvious main subject or is very busy, it is useful to include a focal point so that the eye has something to rest on. A focal point usually only occupies a small amount of the frame, but to be immediately noticeable it must contrast in some way with its setting.

The simplest form of focal point in a photo is an isolated object, seen from a distance, against a plain background; and where you position the point is very important in such compositions.

If you place an object in the centre of the image it tends to look rather dull and static. An off-centre point is much more dynamic, but place it too near the edge of the frame and you need to justify its position.

You can use colour to control where the emphasis falls in a picture. For example, a splash of red in a predominantly green image can give unexpected importance to a small element of the scene.

placing the tree off-centre gives a much more dynamic image than if it had been centrally located

broken horizon prevents the scene from looking static

diagonal bands of colour occupy the eye when it moves from the focal point

▼ RULE OF THIRDS
The stark, graphic beauty of this landscape would be visually pointless were it not for the inclusion of the tree – carefully placed off-centre – as the focal point.

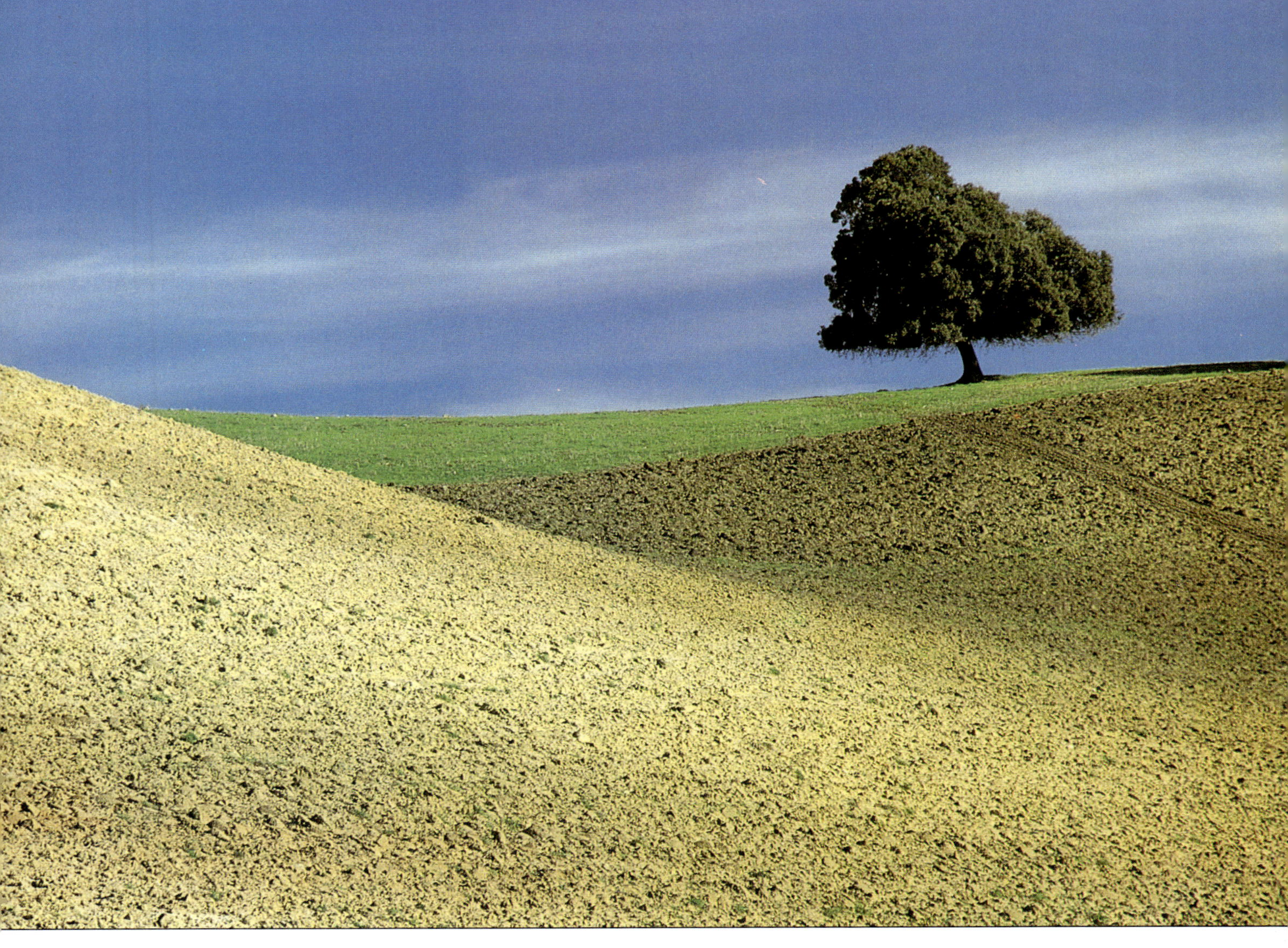

Directing attention

When there is no obvious focal point to emphasize, through colour contrast or isolation, there are several other devices you can use to direct the eye. Land and cityscapes, and groups of similar objects, in particular, benefit from the following techniques.

Selective focusing

When you look at an image you immediately notice the difference between areas that are in sharp focus and those that are not. So when you photograph a group of similar objects it is often more effective if just one, or a few, of them is sharp and the rest are out of focus. It helps to provide the scene with a focal point.

A telephoto lens has less depth of field than shorter focal lengths, so it can help draw the eye from unsharp to sharp elements. With other lenses you can reduce the depth of field by using a wide aperture.

Using exposure

Exposure can play a similar role to focusing in a photo – you can manipulate it to place the emphasis on a narrow band of interest.

For example, in a scene where an object is indistinct because the colour of the sky is diverting attention away from it, you can underexpose the sky, so that the point of interest is highlighted, and the viewer knows exactly where to look.

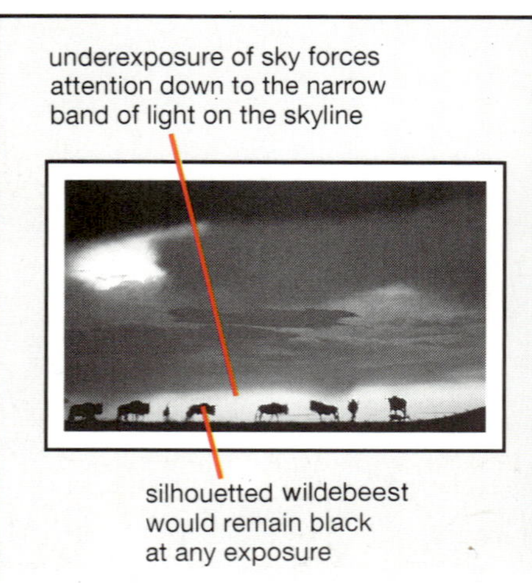

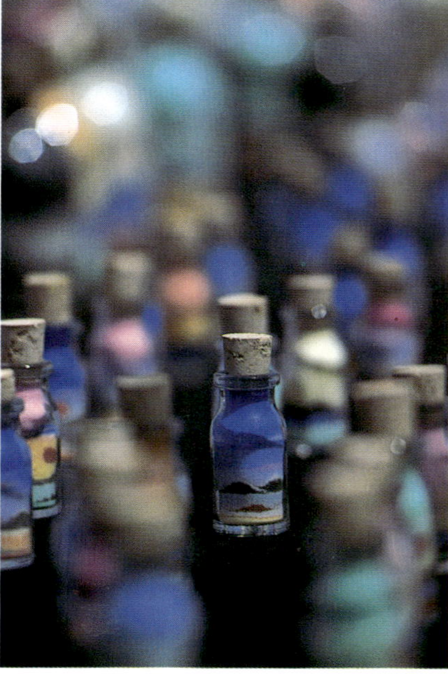

▲ **BOTTLED OUT**
The photographer used depth of field creatively to highlight only two bottles in the frame, providing the picture with a focal point.

Light source

You can use light to create a focal point, too. For example, a small shaft of light streaming through a high window, or the solitary lamplight of a distant farmhouse in a landscape, direct the viewer's attention.

A patch of late afternoon light picking out the highest building of a mountain village, or the reflection of sunlight on a glass skyscraper in a cityscape, provide focal points because of the contrast between light and shade. You can recreate a similar effect indoors using a spotlight.

▶ **MAKING LIGHT WORK**
Waiting for a shaft of sunlight to break through clouds can be a slow process – but it's well worth the wait. The shaft of light draws your attention down to a small area of firs and the dark colours of the trees and stormy sky further emphasize the stream of light.

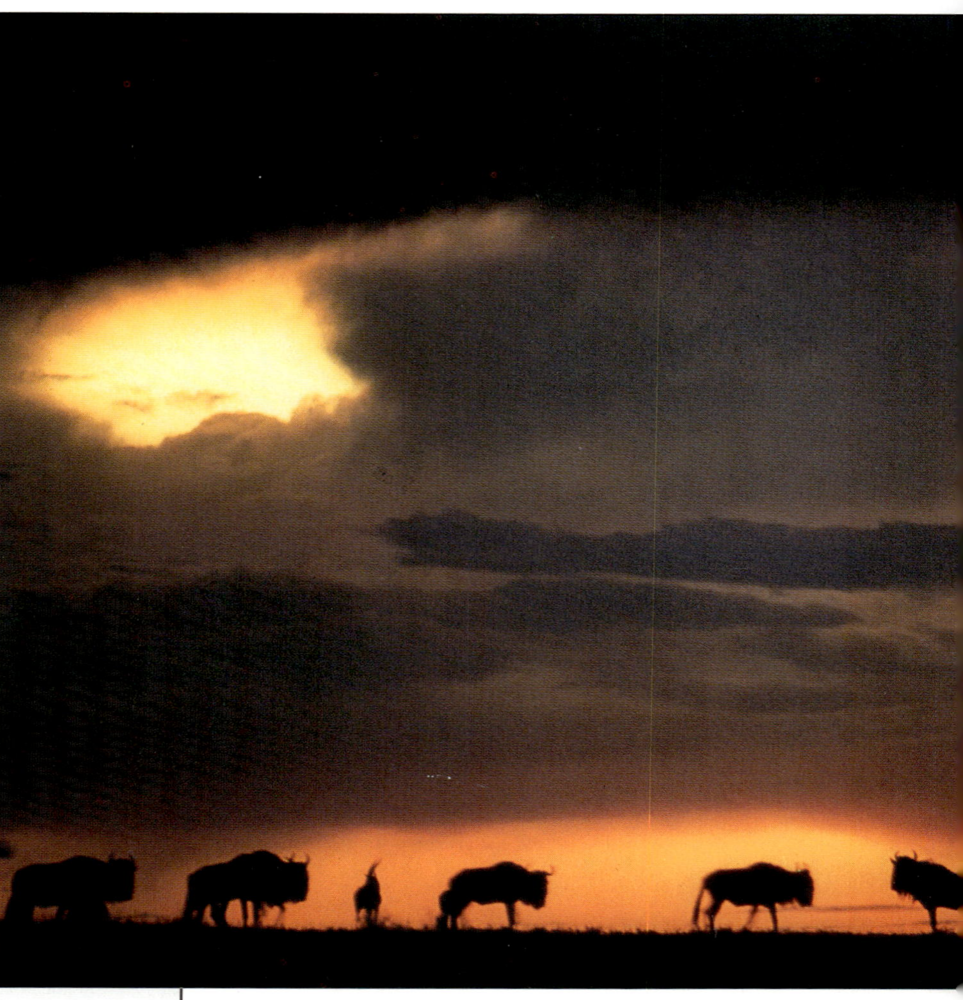

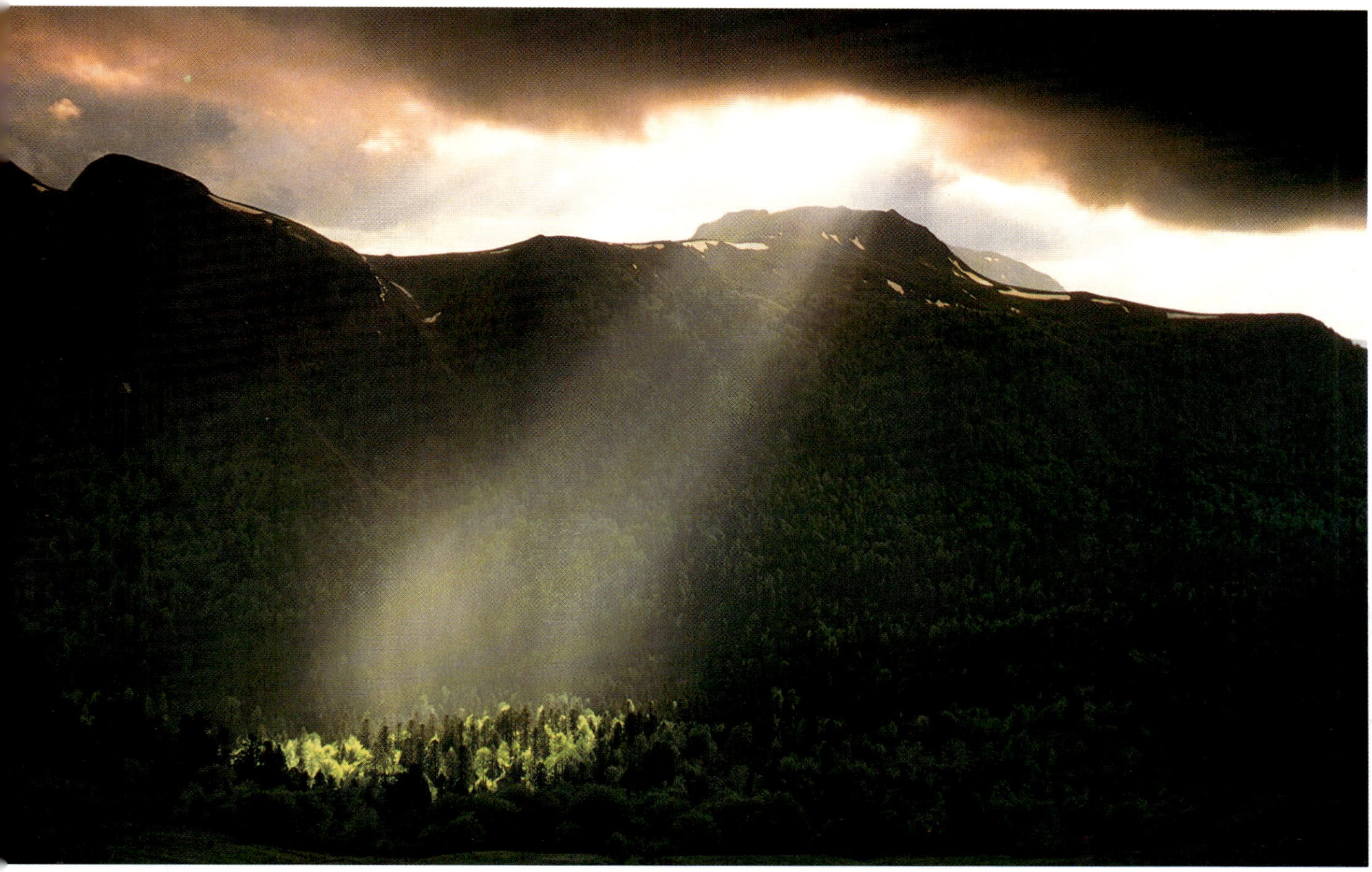

The eyes have it

A more unusual, but very effective, way of providing a picture with one or more focal points is to make use of a person's gaze or eyeline.

Imagine a scene where a woman is looking down on a child, who has turned to take a longing look at a playground in the distance. Your eye follows the downward gaze of the woman, then the backward glance of the child before finally coming to rest on the playground.

▼ **FOLLOW THE GAZE**
This image uses the gaze of both the man and the boy to direct your attention around the frame.

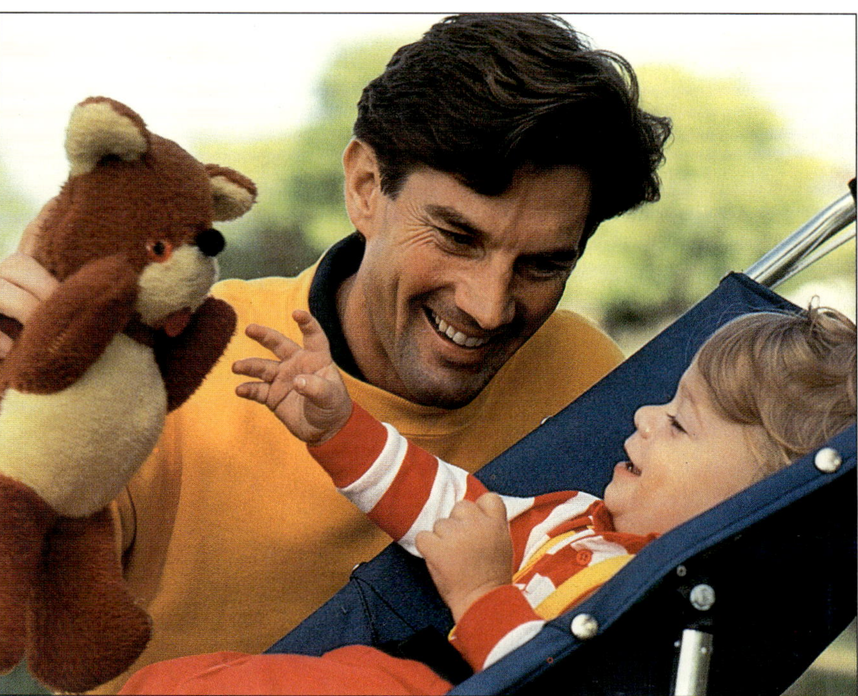

Two focal points

As soon as you include more than one focal point in an image, your viewer's attention is divided. In such cases you need to make sure that the objects differ in size and position so that the eye comes to rest on one of the points rather than constantly flitting between the two.

If you think of the centre of the frame as a fulcrum, then a large object close to the centre will counteract a smaller one located near an opposite edge.

For example, if you take a picture of a small and large yacht with the sea as the background, try to position the two vessels diagonally in the frame, with the larger yacht nearer the centre. The size difference makes your eye look from the larger yacht to the smaller, utilizing the space in between.

Two well-balanced points, similar in position and size, leave the eye undecided as to where to look. This 'lack of resolution' creates tension in the image. Use this technique occasionally to add a feeling of suspense to a picture, or to further emphasize the similarity between two identical objects.

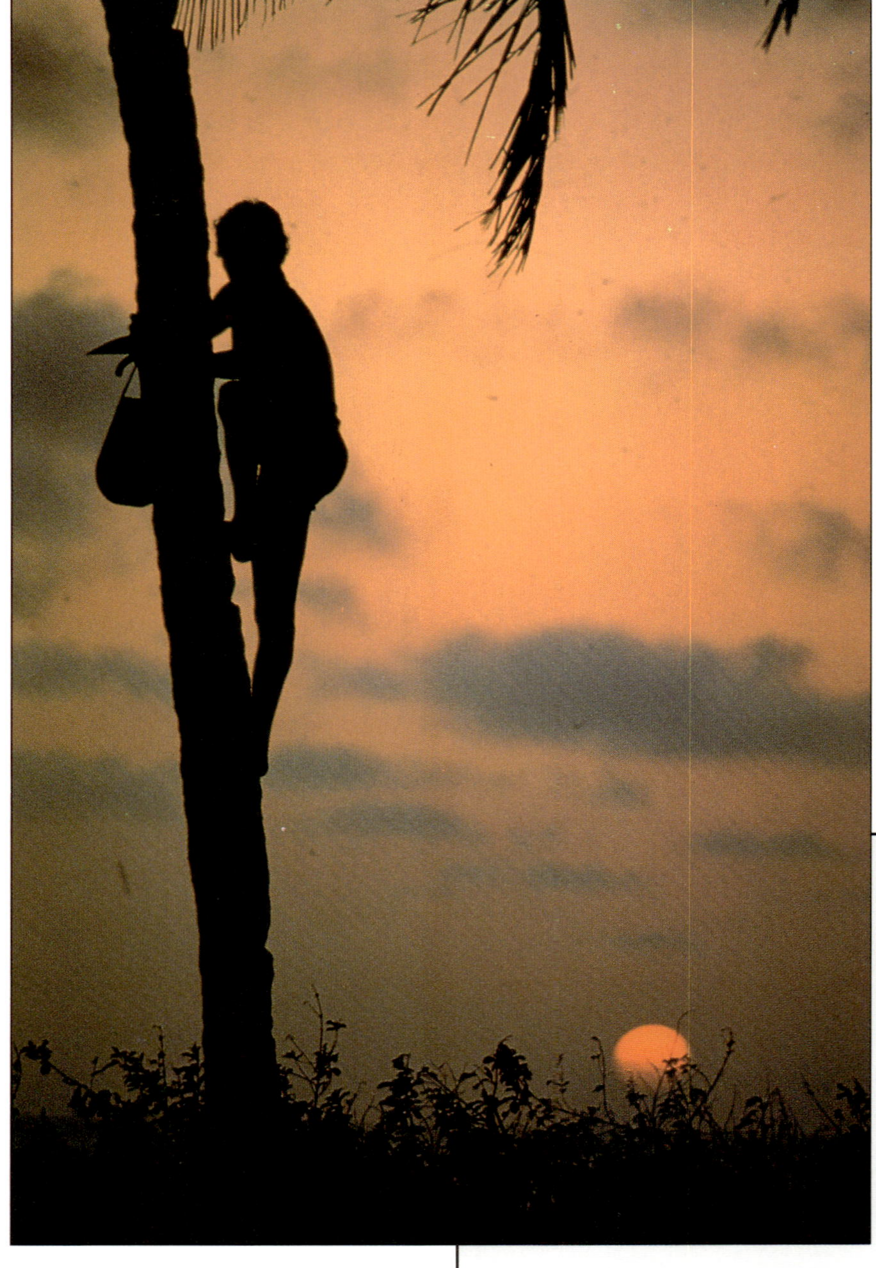
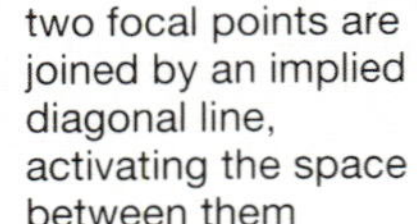

▼ TWIN TENSION
Even though the design is symmetrical, with the two similar looking girls taking up equal space in the frame, your eye doesn't know on which of them to finally rest, creating an 'unresolved tension' in the image.

▲ THE RIGHT BALANCE
In this scene the difference in size and position of the silhouetted boy and the setting sun is essential so that your eye finally rests on the sun, rather than to-ing and fro-ing between the two elements.

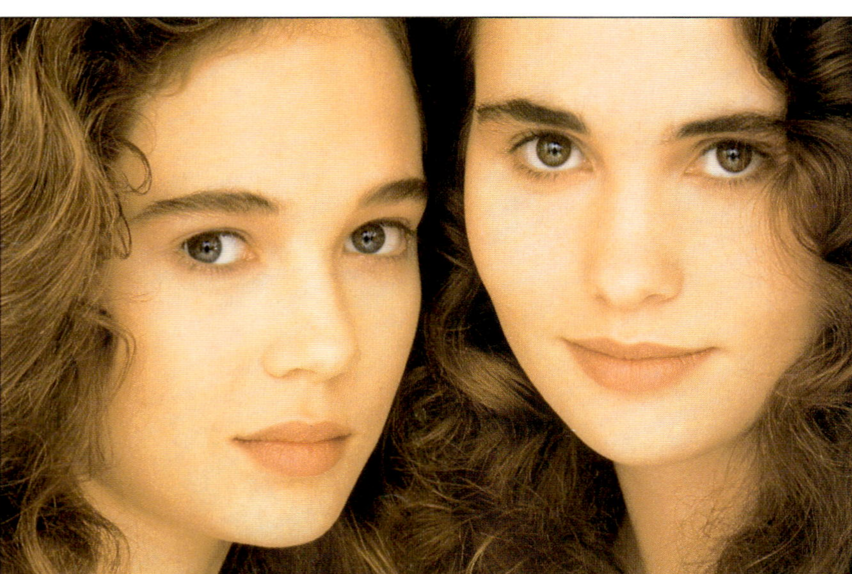

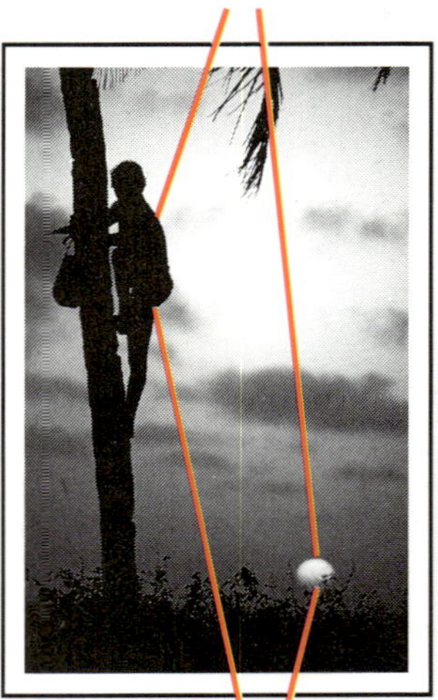

Perspective and viewpoint

In everyday life you take the space, depth and solidity of objects for granted. But in photography, how do you illustrate a three dimensional subject using a flat piece of paper or film?

Most photographs contain clues which help you to determine the depth and form of objects as you see them in real life. One of the most important of these is perspective – how deep photos look. Understand how perspective works and your photos gain the impression of a third dimension.

Of course, depth is not an essential requirement of every good photograph. For instance, abstract patterns of flat shapes or colours make impressive two dimensional pictures.

However, there are many subjects where a flat image would be disappointing. Elsewhere in this book, we look in more detail at the different kinds of perspective, but here we are primarily concerned with perspective and viewpoint. Once you know how, try making better use of perspective as an element of design and composition in your pictures.

This landscape combines several devices to create a tremendous feeling of distance. The more you learn about the tricks of perspective and how to use them, either together or separately, the greater the 3-D effect.

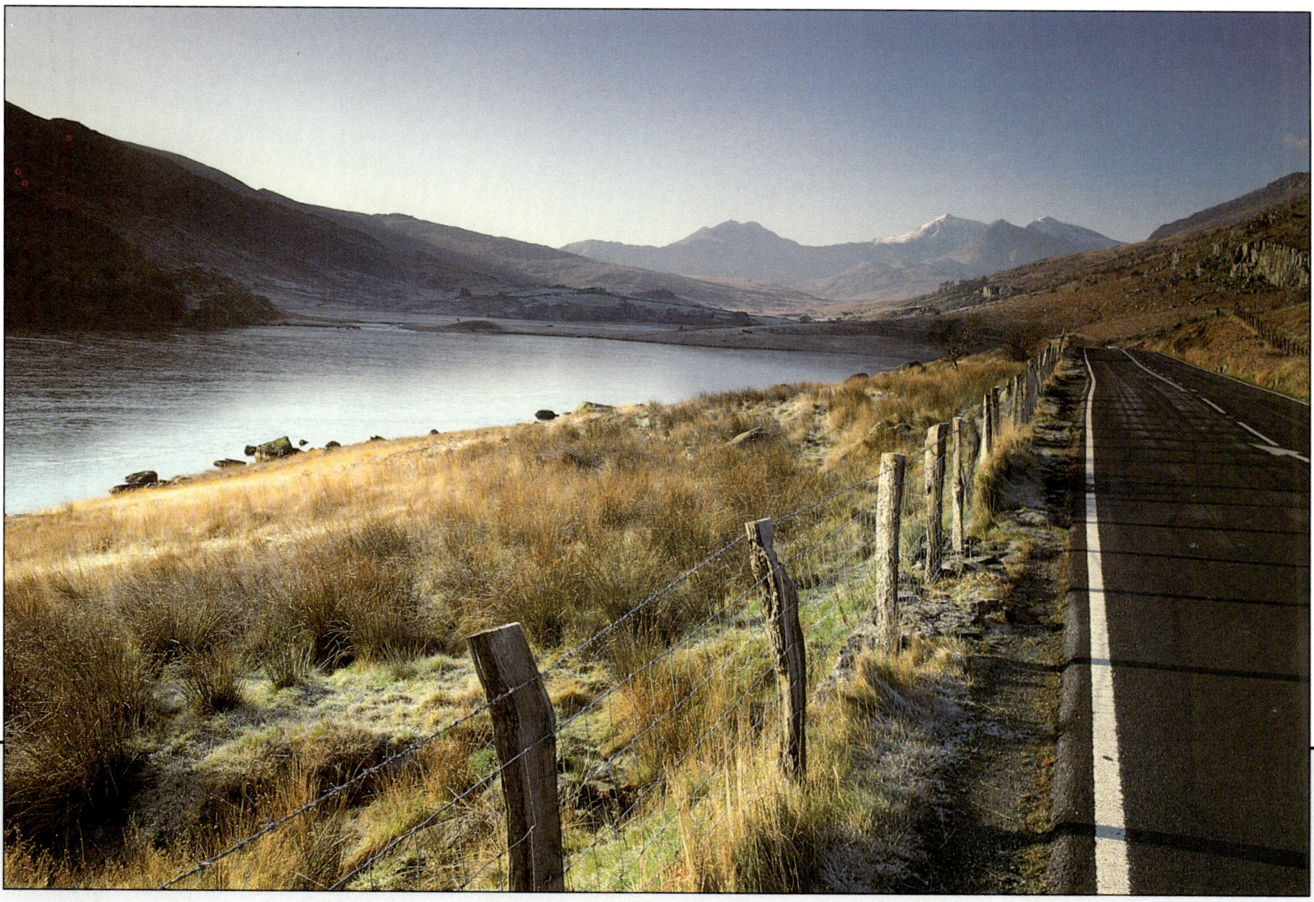

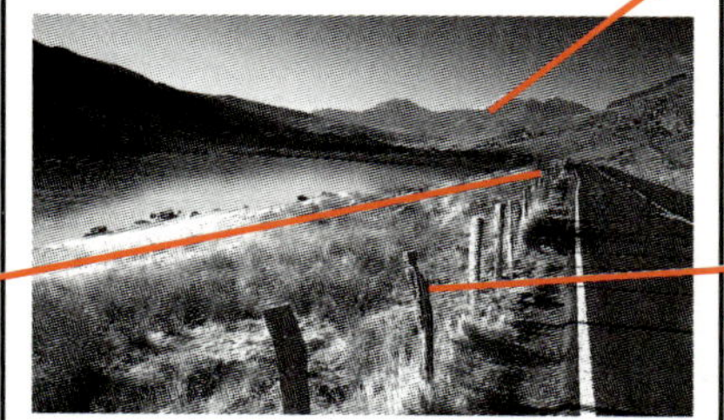

VIEWPOINT
Your choice of viewpoint, whether near or far, looking up or down at your subject, can greatly affect the perspective of a photograph. On the next few pages you can see how a low viewpoint exaggerates perspective, while a high viewpoint minimizes perspective.

LINEAR PERSPECTIVE
Linear perspective is one of the simplest ways to create an illustion of distance. Here, the road, river and fence draw your eye to the back of the picture, allowing you to explore every part of the composition.

AERIAL PERSPECTIVE
In landscape photography, the influence of aerial perspective on the feeiling of depth can be considerable. In this example, the pale mountains seem very far away. Later we shall look at how to control and emphasize this effect.

DIMINISHING PERSPECTIVE
Shapes of identical or similar size receding into the distance are yet another way of adding depth to an image. See how the fence posts get smaller the further away from you they are. Because you know the size of the fence, a sense of scale is added to the whole scene.

Understanding perspective

There are a number of basic elements you can use to add depth to your pictures:

Linear perspective is an easy way of indicating depth. It describes the way parallel lines seem to converge towards the back of the picture.

Think of railway tracks and roads – you know for a fact that such lines are the same distance apart all along. But viewed receding from the camera these lines get closer and closer together until they appear to meet on the horizon.

Diminishing perspective If you look along a street of houses, they seem to become narrower and less deep as they get further away. This is known as diminishing perspective and happens when the objects are identical or similar in size. Things of recognizable size such as people, animals and cars help add an element of scale to your pictures too.

Selective focusing You can exaggerate perspective in a photo by using selective (differential) focusing. A picture which is sharp throughout has less apparent depth than one where the background is out of focus. This is because your brain always assumes that sharply defined objects are at a different distance from blurred ones.

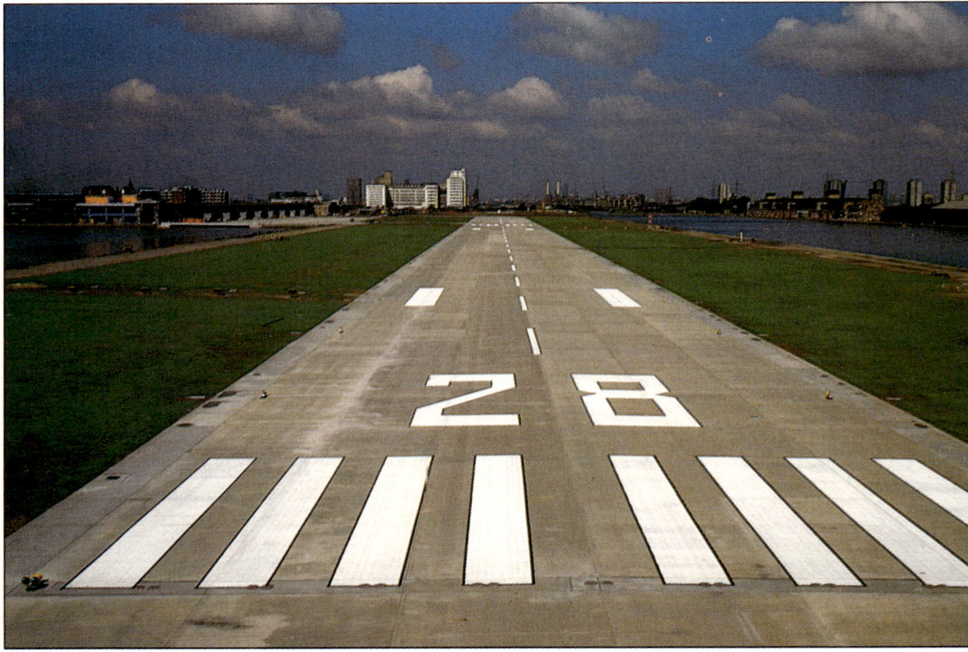

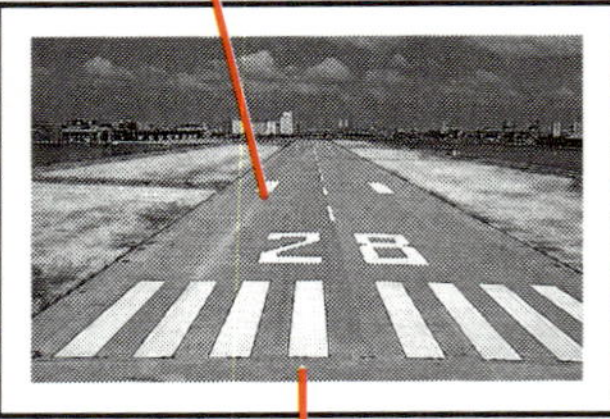

both the white markings of runway and green verges help to draw your eye into the distance

sense of depth exaggerated by central viewpoint

▲ MEETING POINT
Converging lines immediately add depth to a photograph. The diagonal lines draw your eye to the tiny buildings at the back of the scene and also introduce movement into the image.

▶ ARCHERY PRACTICE
The diminishing targets are identical in size, and because they form a line which leads your eye into the picture, the sensation of distance is very strong.

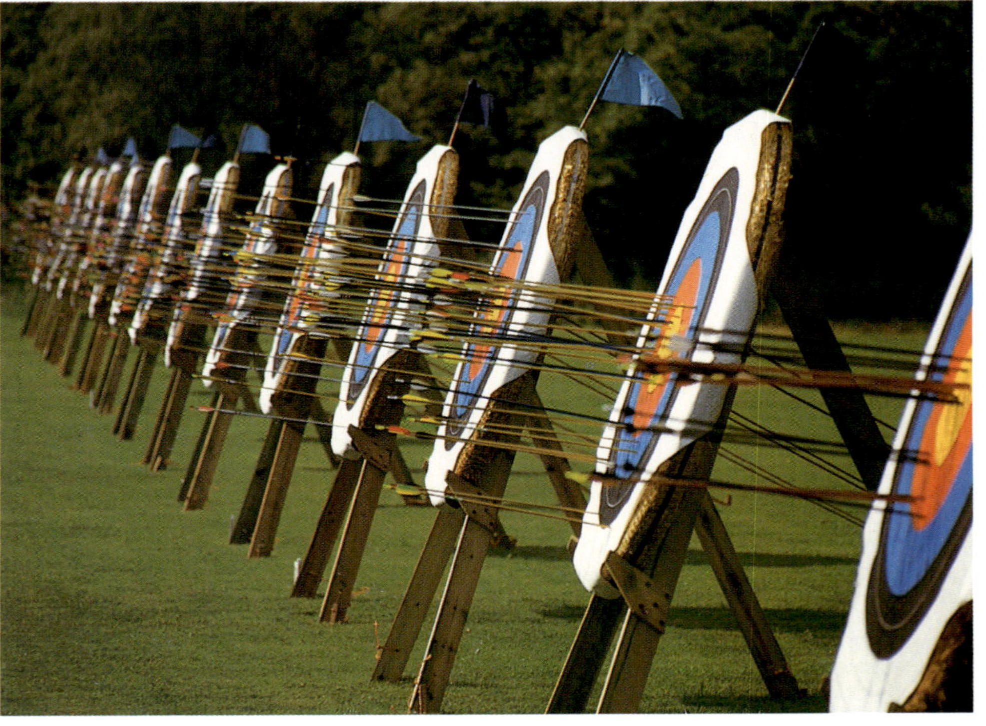

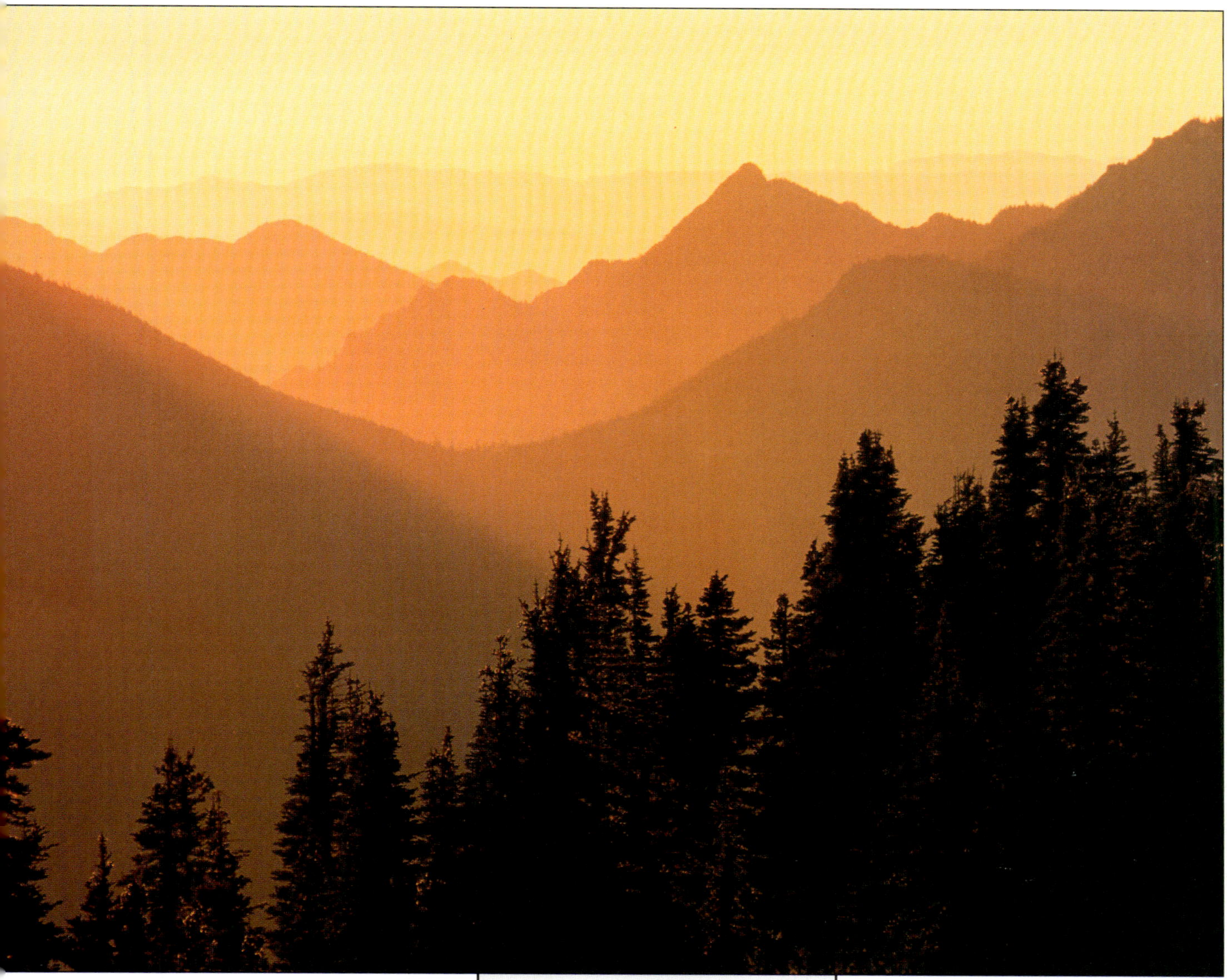

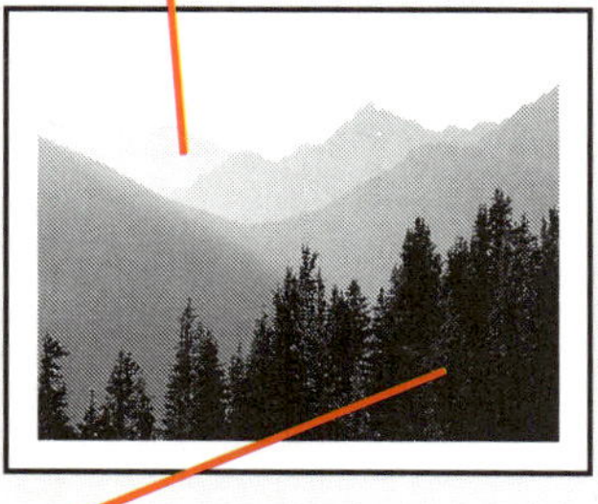

Aerial perspective You can increase the illusion of depth in landscape photographs by using aerial perspective. However, the term is misleading since it has nothing to do with aeroplanes or observing things from the air.

Aerial (atmospheric) perspective describes the fact that things which are far away appear hazier, bluer and lighter in tone than the same objects viewed close to. This is a natural phenomenon created by the effect of water droplets in the earth's atmosphere on light waves travelling over long distances.

Colour and tone Your choice of colours can affect the apparent depth of an image. Warm colours advance out of a picture while cool ones recede. For example, a red poppy stands out against a green background in a photo, increasing the sense of depth between them.

You can achieve a similar effect using tonal differences. Light, bright tones come forward and dark ones naturally fall into the background. Tonal perspective is particularly effective for black and white shots.

▲ HAZY DAYS
Considerable depth stems from the way the mountains get paler and more indistinct the further they are from the camera. The foreground silhouettes heighten the effect.

▼ STANDING OUT IN A CROWD
By blurring the hockey players in the foreground and background, the sharp, main subject stands out from the rest of the picture.

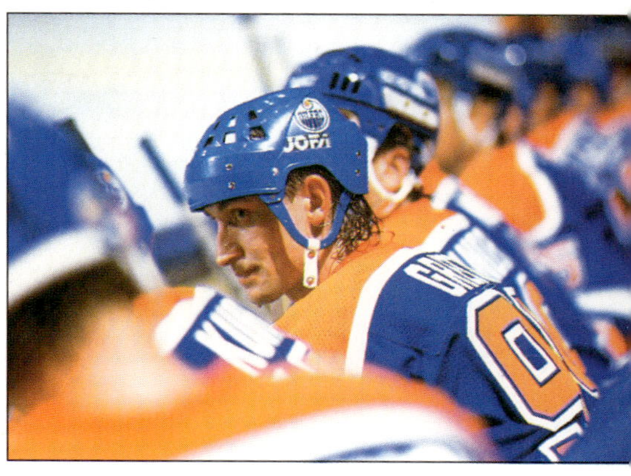

Choosing a viewpoint

Your choice of viewpoint is very important, since by varying your position you alter the perspective of a scene. You can learn a great deal about the rules of perspective by looking at how the size of an object changes the nearer or further, higher or lower you are from it.

For example, visualize a fountain in front of a building. From a distance the fountain looks small and the building large, but as you move closer, the fountain dominates the scene and the building loses prominence.

Unusual viewpoints can produce pictures that have a great deal of impact. Shooting from ground level looking upwards (worm's eye view) or looking down on a subject (bird's eye view) can help you to create interesting shots out of ordinary subjects.

Generally speaking, low, close viewpoints exaggerate perspective and high, distant ones minimize it. Also, a wide angle lens adds depth to images by making foreground objects seem larger and distant ones smaller. A telephoto lens has the opposite effect.

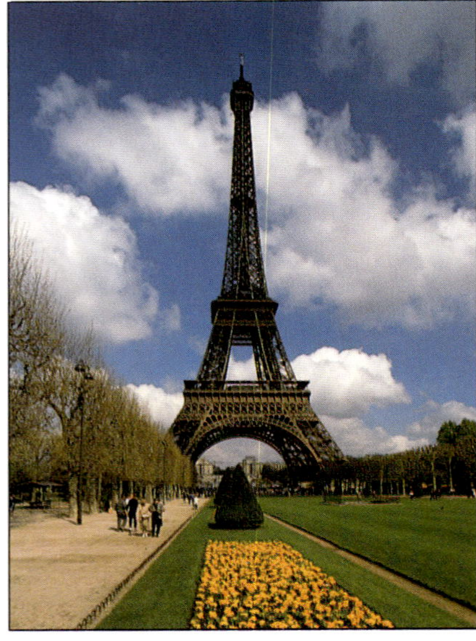

▲ **POINTS OF VIEW**
A new viewpoint combined with a change of lens makes a huge difference to scale and perspective. Although the picture above includes the whole of the Eiffel tower, the flowerbed in the foreground competes for attention.

▼ *By changing to a close, low viewpoint and using a wide angle lens the image gives a greater impression of the tower's height.*

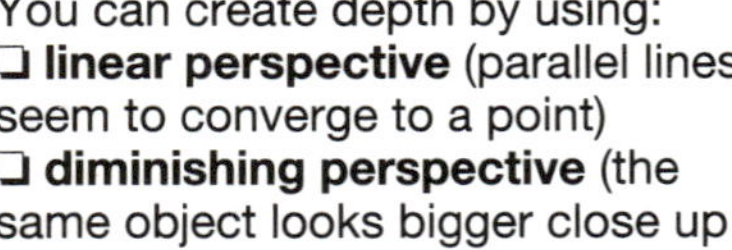

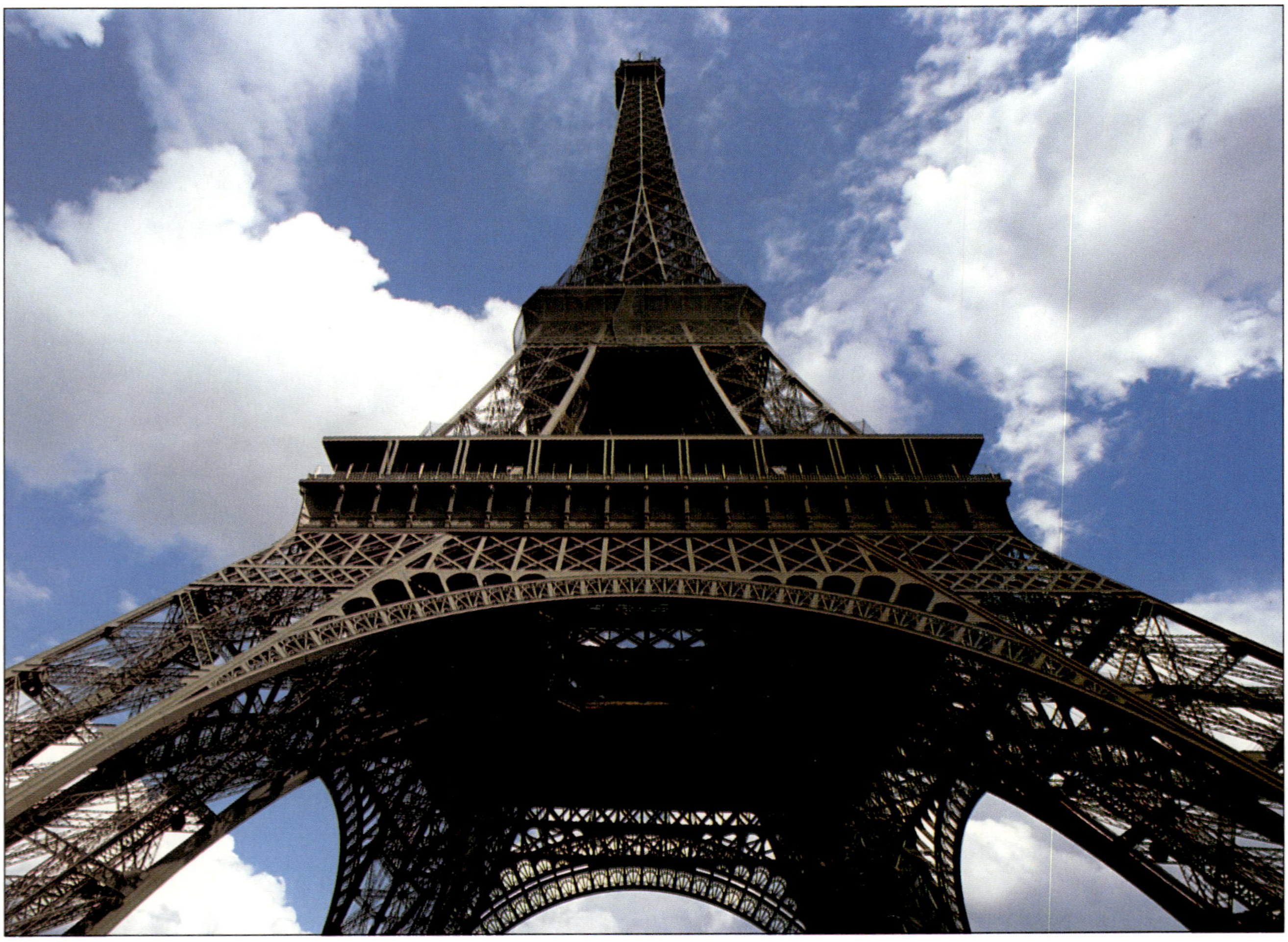

You can create depth by using:
❑ **linear perspective** (parallel lines seem to converge to a point)
❑ **diminishing perspective** (the same object looks bigger close up and smaller further away)
❑ **selective focusing** (something pin sharp stands out, anything blurred recedes)
❑ **aerial perspective** (mountains look paler as they recede)
❑ **colour and tonal perspective** (warm and bright advance, cold and dark recede)

Filling the frame

Sometimes the subject of a composition can appear disappointingly small in a photo. But by simply filling the frame with your subject your picture has instant impact.

When you begin to take photographs one of the first things you learn is where to place your subject in the frame. The most obvious choice is to place it around the centre of the image, so that the edges of the subject are not in danger of being accidentally chopped off.

But such pictures often look very ordinary because the frame is not filled sufficiently. The result is the all too common mistake of the subject looking too small in the final print. The easiest way to avoid this problem is to fill the whole frame with your subject.

For example, when you take a portrait the head and shoulders of your subject should dominate the frame. The rest of the picture should be as simple as possible so as not to distract from your model's face. If you crop in tightly so that just the face is in the frame the image looks even more dramatic.

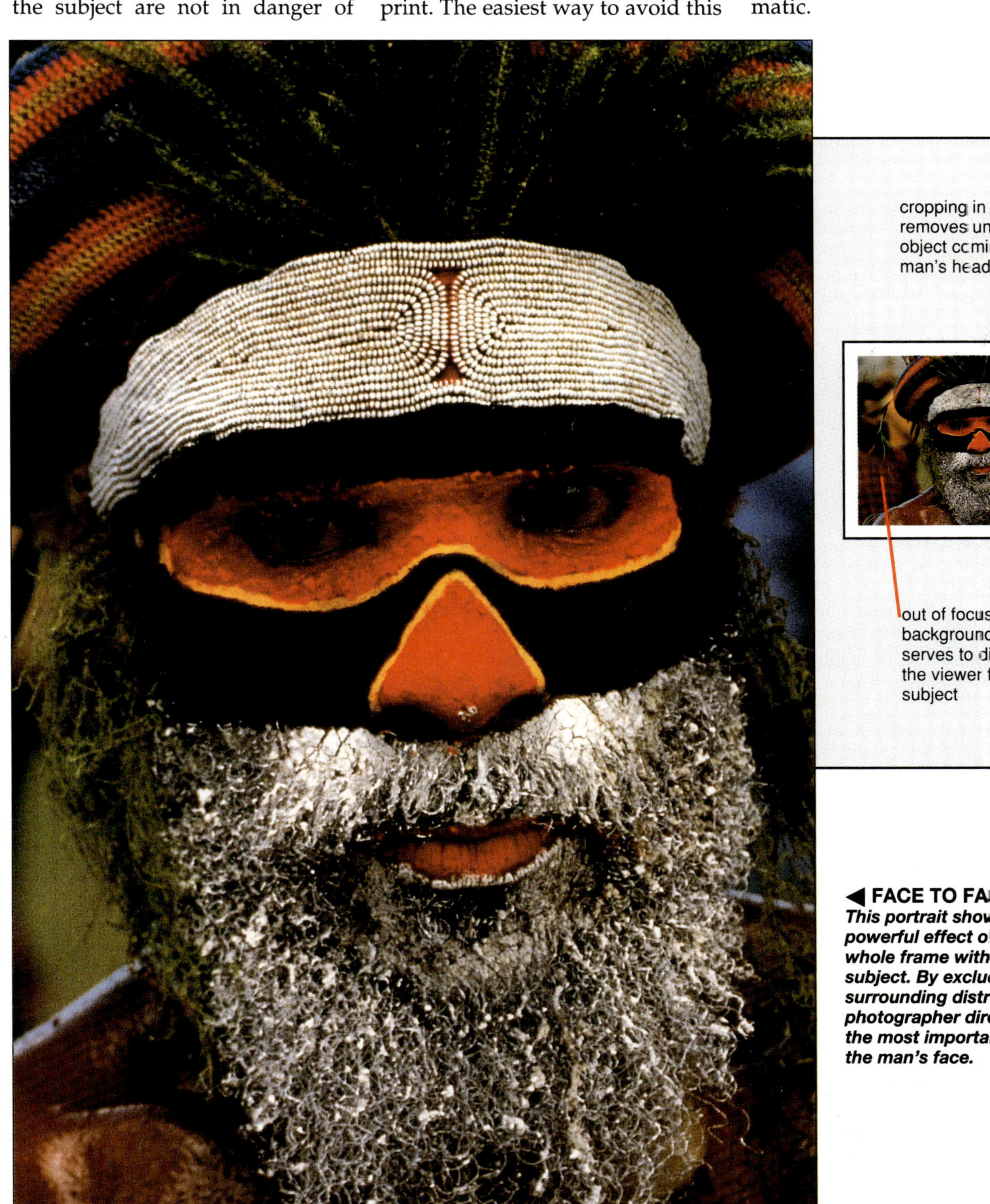

◀ **FACE TO FACE**
This portrait shows the powerful effect of filling the whole frame with your subject. By excluding surrounding distractions the photographer directs you to the most important thing – the man's face.

Why fill the frame?

Obviously you won't always want to fill the frame with one object, so before taking a photograph you need to decide whether to close in tightly on your subject or to show some of its surroundings. For example, including other objects in the frame helps to put your subject into context or you can use the space to add a sense of scale.

However, pictures in which the subject fits the whole frame have an immediate impact on the viewer. There are several reasons why filling the frame is such a useful option:

❏ **Detail** – the larger the subject appears in the frame the more detail is recorded.

❏ **Mood** – if you want your subject to look imposing/dramatic, filling the frame is the best choice.

❏ **Background** – if the surroundings are irrelevant or distracting, crop in tightly on your subject.

❏ **Scale of reproduction** – the smaller the final print is going to be the larger the subject needs to be in the frame.

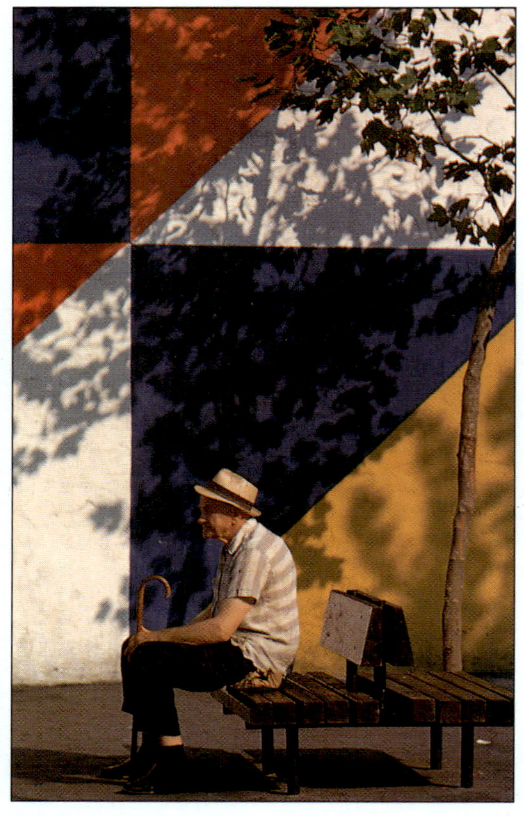

Isolated cases

There are several occasions when deliberately not filling the frame can create successful photographs. Leaving plenty of space around a subject helps to emphasize feelings of loneliness.

In this image, the photographer made the man appear small in the frame to evoke a feeling of solitude. The bright, graphic designs of the wall contrast with the earthy colours, and curved back of the old man, isolating the subject even more.

Varying the size in the frame

Once you have decided that your subject would benefit from being the sole interest in the image, just how large should it be in the frame?

Find a simple subject against a plain background, for example a toddler or pet sitting on some grass, and take a series of shots, increasing the subject's size in the frame each time.

Compare your pictures with the ones on this page and see if you come to the same conclusions as to which one(s) works best.

Don't worry if you only have a compact camera – even the simplest cameras can focus on subjects as close as 1½ metres, and SLRs can focus down to a metre, or often less, using a standard lens.

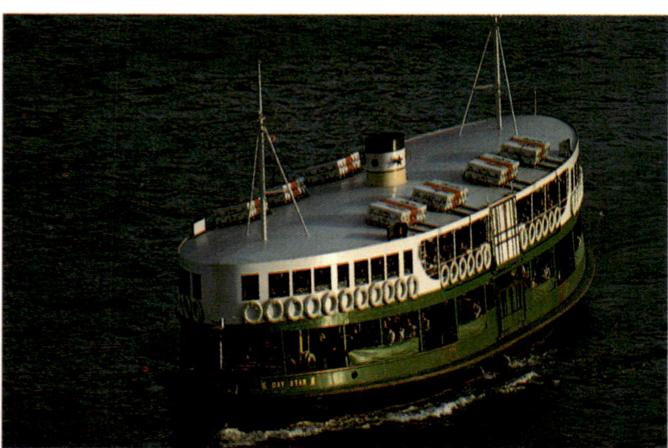

▲ **A SENSE OF SPACE**
The photographer placed the boat off centre in the frame and included a reasonable amount of space around it. But the water doesn't improve the picture and the resulting image is rather ordinary.

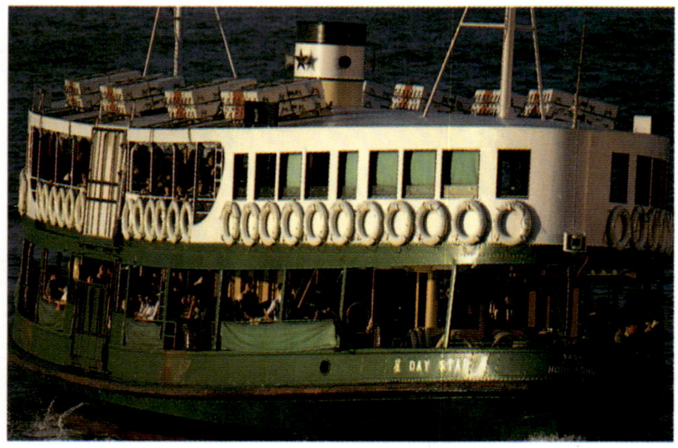

▲ **EDGE TO EDGE**
Here the photographer got his timing just right – a second sooner or later and part of the boat would have been cut off. With the boat fitting the frame exactly, this image has instant appeal.

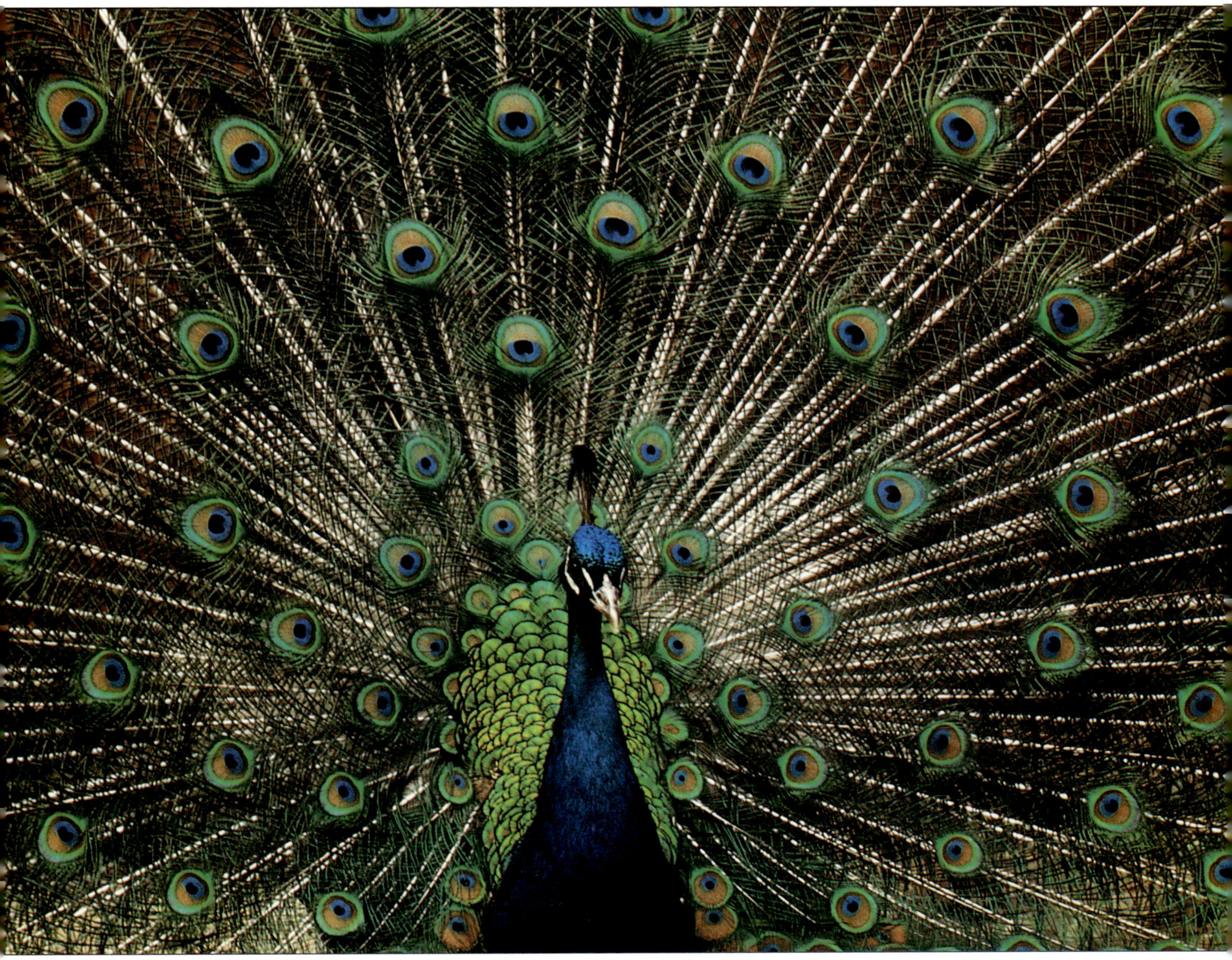

▲ A COLOURFUL SPREAD
The photographer used a close viewpoint to fill the frame and reveal the pattern and vibrant colours of the peacock with greater clarity.

Small scale detail

Most telephoto lenses only have a minimum focusing distance of 1-2m, so if your subject is very small and you want it to fill the frame, there are several accessories you can use. Macro lenses produce excellent quality close-up pictures. They don't distort the subject and are convenient to use.

A cheaper alternative is to fit extension tubes to your lens. Or you can use extension bellows which allow you to fill the frame with subjects ranging in size from about 2cm to 15cm in diameter.

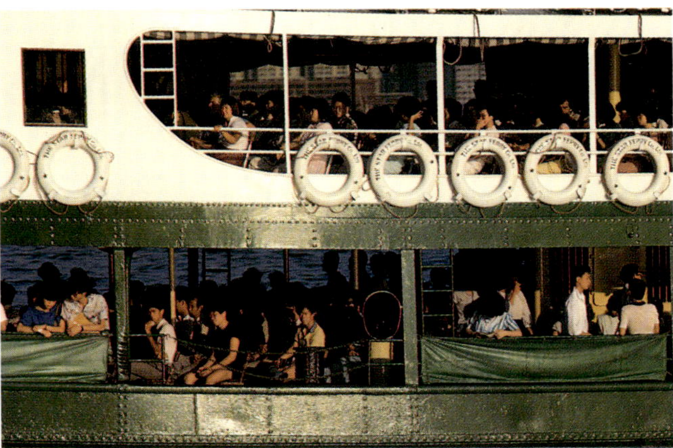

▲ OVERFILLING THE FRAME
For the final shot the photographer used a telephoto lens so that just a section of the ferry is captured. A lot more detail is included and the viewer's interest shifts to the people, rather than the boat they're sitting on.

A change of lens

When you are limited to a fixed viewpoint a telephoto lens enables you to exclude irrelevant detail and fill the frame from quite a distance.

A zoom telephoto is particularly useful for sporting subjects where the action moves rapidly closer and farther from the camera. It means that you can fill the frame with the precise piece of action that interests you.

Of course it's not always possible to close in tightly on a single object, but you can fill the frame by including other elements around it, as long as they are relevant to your main theme.

A wide angle lens allows you to include objects outside the eye's range of vision. Use this to your advantage to include details that contribute to the composition and fill up the frame.

▶ AERO-DYNAMICS
It wasn't possible to make the aeroplane any larger in this picture because of the distance involved. So the photographer included the plane's smoke trail to fill up the frame and add interest.

▼ FOCUSING ON DETAIL
From a fixed viewpoint, the photographer used a telephoto lens to fill the frame with Big Ben's clock face. With the clock so large in the frame a great deal of architectural detail is recorded.

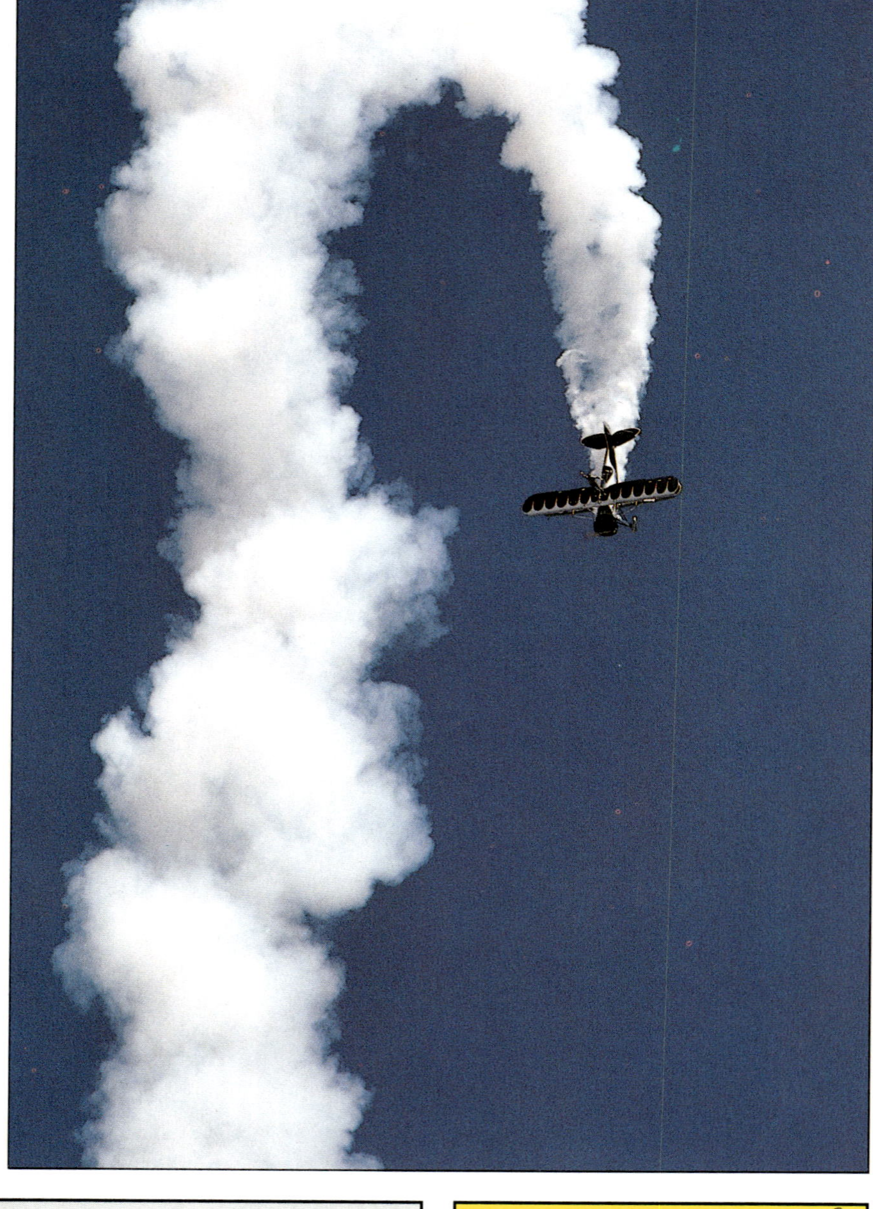

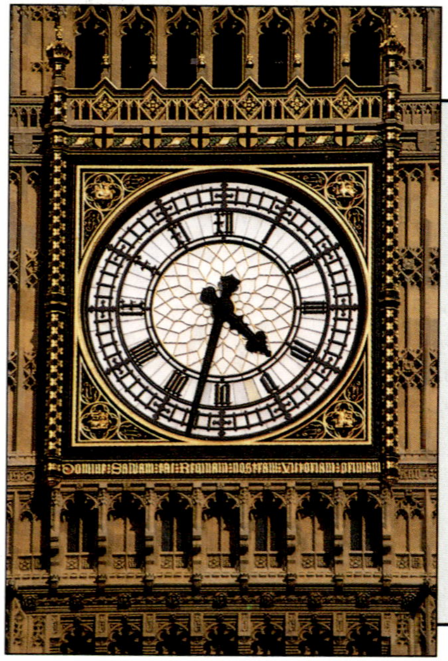

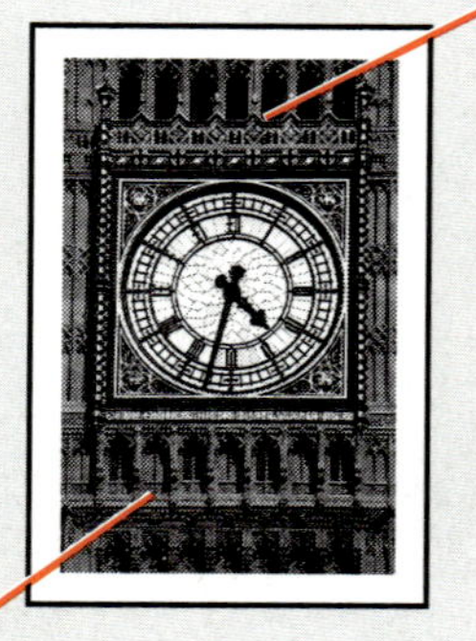

vertical format means that entire frame is filled, heightening the composition's impact

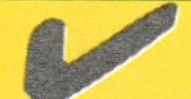

combination of telephoto lens and frontlighting maximizes architectural detail

Points to remember:

❏ Filling the frame with a single subject allows you to include a great amount of detail, and produces simple, dramatic images
❏ Use a telephoto from a fixed viewpoint to fill the frame with your subject
❏ If you don't fill the frame with a single subject, use the space around it constructively
❏ With a wide angle lens the extra space in the frame should be used to support the theme of the composition

Dividing the frame

We have already looked at some of the basic elements of composition; this section unites them, and adds some more.

How you divide a picture, what you include, and where, are some of the most basic elements to consider before taking a photograph. Your choice of subject, viewpoint and framing are important for dividing the picture into balanced areas of tone, colour and detail.

The first question is where to position the horizon, the simplest way to divide the frame. Should it be high, low or in the middle?

The edges of the picture are often neglected but can do a lot to make or break your subject. The sides of the frame can even provide the main interest in a photo too.

How well you fill the frame is also an important consideration, as we saw in the previous section. And, of course, one of the first things we looked at was the focal point, on pages 17-20. Of course, none of these "rules" are unbreakable but it is surprising how often you can use them to add impact to a picture.

▶ **THE COMPLETE PICTURE**
This image combines several devices to fill the frame and divide it into balanced areas of tone and detail. The horizon, splitting the scene into two equal halves in this example, is the most important division in a photo.

Basic visual elements

EDGES OF THE PICTURE
It is easy to ignore the edges of the picture, but they can contribute a great deal to your composition. One way of utilizing the edges of the image is to use a frame within the frame. In this example the palm trees provide a natural foreground frame, drawing your eye towards the island.

HORIZON
Often the most important division in a picture is the horizon. In this picture it cuts the image into two equal halves, but you can choose to place it lower or higher within the frame.

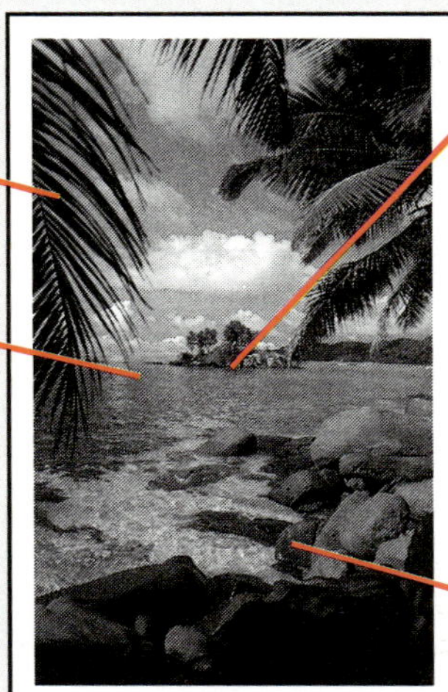

FOCAL POINT
A stumbling block for many photographers is where to position the focal point within the frame. If this scene had not included the small island on the horizon, your eye would not have had a final resting point.

FILLING THE FRAME
If the subject of your picture is fairly small you often need to fill the frame with other elements to create a satisfying composition. In this example, the foreground rocks and palm trees fill the frame and support the main theme of the picture.

Placing the horizon

For most photos, particularly landscapes, the position of the horizon within the frame needs a great deal of thought. And the less activity there is in a scene, the more important its role becomes.

There are no hard and fast rules as to where you should divide the frame – it all depends on which part of the scene you want to emphasize. A safe, but predictable, method is to set the horizon "on the thirds" (one third land/two thirds sky or one third sky/two thirds land). Another is to balance tones or colours according to their brightness or density.

Alternatively you can divide the frame in favour of the land or sky, depending on which is more important. Much depends on the mood you want to convey and how dramatic you want the picture to look.

In the middle

A central horizon runs the danger of splitting the scene into two areas of equal weight with neither dominating. This tends to create a static image, leaving the eye undecided as to where to look.

However, you can use it for those rare shots when complete symmetry is called for. Reflections, for example, can look stunning with the horizon in the middle.

High horizon

Your eye assumes that the larger of the two areas in a picture is the more significant. So if the interest in a scene lies in the land rather than the sky, place the horizon high in the frame.

When most of your image is taken up with land there is a tremendous feeling of depth because of the difference in scale between objects in the fore and background. But make sure that the landscape contains enough variety, otherwise the scene can look rather heavy.

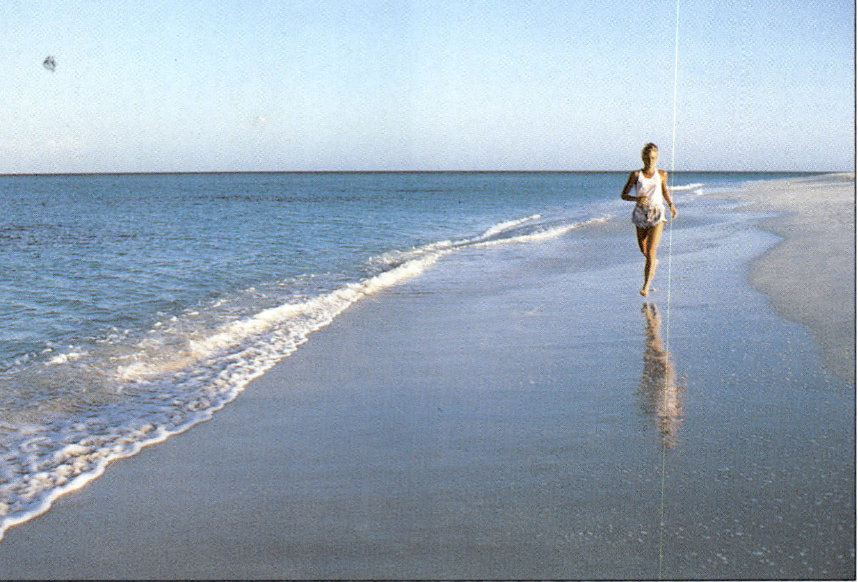

▲ RULE OF THIRDS
The photographer used the classic ratio of two thirds land and a third sky to allow enough space for the woman to run into and for her reflection to be seen clearly. The water's edge helps to lead your eye to the figure.

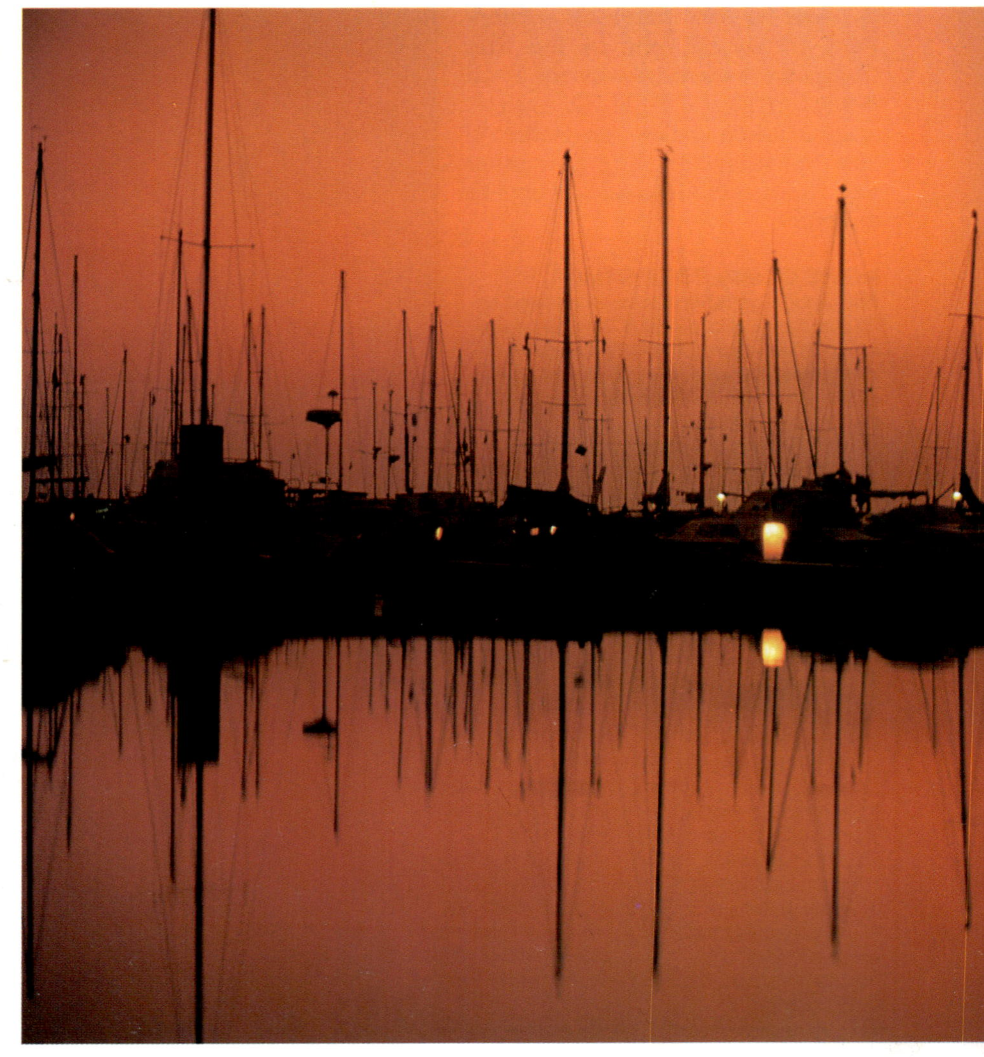

▶ BALANCE AND SYMMETRY
With the waterline positioned across the middle of the frame, the subject and its reflection produce a stunning symmetrical image. Even the solitary light is carefully placed in the centre of the frame.

Horizontal or vertical?

Pictures with a horizontal format draw the eye from left to right across the frame, giving the viewer a sense of wide open spaces. Use a low horizon to make the most of this sweeping effect.

A vertical format is ideal for emphasizing depth in an image, because your eye moves from foreground to background. With a high horizon a great deal of detail can be included in the composition of the picture.

| ²⁄₃ |
| ¹⁄₃ |

| ¹⁄₃ |
| ²⁄₃ |

▲ a sense of space

▶ a sense of depth

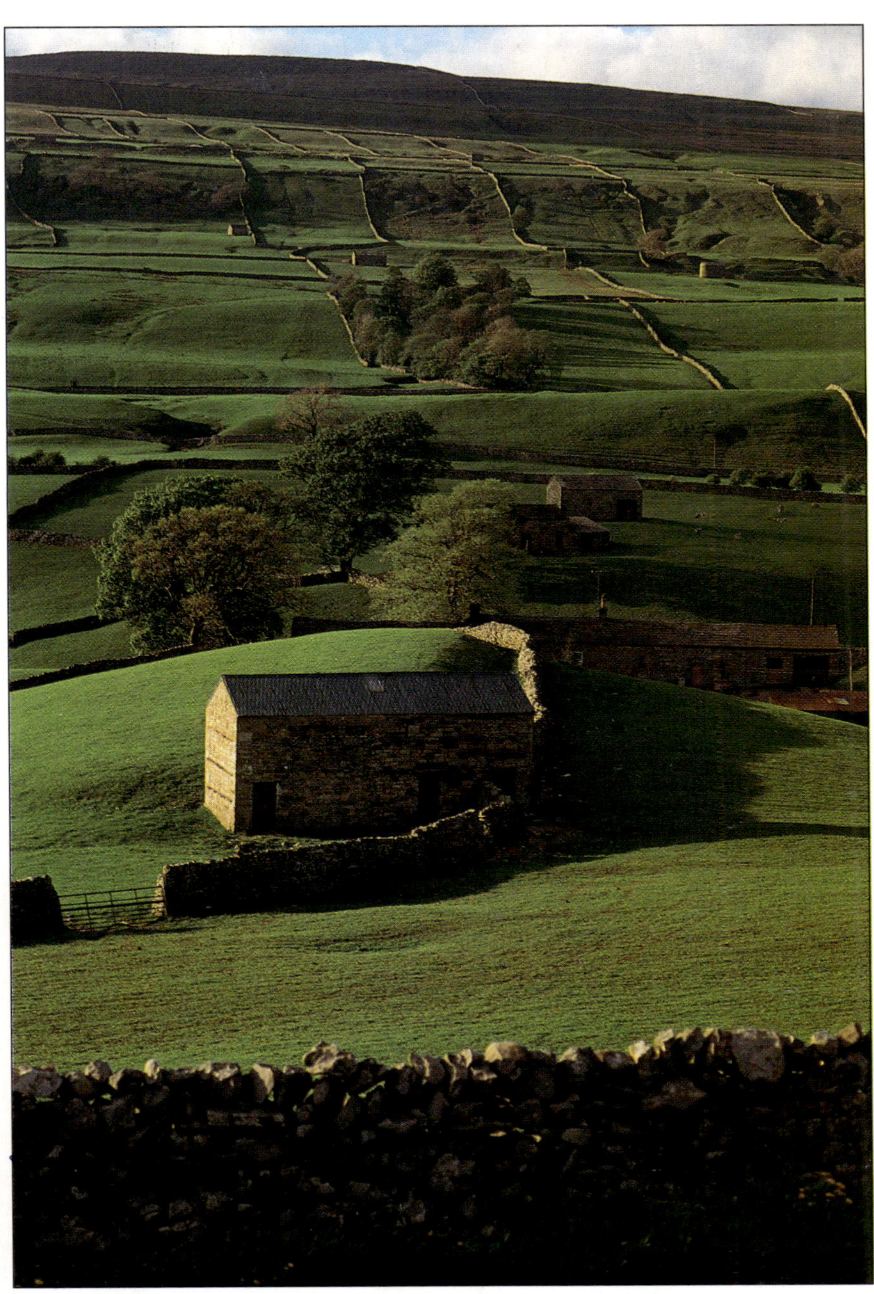

▲ **GREEN AND PLEASANT LAND**

A high horizon means that the colours and details of the land dominate the shot. The large expanse of land, the foreground wall and diminishing sizes of the barns, all give the image a tremendous feeling of depth. A small band of sky helps to prevent the rich greens of the rolling hills from being too overpowering.

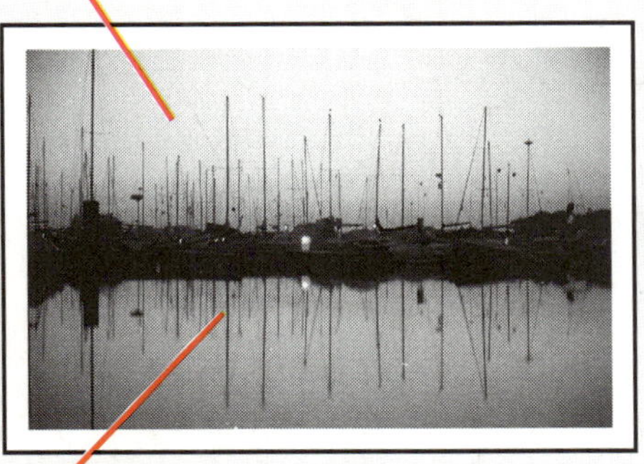

a warm up filter was used to enrichen the colour of the evening sky

the masts and their reflections widen the band of interest, filling most of the frame

Low horizon

When the sky is filled with interesting cloud formations or unusual colours, you can make it the subject of your image by placing the horizon low in the frame.

Picture the purple swirls of a stormy sky, or the pattern created by a flock of birds, for instance. With most of the picture area filled with sky such scenes have a very spacious feel to them.

A low horizon is also useful for cutting out a foreground which is boring, distracting or of little relevance to the shot.

Have a go

To compose each picture with the horizon in the same place is unimaginative. Try taking a series of pictures with the horizon in a different place each time, and decide for yourself which ones are successful and why.

No horizon

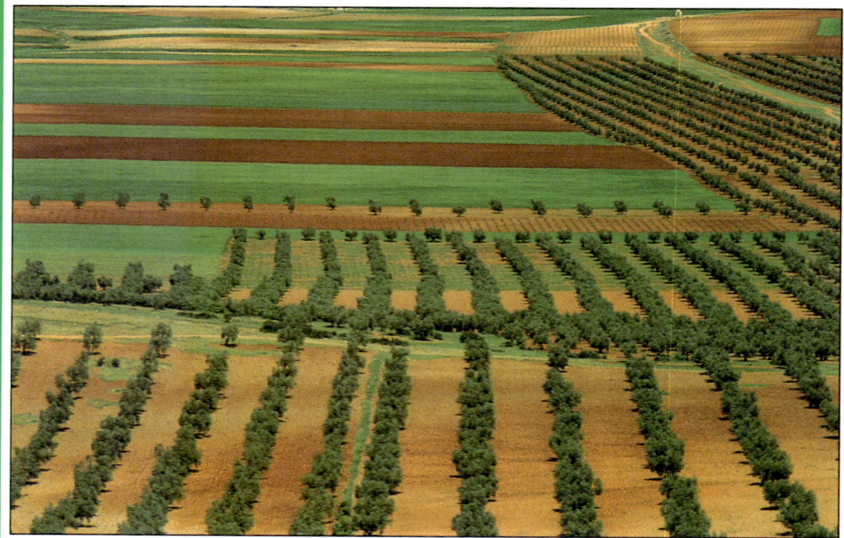

Excluding the horizon altogether from your shot can also produce successful pictures, especially when colour or pattern is the subject of the image. Pictures with no horizon look flat and two dimensional, and any object in the scene, for example a tree, is isolated and given prominence. A telephoto lens flattens perspective further, and helps you select the degree of abstraction you're after.

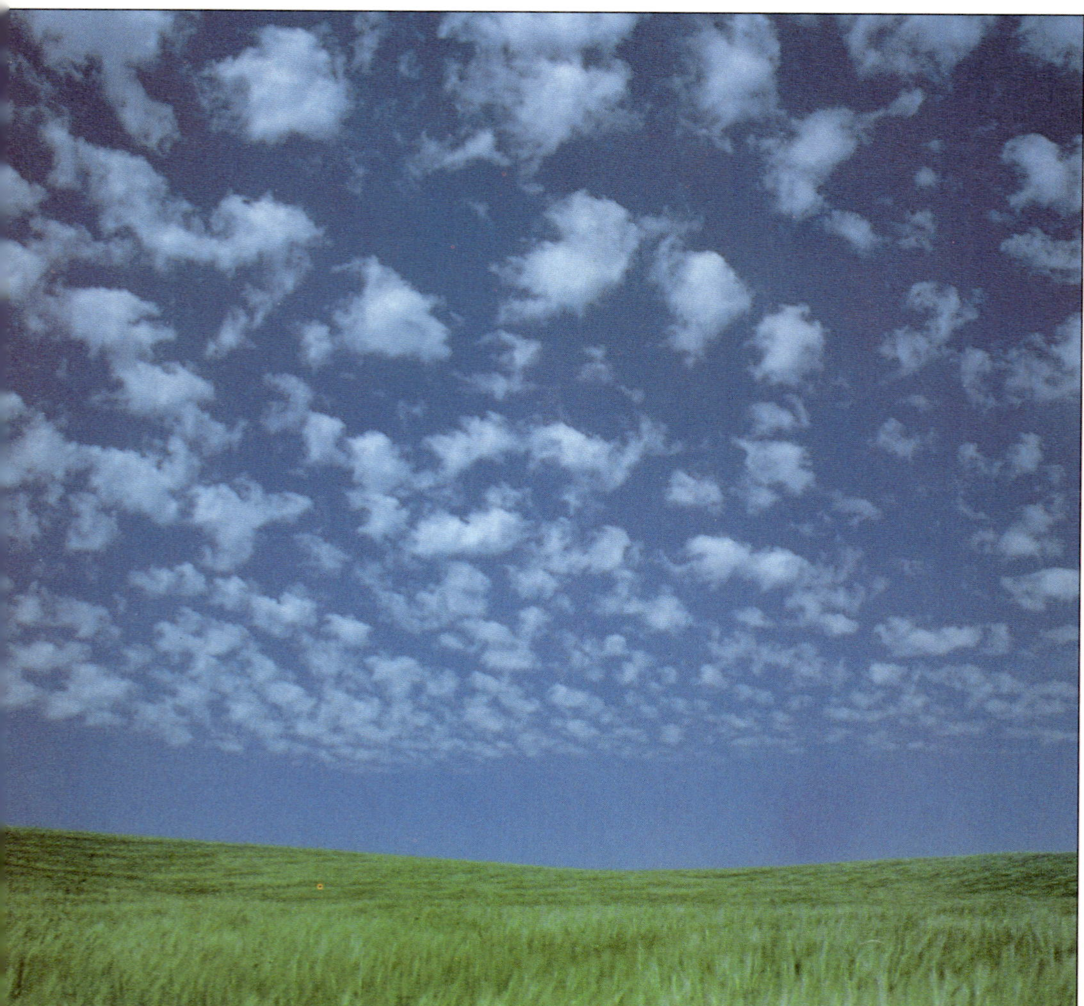

◄ CLOUDSCAPE
In this image the low horizon places the emphasis on the sky, conveying a strong feeling of space. The photographer used a polarizing filter to bring out the shapes of the clouds and improve colour saturation.

Looking at balance

In photography, the word "balance" can mean a lot of things: but what we are concerned with here is the often-forgotten art of composing symmetrical and near-symmetrical pictures.

A great deal of the secret of composition lies in balancing the different picture elements inside the frame. Some arrangements look "right", and others do not. Also, the frame does not have to be dictated by the camera: you can crop or mask the image to a square, a rectangle, or even a circle, though this is something we shall return to on page 91.

Symmetry

Children love symmetry, but as we grow more sophisticated we often reject it as too dull. While you can have too much of a good thing, this very predisposition against symmetry means that if you do compose a picture symmetrically, it can have a certain "shock value" which adds to its impact and re-awakens a child-like freshness of vision.

Diagonals

A totally symmetrical picture is normally calm and stable, but by "tilting" the composition and introducing diagonal lines, it becomes much more dynamic. This is probably connected with the way in which we learn to read: side to side, and up and down, in a regular pattern. "Jumping" from one part of a composition to another is not ordered, so a diagonal movement is more exciting. This sense of movement and dynamism exists even where the subject is totally motionless, like the picture of the cloisters below.

Basic visual elements

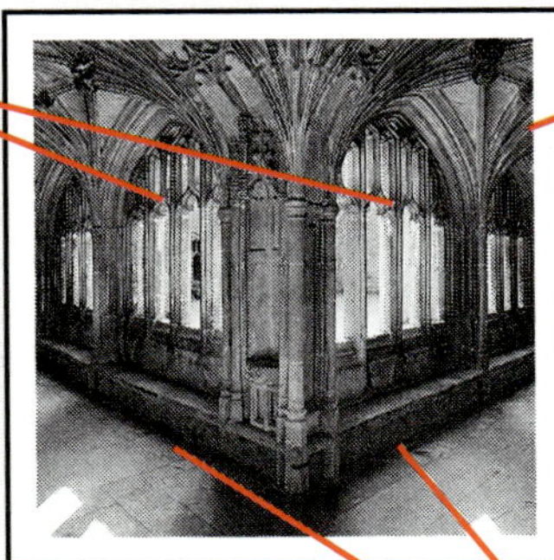

SYMMETRY
The precise dimensions of certain subjects, such as buildings and patterns, can look stunning if positioned symmetrically in the frame. In this example, symmetry emphasizes the architectural detail of the cloisters.

UNUSUAL FORMATS
Choosing a format to suit your subject is one of the most important decisions to make before taking a photograph. In this picture a square frame was used to echo the precision of the stonework.

DIAGONALS
Lines are an integral part of every composition, and the way you arrange them in the frame affects the mood of the picture. Here, the photographer chose to make the lines diagonal in the frame to inject movement into the scene.

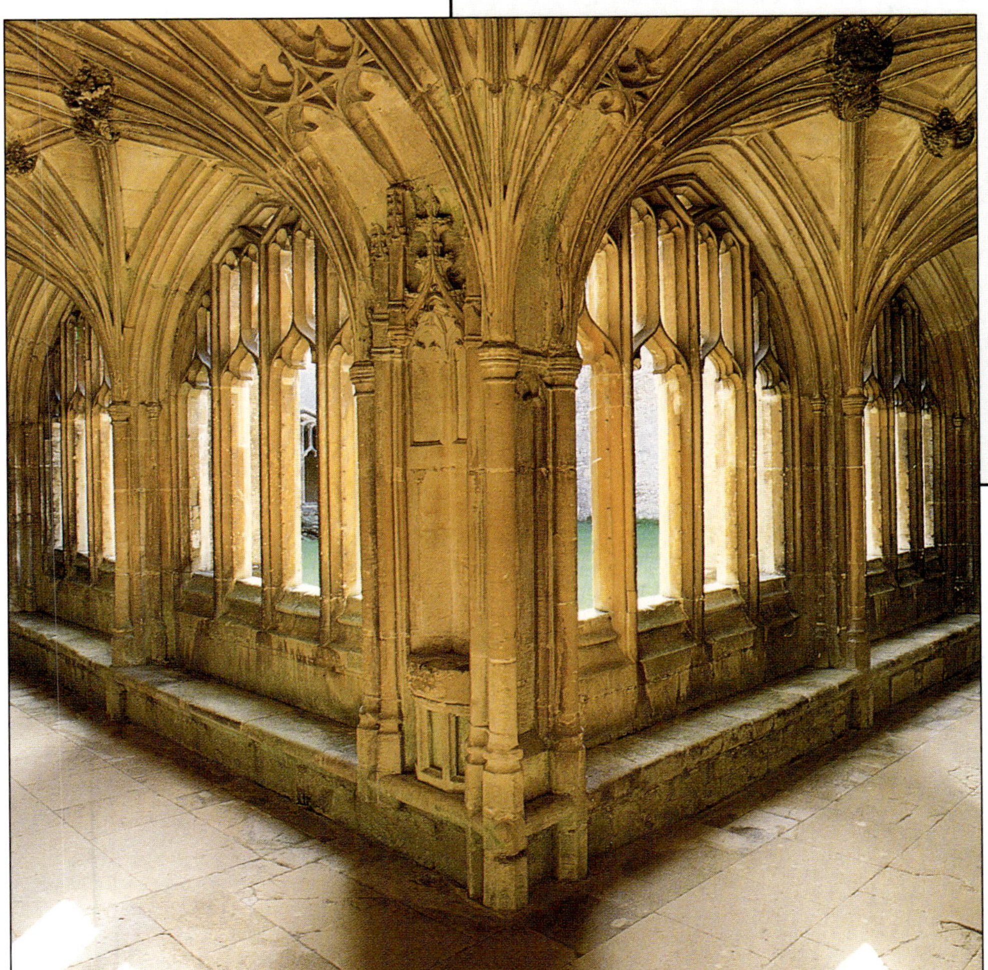

◀ UNDERNEATH THE ARCHES
The precision of the architectural detail is reinforced here by the square format. With the cloisters positioned to create diagonals with the edges of the frame, a sense of energy and depth are also added to the scene.

Symmetrical compositions

A symmetrical picture is one which can be divided either horizontally or vertically so that if folded, one half would fit exactly over the other. Even rarer, it can be an image that is symmetrical around one central point, like a wheel, so that you could fold it across any axis to give two matching halves. Such compositions have an equal and balanced feel to them.

True symmetry is hard to find in nature – the majority of symmetrical subjects are man-made, such as buildings or cars. A lot, too, depends on your viewpoint and how you position the subject within the frame.

For example, if you are shooting a Georgian house with a straight path leading to a central door, the best viewpoint would be dead centre of the path, to emphasize the precision of the architecture. Front-lighting also helps to enhance the effect of symmetry, since no shadows are thrown to off-balance the scene.

The perfect balance of symmetrical scenes means that there is less to stimulate the eye to move around the frame; and for this reason patterns are good subjects to choose. Repeated shapes such as furrows in a field, brickwork, a wrought iron gate or a pile of oil drums, can all be used to make symmetrical images.

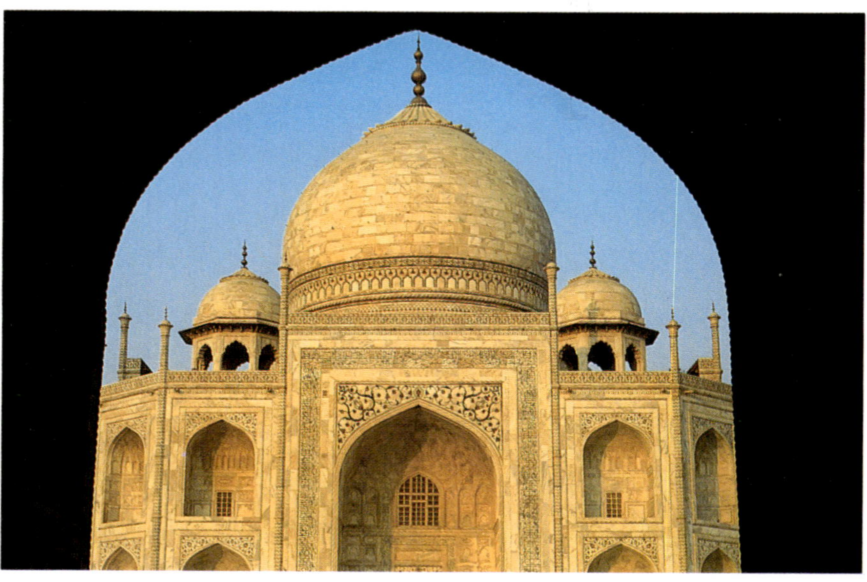

▲ ARCHED BEAUTY
Buildings provide a wealth of symmetrical subjects, and the Taj Mahal must be one of the most photographed of them all. The photographer further enhanced symmetry by choosing a camera position in the exact centre of an overlooking arch.

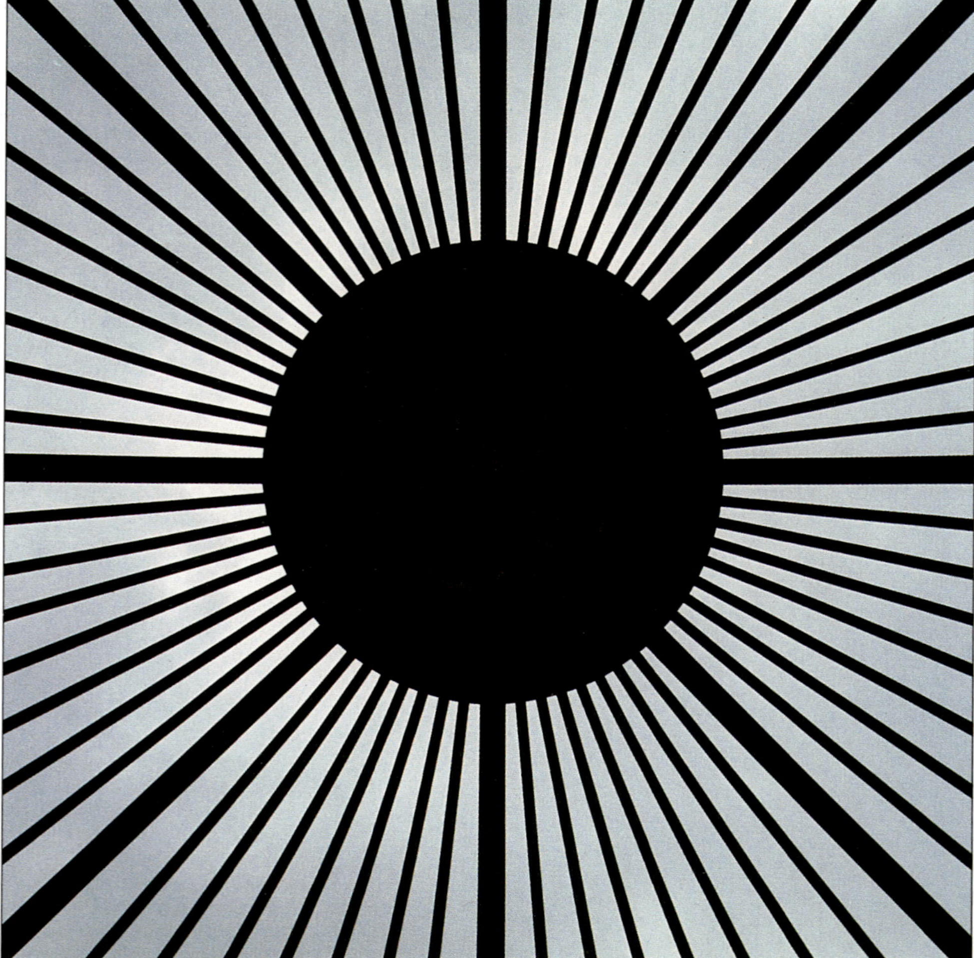

◄ DRIVEN TO ABSTRACTION
Perfect symmetry, a picture that can be folded across almost any axis to give two matching halves, is rare to find, so grab the chance. In this abstract pattern of a roof skylight your attention goes directly to the centre of the frame.

Creating symmetry

There are more ways of taking a symmetrical picture than simply finding a subject which is symmetrical:

Reflections in plate-glass windows and in still lakes and ponds form natural mirror images, creating symmetry out of asymmetrical subjects. Mirrors can be used to create this effect artificially, too. You can lift a portrait out of the ordinary, for example, by placing a well-polished mirror beside your subject to give an illusion of identical twins.

Double exposure allows you to create an interesting picture with symmetry by superimposing two identical images on a single frame. For instance, if you want to make a symmetrical picture of some flowers, shoot them once so that they fill one half of the frame, then reshoot the same image on the unexposed half of the frame.

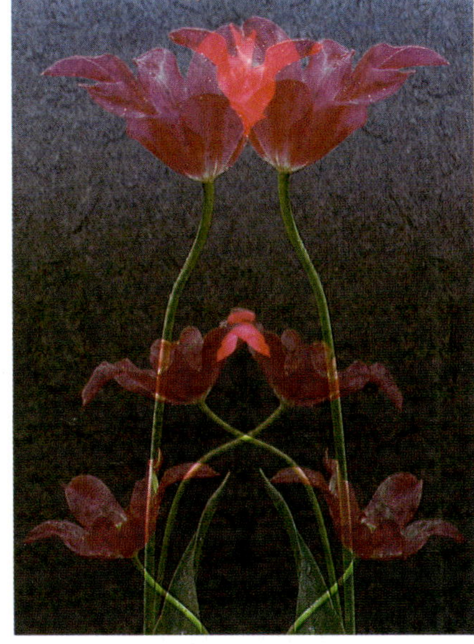

▲ DOUBLED UP
This unusual still life was produced using the technique of double exposure. After taking one shot of the flowers, the photographer turned the arrangement around for the second shot, producing a mirror image.

▼ MIRROR MAGIC
The photographer used a mirror to create this stunning symmetrical image of Ayer's Rock in the Australian outback. You can re-create this effect either with Cokin's purpose-built attachment or by holding a mirror in front of your camera lens.

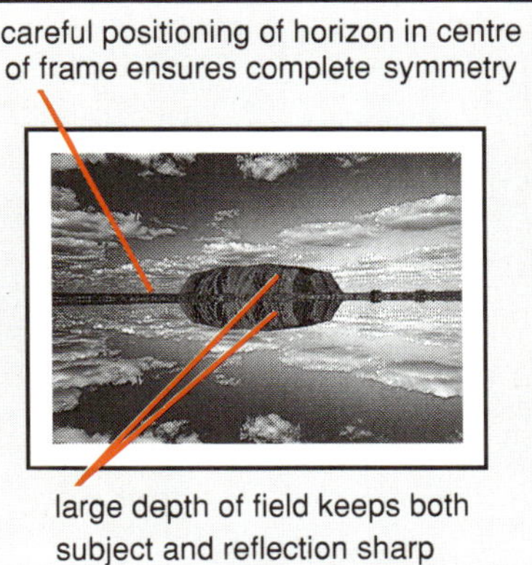

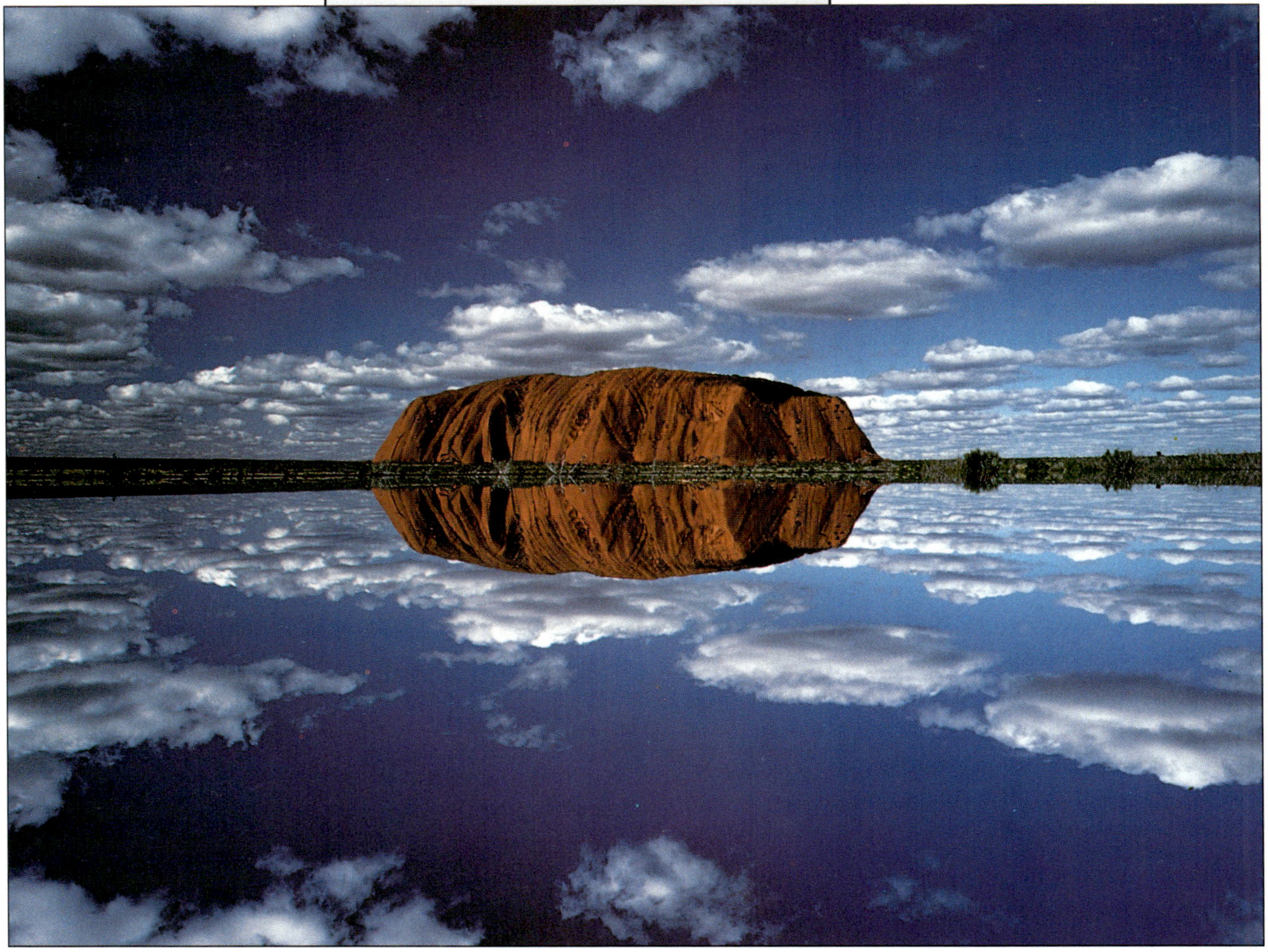

Breaking symmetry

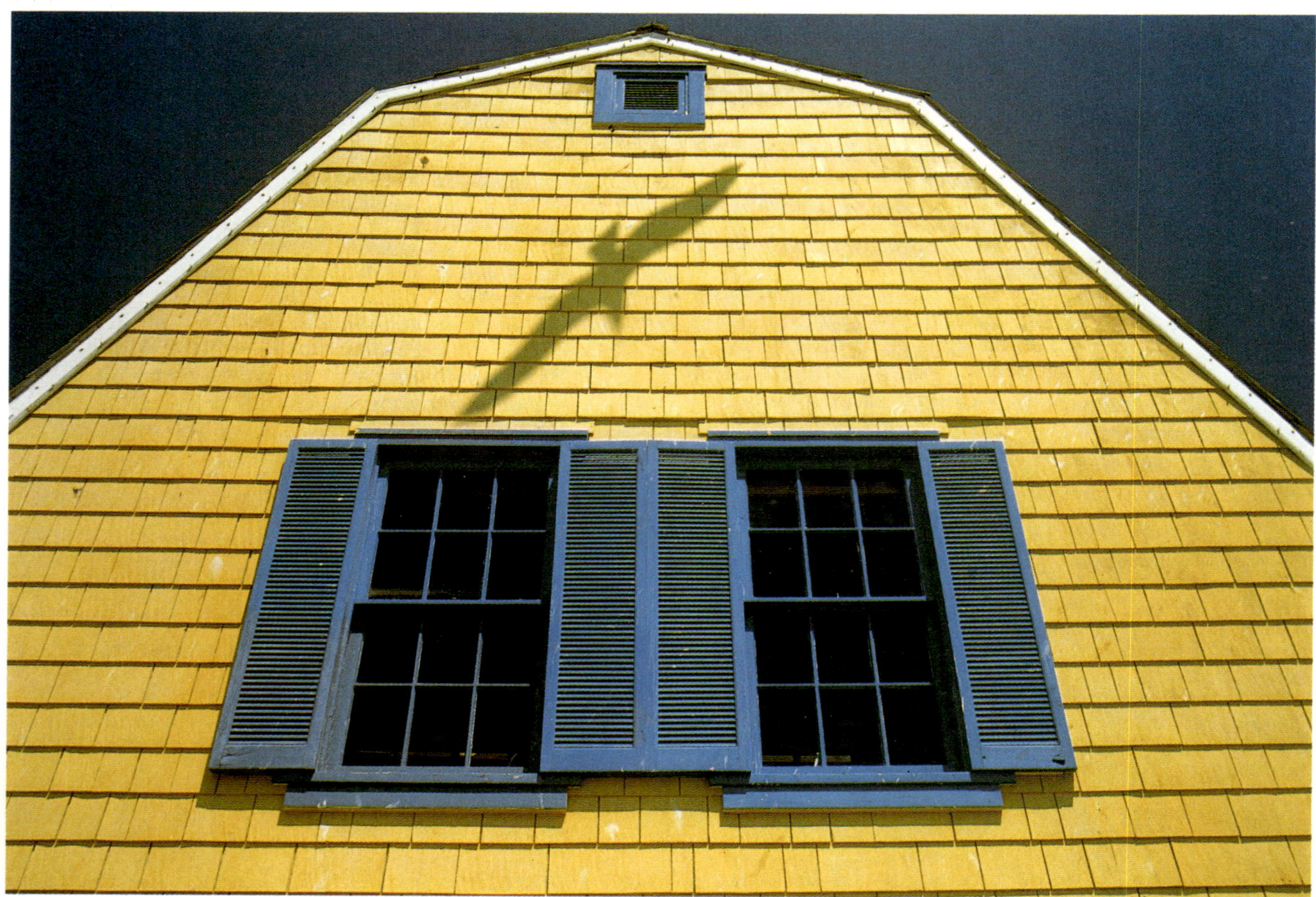

The line between symmetry and asymmetry is a very fine one. If you are aiming to produce a symmetrical composition then it must be exact in order to succeed. If not, the smallest misalignment will stand out immediately.

Sometimes, however, there is the danger that symmetrical pictures are too predictable and, therefore, look dull. In such cases you can create impact in a scene by disturbing the symmetry in some small way. If you are shooting a pattern, say, try adding a splash of accent colour – even a tiny area of red or orange will draw the eye.

People attract a great deal of attention, too. Even if they only appear fairly small in the frame, they help to break the symmetry quite strongly.

Shadows are also useful for disturbing the perfect balance of a composition. If you photograph a skyscraper which is sidelit, the shadows which fall across it off-balance the symmetry of the architecture.

▲ **BIRD ON THE WING**
This picture has a great deal of impact because the shadow of the bird on the building adds an element of surprise to an otherwise static scene – even the sky is polarized to almost match the colour of the windows.

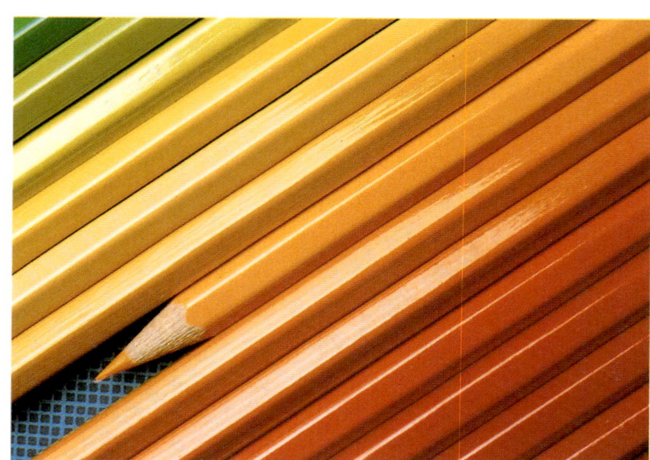

▲ **A LITTLE TIP**
You can often create more impact in a symmetrical scene by disturbing it in some way. This diagonal pattern of pencils was broken by showing the tip of the orange pencil.

You can find symmetrical subjects in:

❏ some natural objects but mostly in man-made things, such as buildings and formal gardens

❏ in naturally occurring reflections

You can create symmetry by:

❏ using mirrors to produce a reflection of your subject

❏ making a double exposure using the same image twice

Composition and depth

A lot of the time the key to composition is including interest in each 'layer' and area of the photo, so the eye wants to linger on the picture and take it all in. This helps the picture look three dimensional – as the world is in reality.

"Picture elements" can be any number of things: physical objects, the placing of those objects in the frame, the relationship of those objects to each other, and more. The way in which you use those elements can give the picture a sense of depth or, occasionally, you may want to forego this and play up pattern instead.

Before you take each picture, you have to ask yourself whether its elements are making a positive contribution. This all sounds rather laborious, but with a little practice thinking about composition soon becomes second nature - like a pilot going through the checks before take-off.

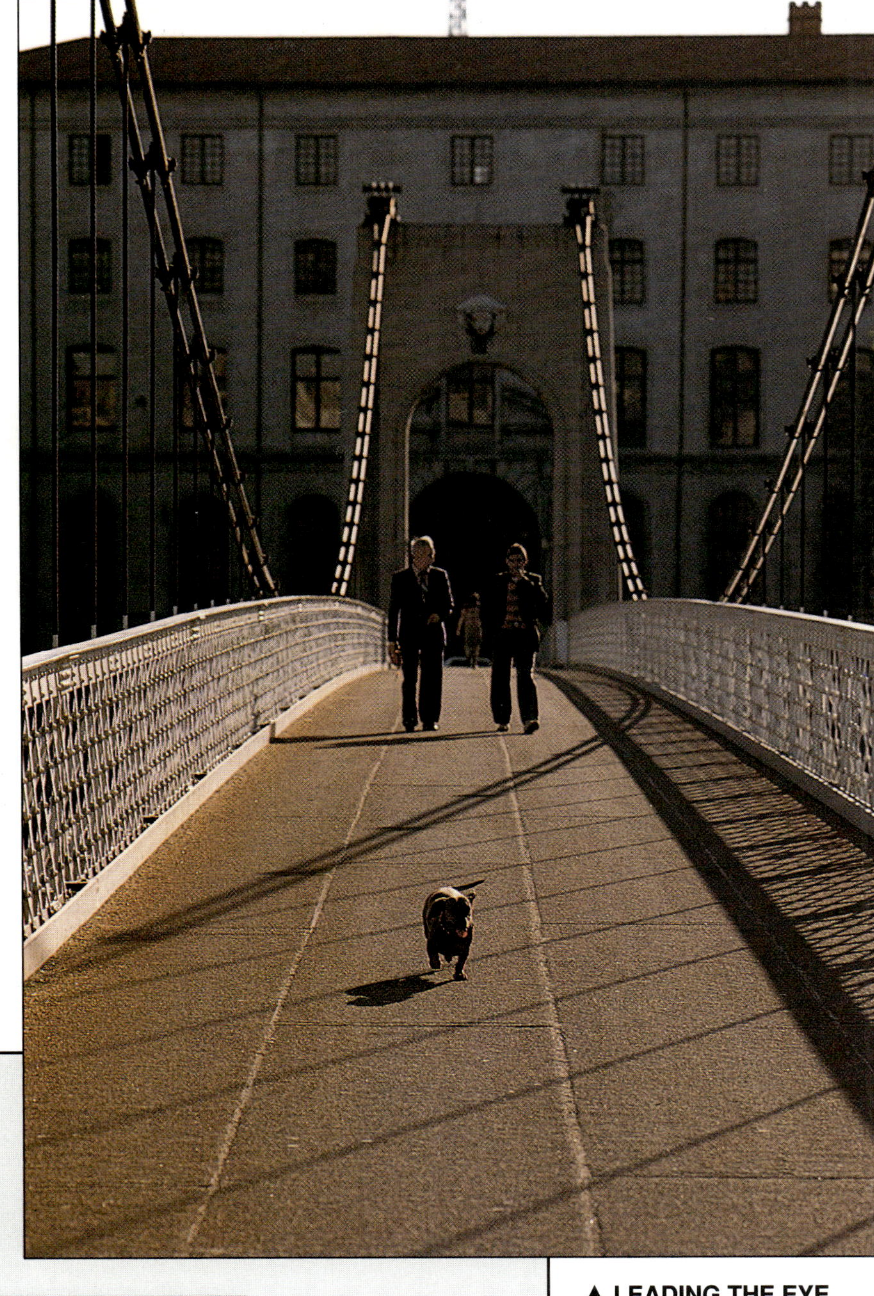

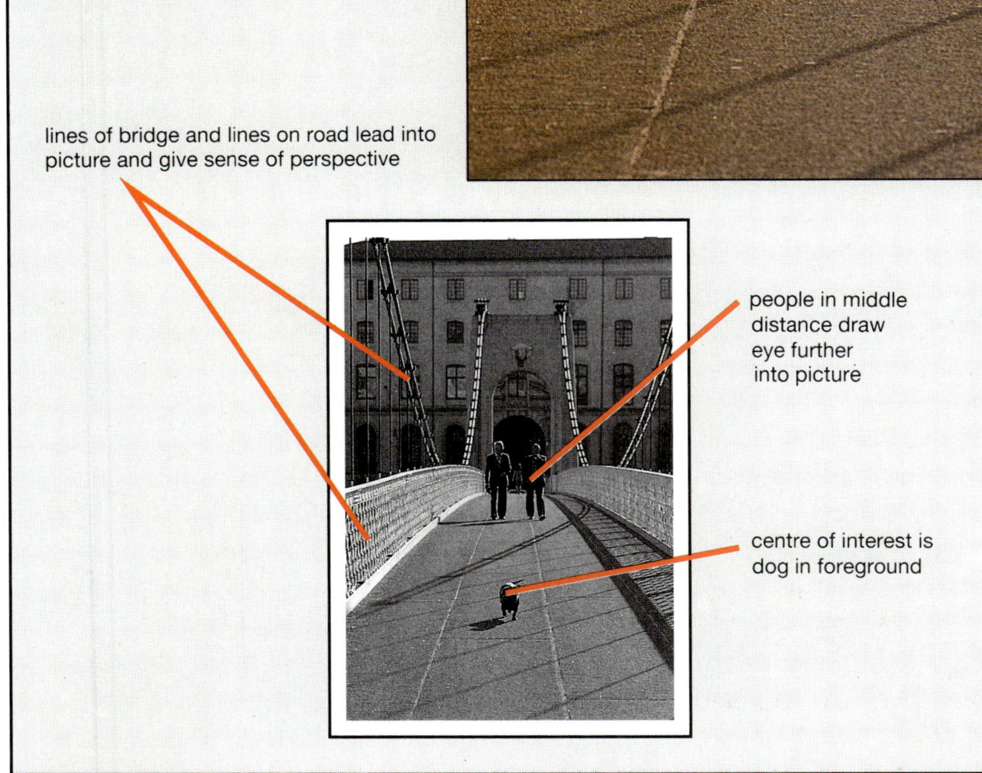

▲ **LEADING THE EYE**
In an improbable setting, the small dog catches the eye and lifts this picture out of the ordinary. The road makes the scene start at your feet and links the foreground to the rest of the picture. The bridge also draws you towards the grand house in the background.

The three zones

A photograph is a two dimensional piece of paper or film on which you usually want to capture a three dimensional subject. To do this it helps to think of the picture in the viewfinder as a theatre set with three zones or planes - a foreground, a middle distance and a background.

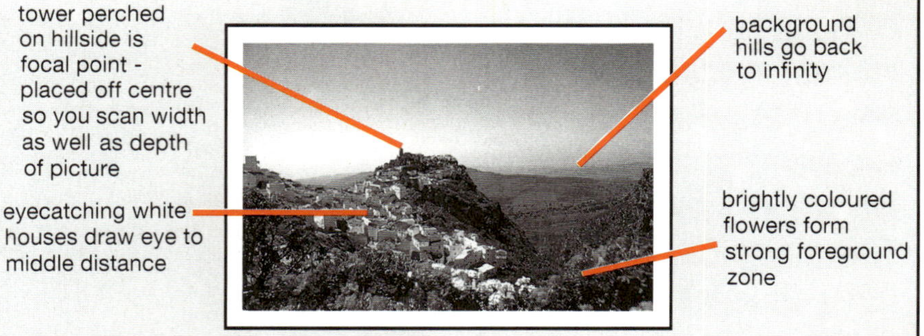

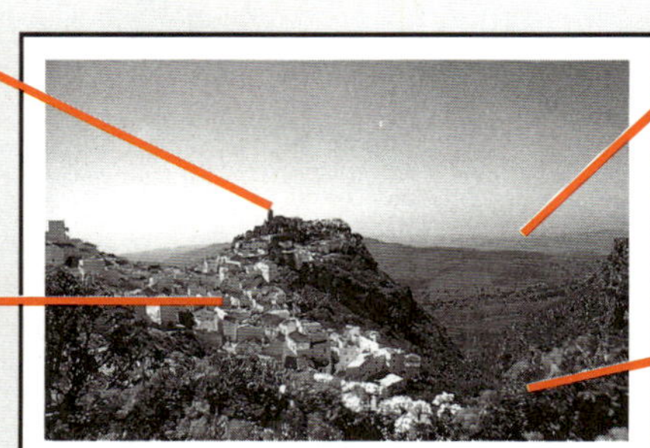

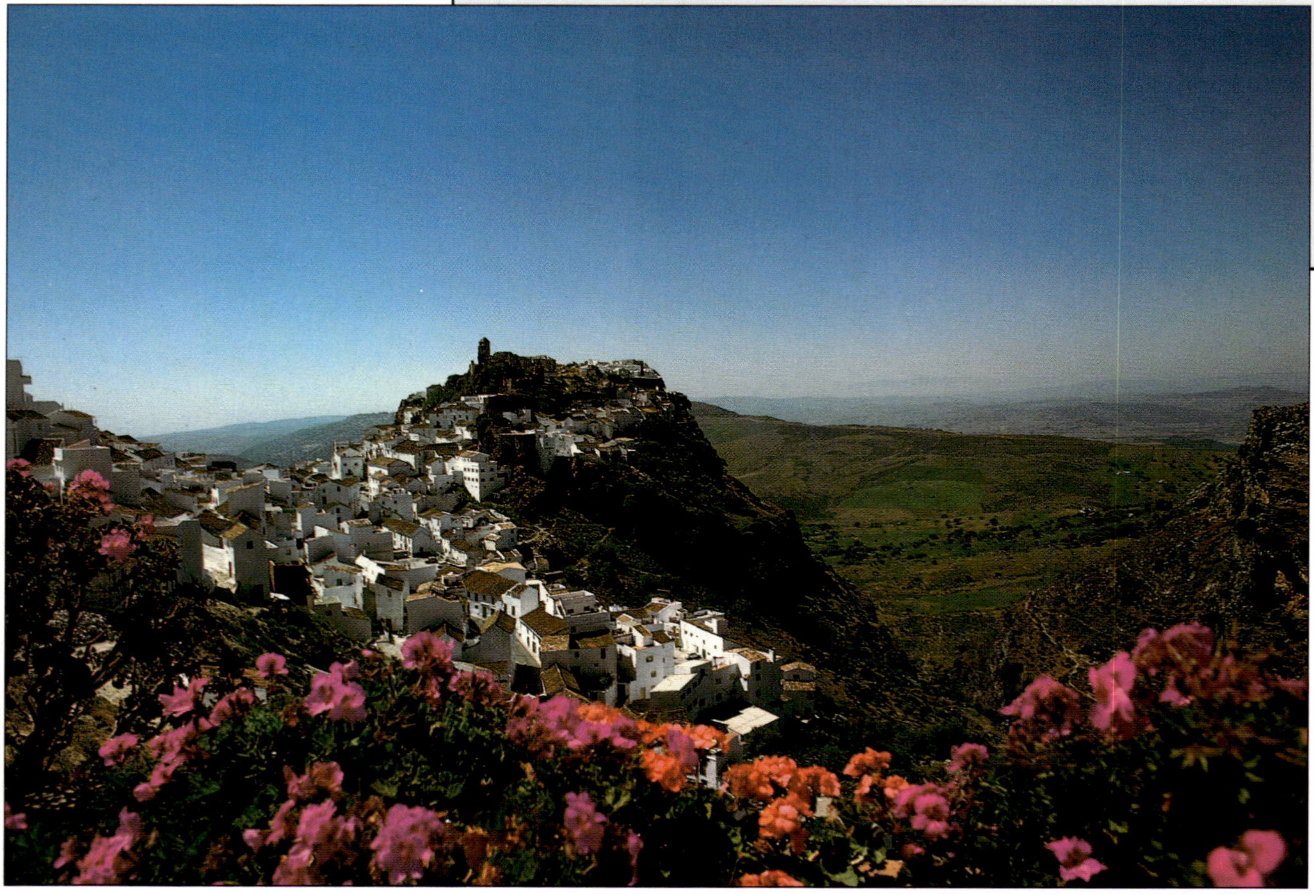

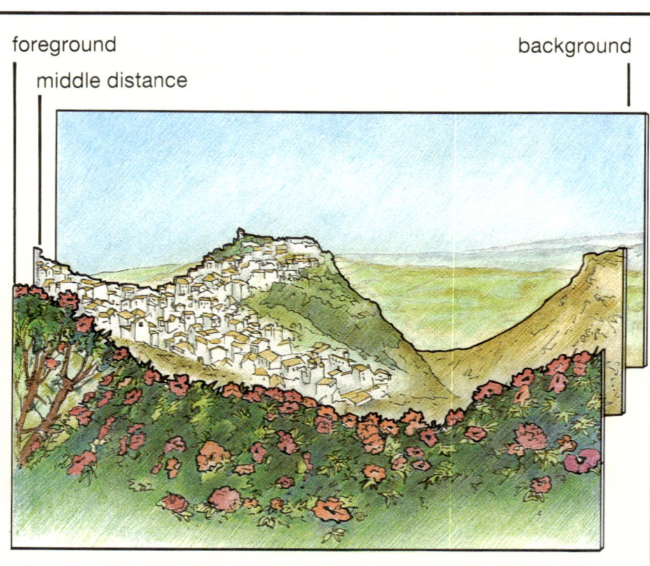

▲ A SENSE OF DEPTH
Striking contrast between foreground, middle distance and background zones makes this a powerful picture. Through a dip in the flowers and a break in the hills in the middle distance, the eye glimpses acres of pasture stretching into the horizon.

Stage effect

For a three dimensional image, think of the zones of a picture as a theatre backdrop - behind each setting a different scene is revealed.

Layering a picture like this is particularly effective in a deep landscape. But you can still include interest in each of the three zones in a more shallow picture, whatever the subject matter - the 'backdrops' are just closer together.

Make sure that each zone has some interesting element to entice you into the picture. By drawing the eye from one zone to the next behind it the photo has a sense of depth.

Think how you can use viewpoint to help you create a three dimensional photo. Choose a viewpoint that gives a clear foreground, middle distance and background as this makes the eye travel over the picture, giving a feeling of space. It may also be effective to include a foreground object that makes the picture start at your feet.

With landscape or townscape shots a line that leads the eye from one zone to the next - for example, a winding path or wall - links the picture zones together.

Placing the subject

The subject can be sited in any of the three zones, but it is usually most effective in the foreground or middle distance.

Rather than a main subject, landscape shots often have a focal point - a small but distinct object such as a white house in green fields - that draws the eye. If you study various landscape pictures you may find the focal point in any of the three zones - foreground, middle distance or background.

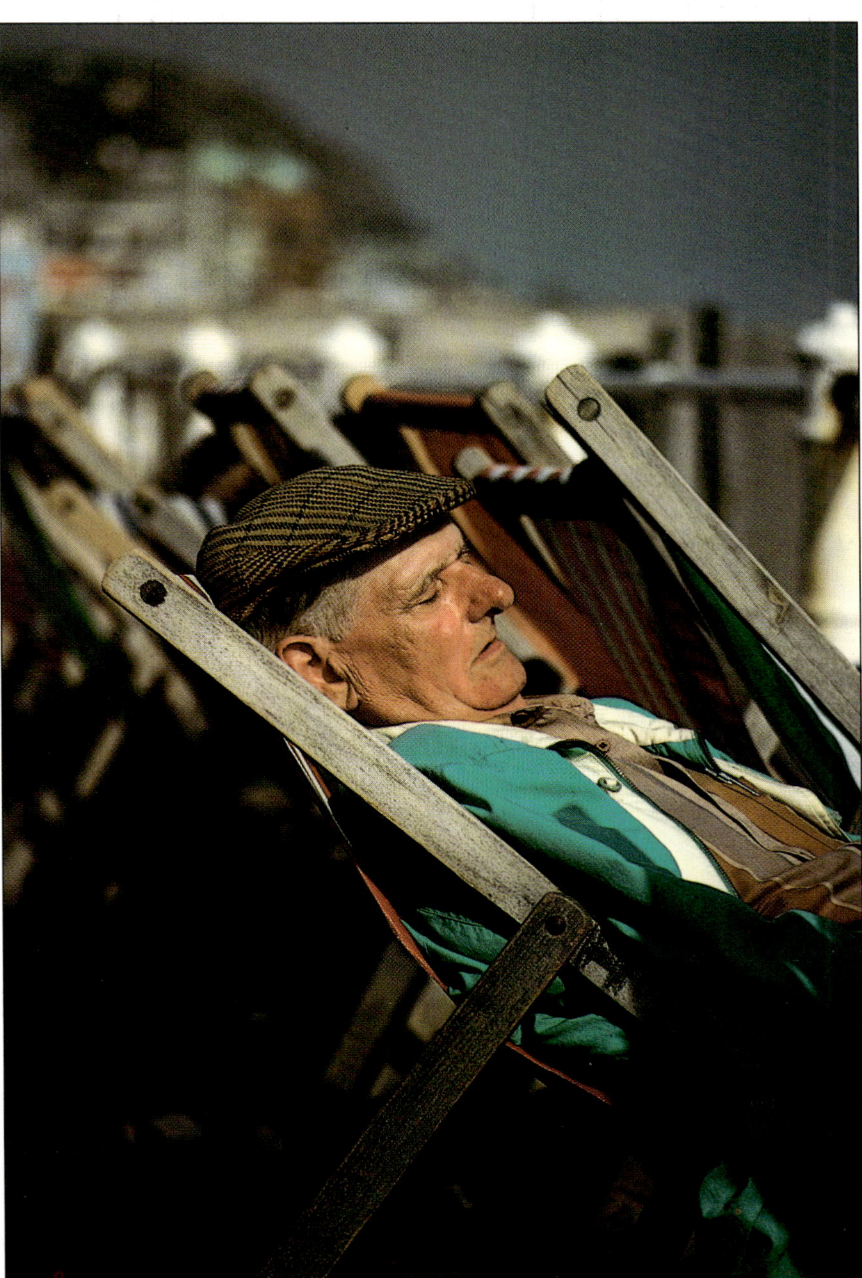

▲ **FOCUSING FOR DEPTH**
The subject is the pin sharp close-up of a man dozing on a beach. He exists firmly in the foreground of his setting of a row of deck chairs, from where the eye moves on to lose itself in a blurred background where objects become unrecognizable.

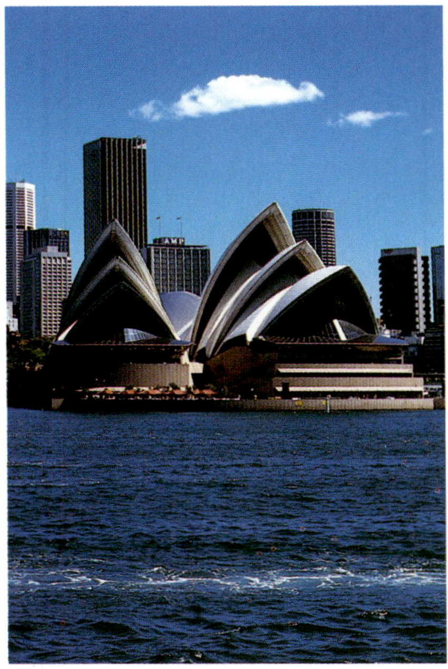

▲ **A TWO ZONE IMAGE**
Without any boats the picture has no middle distance interest and the eye skims over this zone - there's only foreground and background. The image is a bit flat and boring.

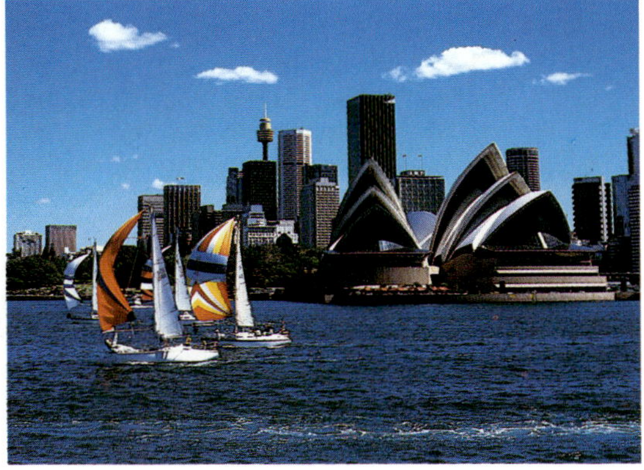

▲ **MIDDLE DISTANCE INTEREST**
The boats in the middle distance add an enlivening ingredient to this picture by giving it a third zone. Their colourful sails attract the eye, which then travels to the background buildings.

Decorative impact

You may not always want to give a sense of depth. Sometimes you may choose to create a deliberately flat image, so that the emphasis is on shape, colour or abstract pattern.

This works well with the right subject matter - for example, a close-up of architectural or natural detail. A beach shot with horizontal bands of sand, sea and sky can also be effective, provided a subject such as a person acts as a strong centre of interest.

▶ BOLD COLOUR AND SHAPE
Here the photographer chooses to give up a sense of depth by throwing the middle distance and background out of focus so as to emphasize the colour and shape of the girl and umbrella in the foreground. The whole image - with the sea and sky now flat ribbons of colour - has great decorative impact.

▼ FLAT PATTERN
A telephoto lens flattens the picture surface so that colour and pattern fill all three zones. The low 'on the level' viewpoint loses the skyline, emphasizing how shallow the picture is, and takes in the bright fishing ropes in the foreground.

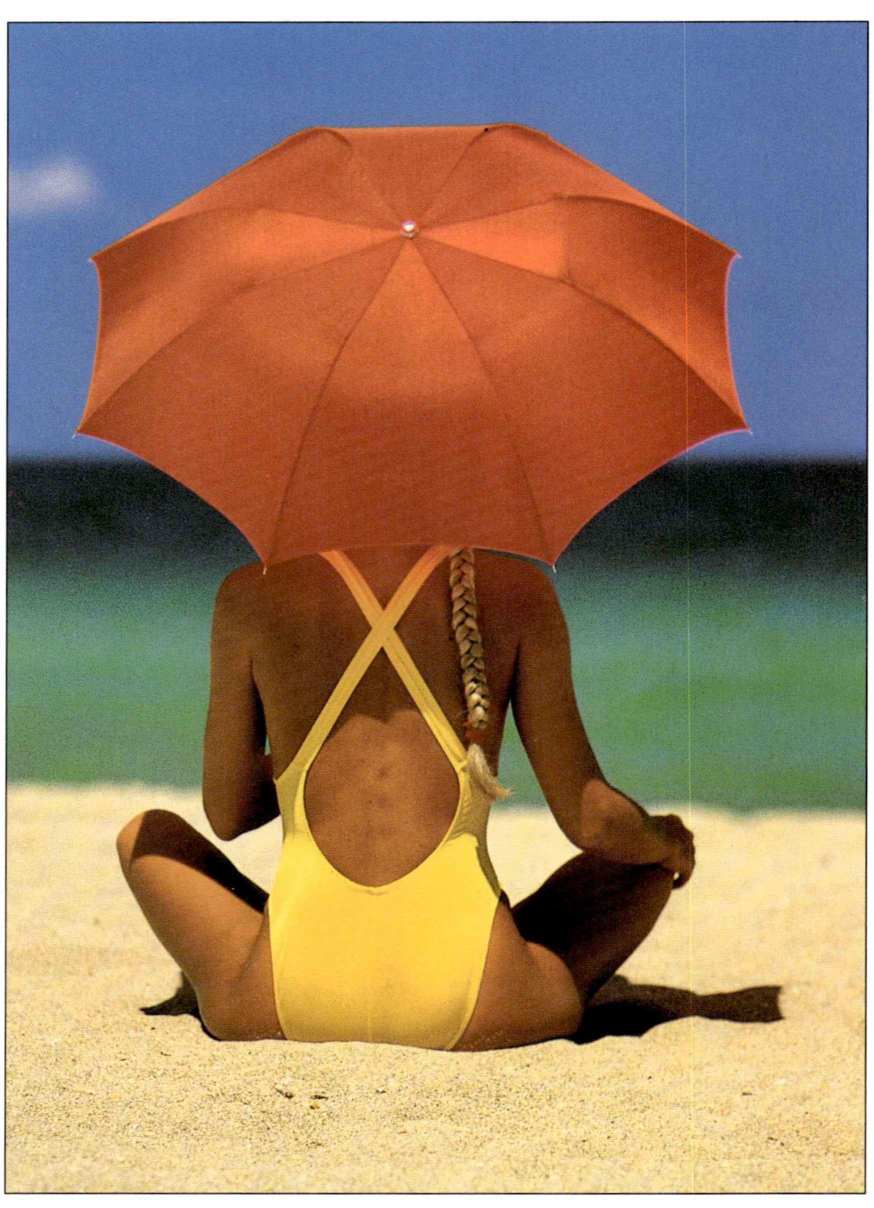

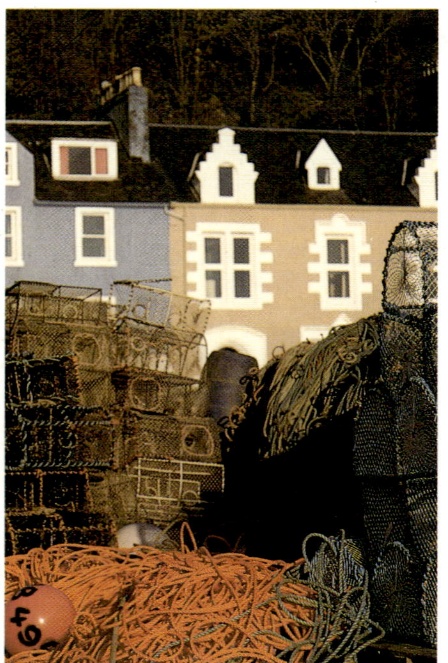

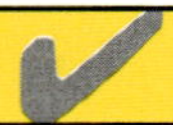

Remember what can make a successful picture:

Subject What is interesting about it: mood, shape, colour, context? Look at it from different angles, try standing further back and moving in closer. Keep in mind top photographer Eamonn McCabe's advice: 'I don't think that equipment makes or breaks a picture. It's the eye that sees it and takes it.'
Think about where to position the subject:
❑ in the centre.
❑ slightly off centre.
❑ roughly on a third.
❑ somewhere else.
Format Try both formats and decide which works best:
❑ for the subject.
❑ for the foreground.
❑ for the background.
Foreground and background
Having placed the subject where and how you want it, double check:
❑ What's going on in the foreground, middle distance and background?
❑ Is the picture interesting in all three zones?
❑ Are there any problems to deal with?
Finally, remind yourself what it was about the subject you want to convey in the photograph - serenity, balance or excitement?
Do you want to create particular emphasis in one area?
   With experience, these thoughts and decisions flash through your mind automatically, in a twinkling!

Linear perspective

When parallel lines appear to converge as they recede into the distance, a strong impression of depth is created. This is known as linear perspective, and you can use it in your pictures to draw the viewer's eye into a scene.

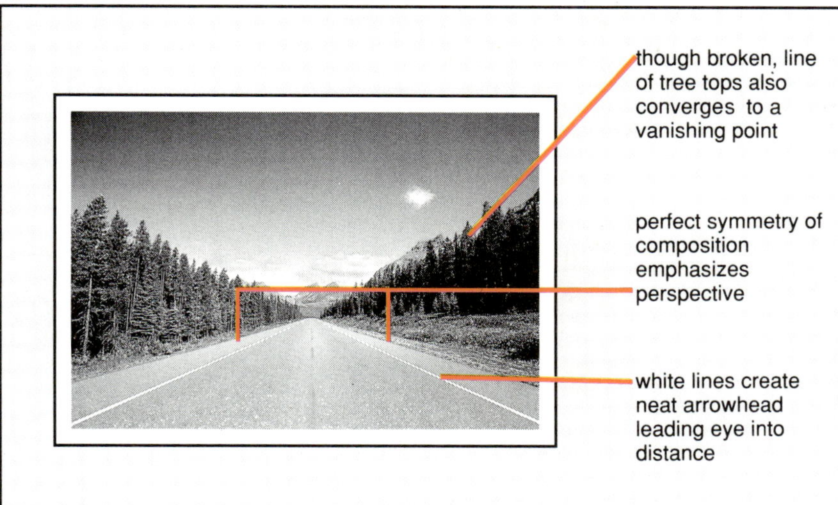

If you look down a railway track the rails seem to get closer and closer together until, at a considerable distance, they appear to touch. The sleepers also seem to get smaller and closer together the further away they are.

Experience has taught you that this is an illusion (called linear perspective) – both the rails and sleepers are really the same distance apart all along the track. But you interpret it as depth.

A railway line is an obvious example, but take a look around – linear perspective is everywhere. Think of roads, furrows in a field, a tree-lined avenue, rivers and canals, the white trail left by a moving ship – the opportunities for conveying depth are endless.

▼ **THE ROAD TO SOMEWHERE**
The sharply converging lines of the road and trees combine to give this image a tremendous feeling of depth.

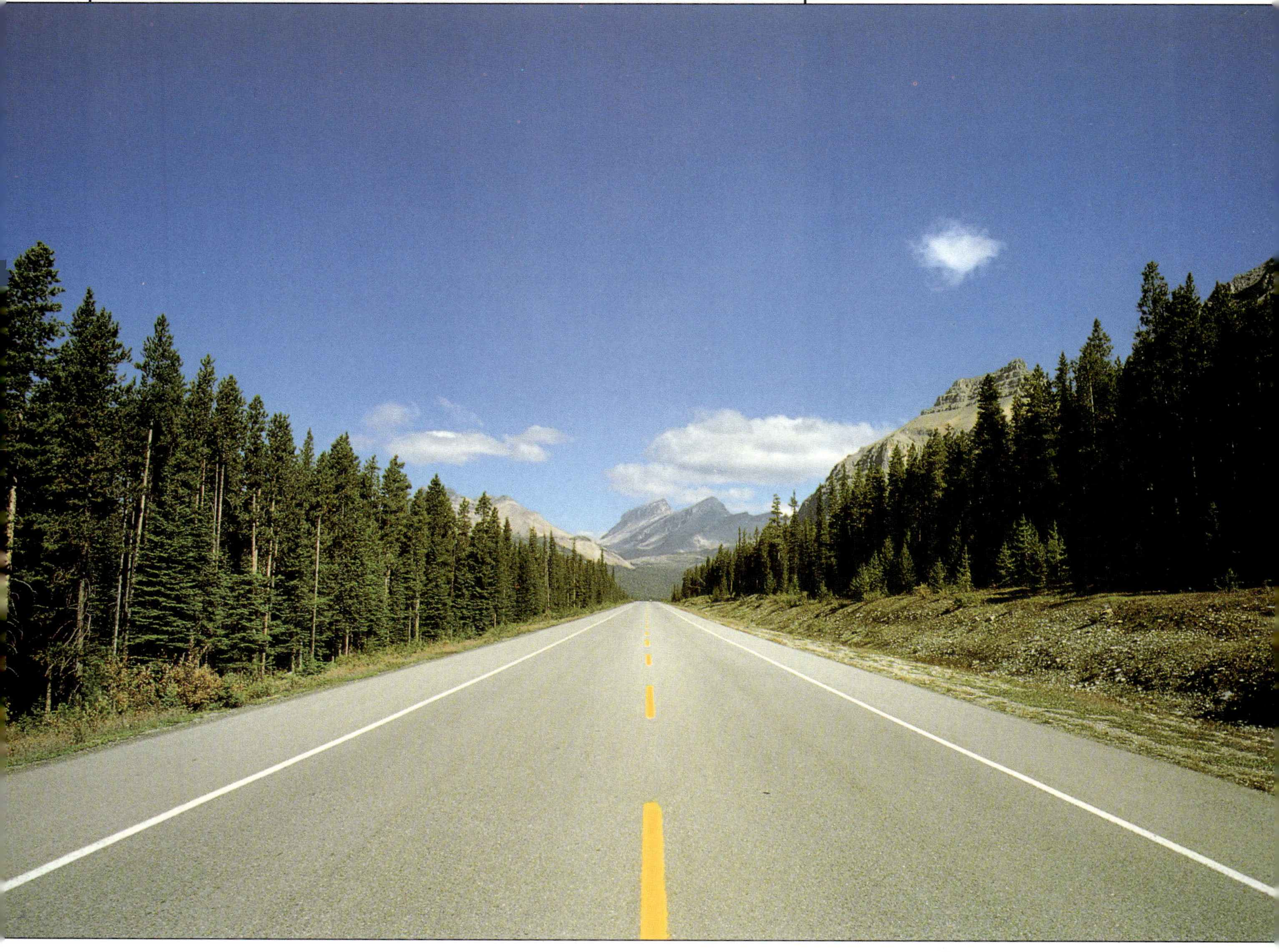

Vanishing points

Looking down the middle of a road, you notice that the parallel edges of the road seem to converge at a point on the horizon. This is known as the vanishing point – an essential element of perspective.

A vanishing point may appear inside the frame of a photo, but more often than not it falls at an imaginary position outside the picture.

For example, if you take a shot of a building you would have to leave a great deal of space around it in the frame for the vanishing points to be included.

Vanishing points add to the three dimensional effect in a photo. The more vanishing points you include, the stronger the effect. If you have three vanishing points in a photo the sense of depth is very powerful.

You can create two or more vanishing points by including surfaces that meet at right angles. For example, if you photograph a house head on, the image looks two dimensional. But, if you position yourself so that two walls of the building can be seen at right angles to the camera, two vanishing points are suggested – one from each wall.

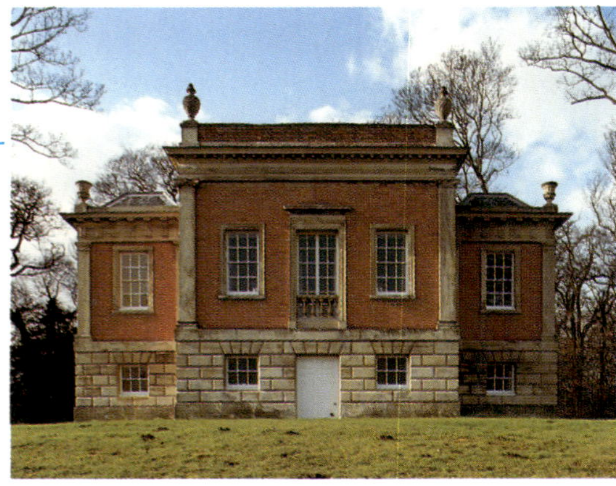

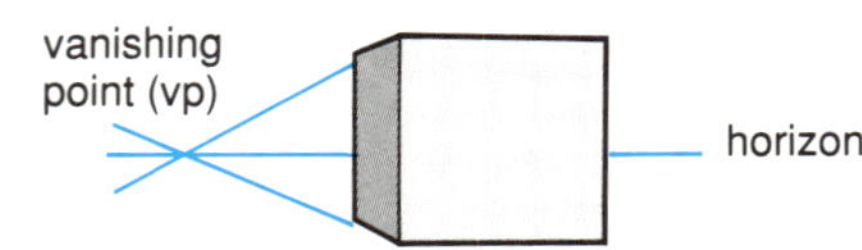

NO PERSPECTIVE
Photographing a building head on so that only one surface is visible produces a flat, two dimensional image because there are no converging lines involved in the shot.

ONE POINT PERSPECTIVE
Face on, but standing to one side of a building, the lines forming the top and bottom edges of the side wall seem to get closer together the further away they are. If you extend these lines they converge and meet on the horizon – called a vanishing point.

TWO POINT PERSPECTIVE
When facing the corner of the building the same rule applies. The lines forming the top and bottom edges of both sides converge and meet, but at two vanishing points, not one.

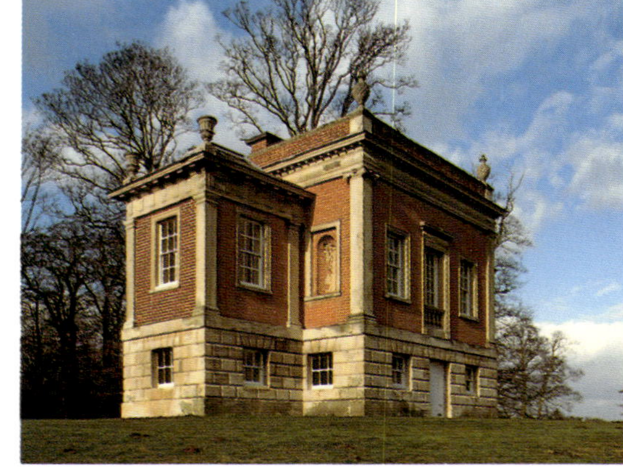

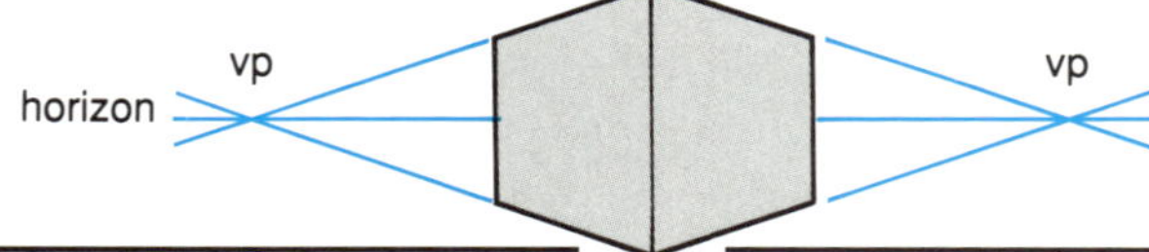

THREE POINT PERSPECTIVE
If you view a building from a low viewpoint you imagine that the vertical lines of the building converge too. This is three point perspective and reveals the greatest sense of depth.

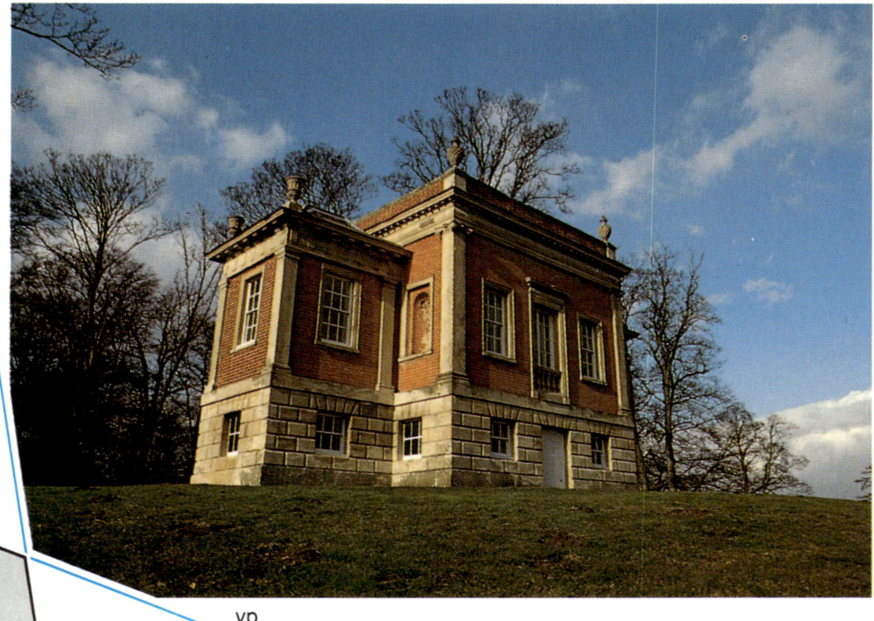

Emphasizing perspective

Your viewpoint and choice of lens are very important for increasing the effect of linear perspective. The steeper the angle of the converging lines in an image, the greater the 3-D effect.

For example, if you take a photo looking down a tree-lined avenue from a close viewpoint, the parallel lines of the trees converge sharply.

By using a wide angle lens you can include more of the foreground too. This exaggerates the difference in size between the nearest and furthest trees, giving a greater impression of depth.

If you opt for a distant viewpoint and a telephoto lens you get the opposite effect. The image is foreshortened and the trees hardly seem to converge at all.

Lead-in lines

A lead-in line is a useful compositional device for directing the viewer's eye from the front of the image toward the main interest. You can use a fence, track, hedge, footprints or even the curve of a hill to draw the eye into a photo-graph and increase the sense of distance.

Place your subject, such as a friend, pet or landmark, in the middle or background of your scene. Then try shooting the image both with and without a lead-in line (the line can come from the bottom, side or top of your frame) and see the difference for yourself.

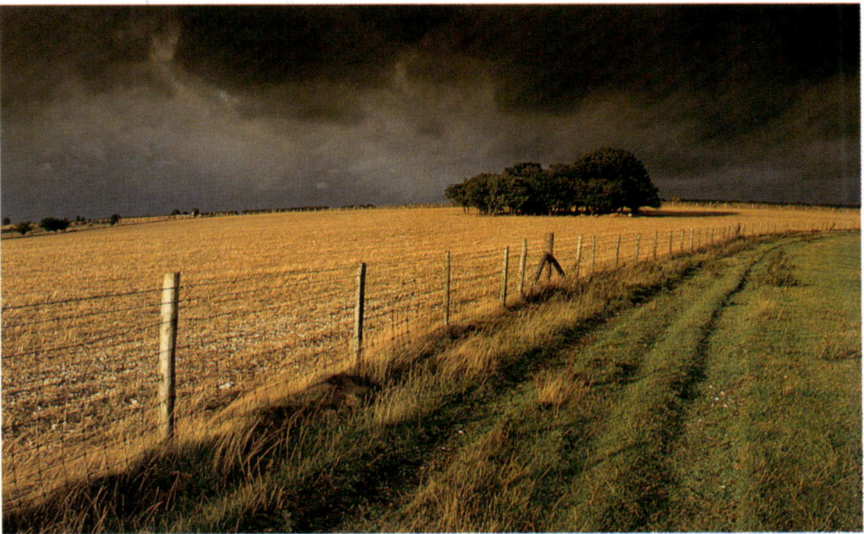

▲ FOLLOW THE LEADER
The fence leads your eye from the front of the picture to the clump of trees and stormy sky beyond. It also forms a boundary between the colours.

▼ LINEAR MANIA
There are so many converging lines in this image that the overall effect is almost overpowering. By using a fisheye lens, the photographer has made the diagonal lines of the carriages seem even steeper.

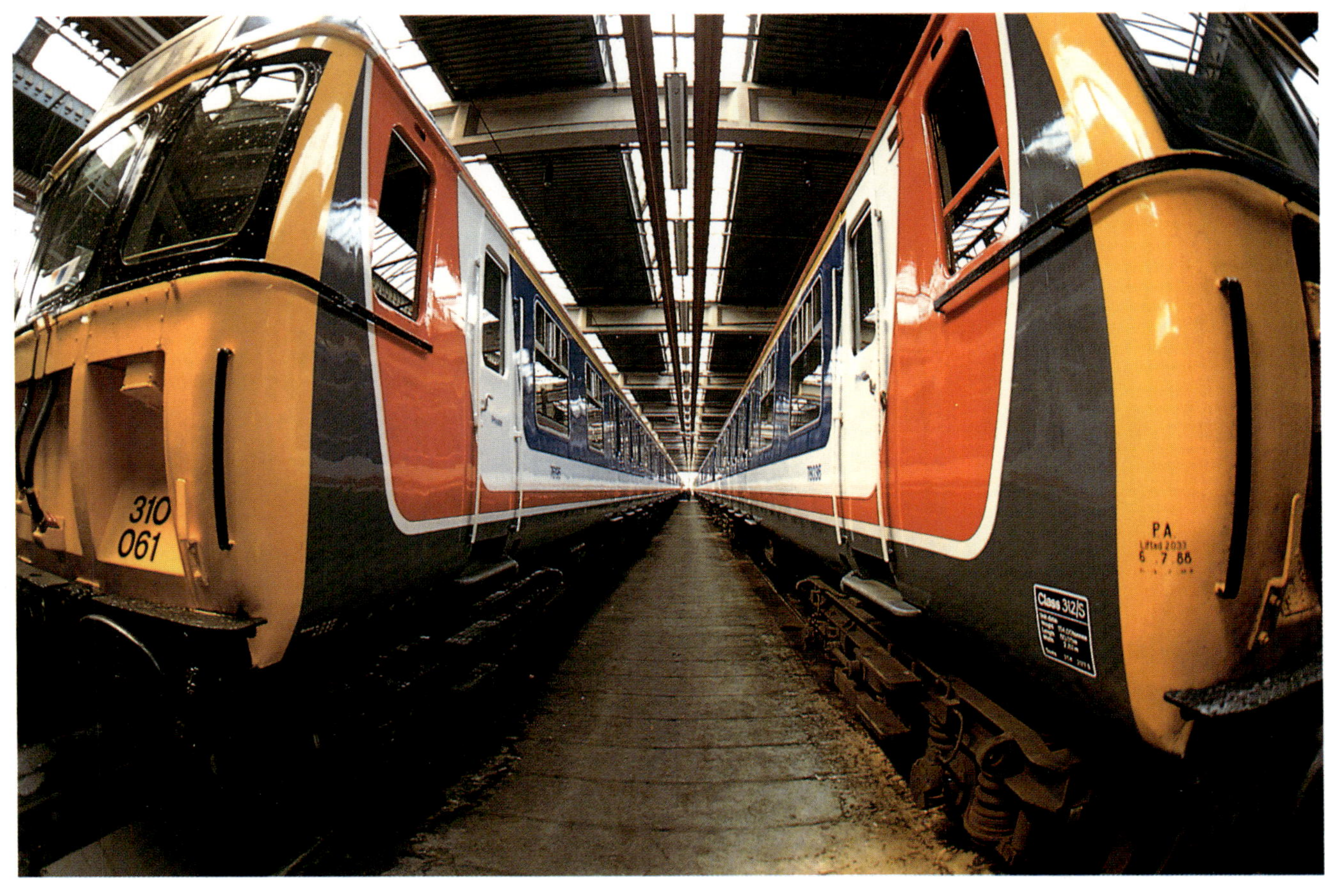

Converging verticals

When the back of your camera is square on to the subject, the vertical lines in the image are reproduced accurately. However, when you photograph a tall building from ground level you usually have to tilt the camera backwards to include the top of it.

This makes the sides of the building appear to converge toward a distant vanishing point, and the structure looks as if it's falling backwards.

The same optical effect occurs when you look up at a building, except that your brain adjusts the image so that you see the lines as being parallel again. This means that you are not aware of converging verticals until your photographs are printed.

Converging verticals can make you feel dizzy, and you can exploit this to produce dramatic photographs. If, however, you want to correct the effect, stand as far back from your subject as you can and use a telephoto lens. This helps you to include the top of the building without tilting the camera.

If this is not possible you could use a perspective control lens (shift lens). It works by moving the whole lens fractionally upwards on its mount while keeping it at right angles to the film. Unfortunately, such lenses are expensive, so you're probably better off moving your feet!

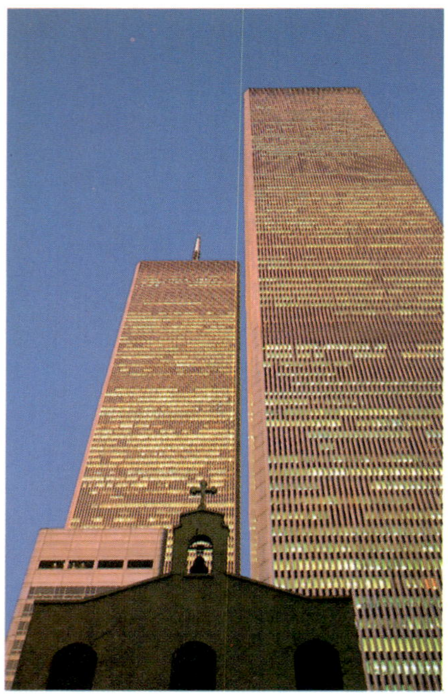

▲ **DIZZY HEIGHTS**
By tilting the camera upwards, the photographer has made the skyscrapers look as if they are falling backwards, creating a dramatic, giddy effect.

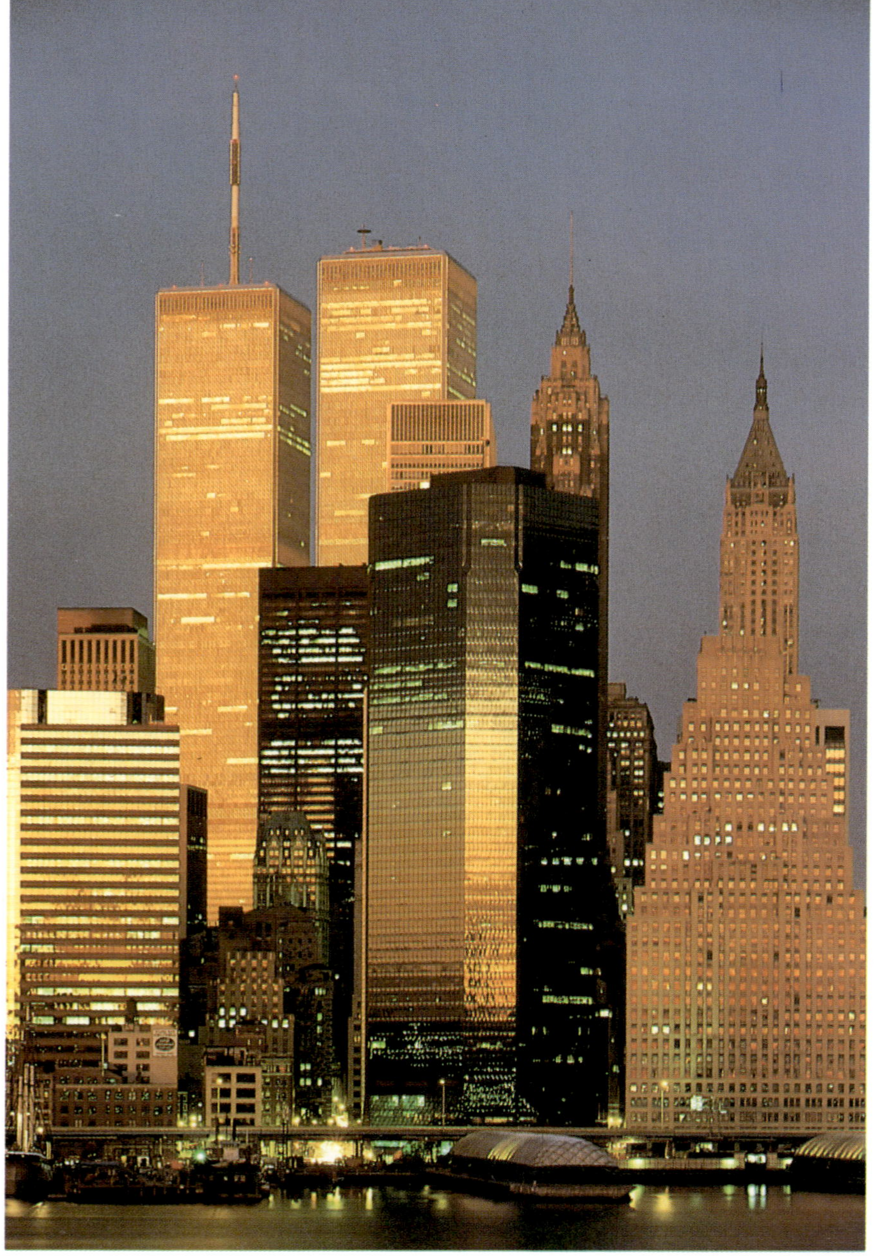

◄ **MANHATTAN SKYLINE**
A more distant viewpoint allows you to include the whole of a building and record the parallel sides of structures accurately. If you don't want converging verticals when you shoot architecture, the answer is to move far enough away so that you keep the camera straight.

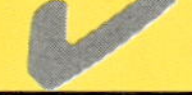

CHECK IT!

You can create an illusion of depth by using:

❏ linear perspective
❏ lead-in lines
❏ a close viewpoint
❏ a wide angle lens
❏ one or more vanishing points
❏ converging verticals

Creating depth

When confronted with the problem of how to convey depth in a photograph, many people immediately think of linear perspective. Although this is a useful device, there are several other effective ways of giving a picture depth.

There are times when two dimensional photographs look stunning because of their flatness (particularly abstracts and patterns). But in most cases, pictures look more realistic when the third dimension has been added.

Take a look at some successful photos in books and magazines – landscapes, people and still lifes – and notice how each shot benefits from having a strong sense of depth. So, what can you do to give your pictures a similar 3-D effect?

Scale, overlapping forms, diminishing shapes and selective focusing are all useful devices for conveying depth. Once you have read the following pages, try taking some shots based on one or more of these elements, and see the results for yourself.

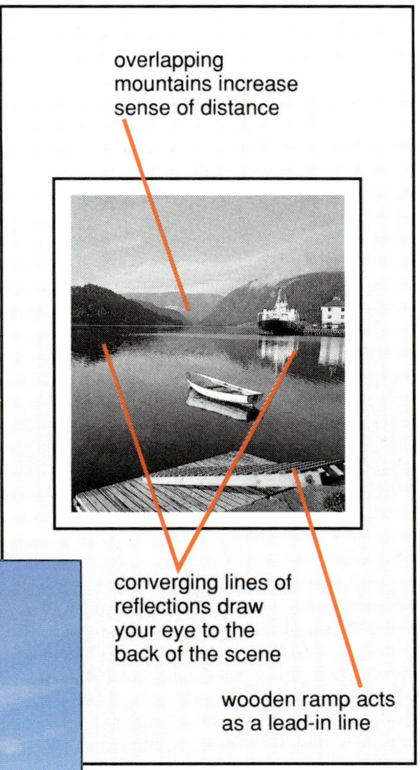

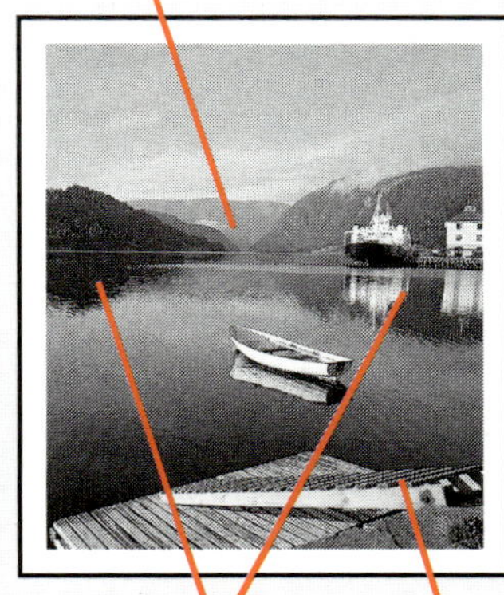

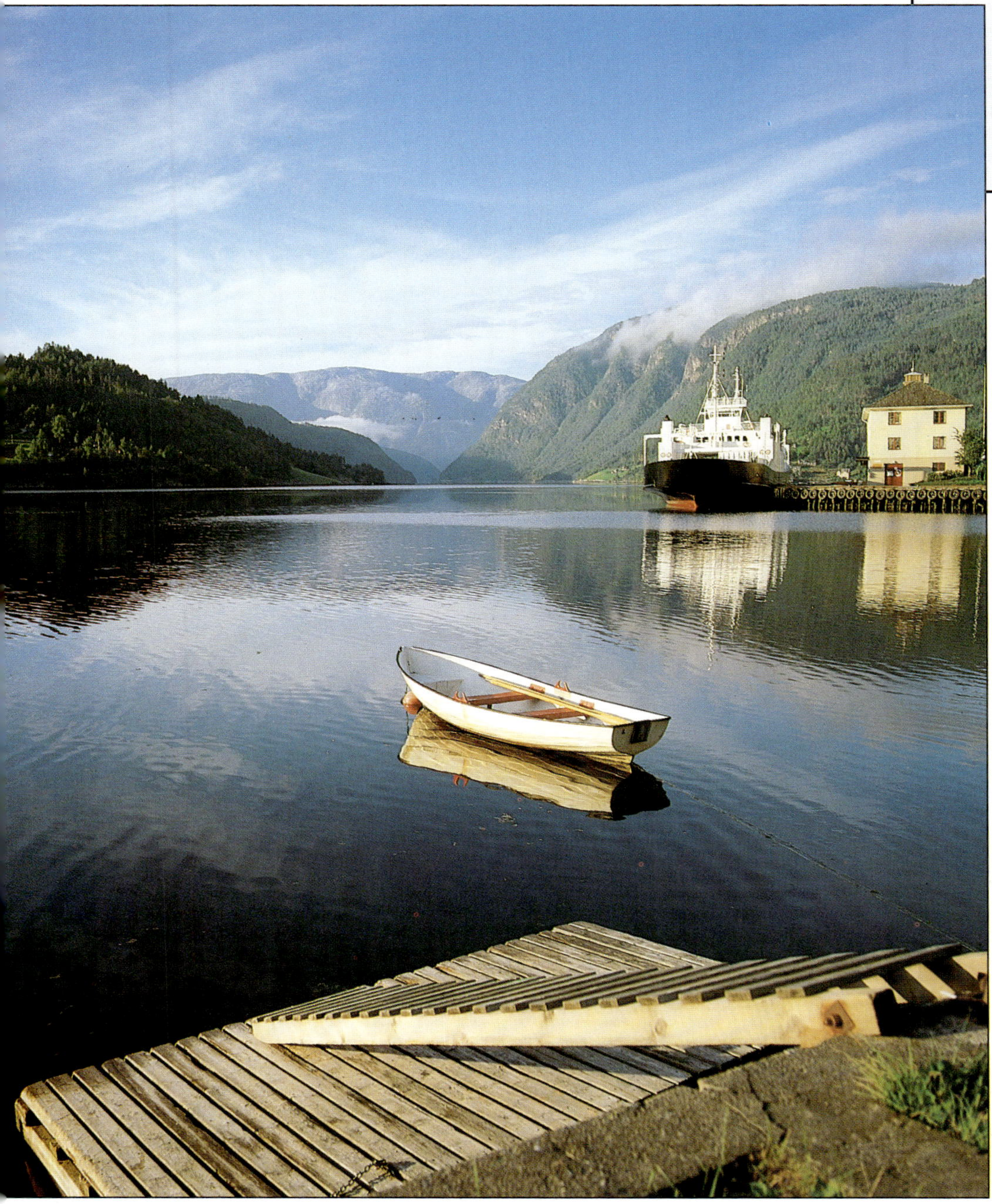

◀ **THE THREE ZONES**
One of the fundamental ways of indicating depth in a photo is to place objects of interest in the fore, mid and background. In this picture your eye is led down the wooden ramp to the rowing boat, across the fjord to the ship and house, before finally coming to rest on the mountains in the distance.

Tricks of perspective

Once you have decided that you want to create a three dimensional design rather than a two dimensional one, there are several tricks you can exploit to give an impression of depth.

Diminishing perspective
When objects further away from the camera look smaller than those near to it, the effect is known as diminishing perspective. The sense of distance is strongest when the objects are either similar-sized or are repeated in a line.

Think of a queue of people, a herd of cows, a fleet of yachts, a group of hot air balloons, a line of lamp posts or a row of beach huts – all appear to diminish in size as they recede into distance.

To emphasize the difference in size between objects, move closer and use a wide angle lens, so that the nearest object looms even larger in the frame.

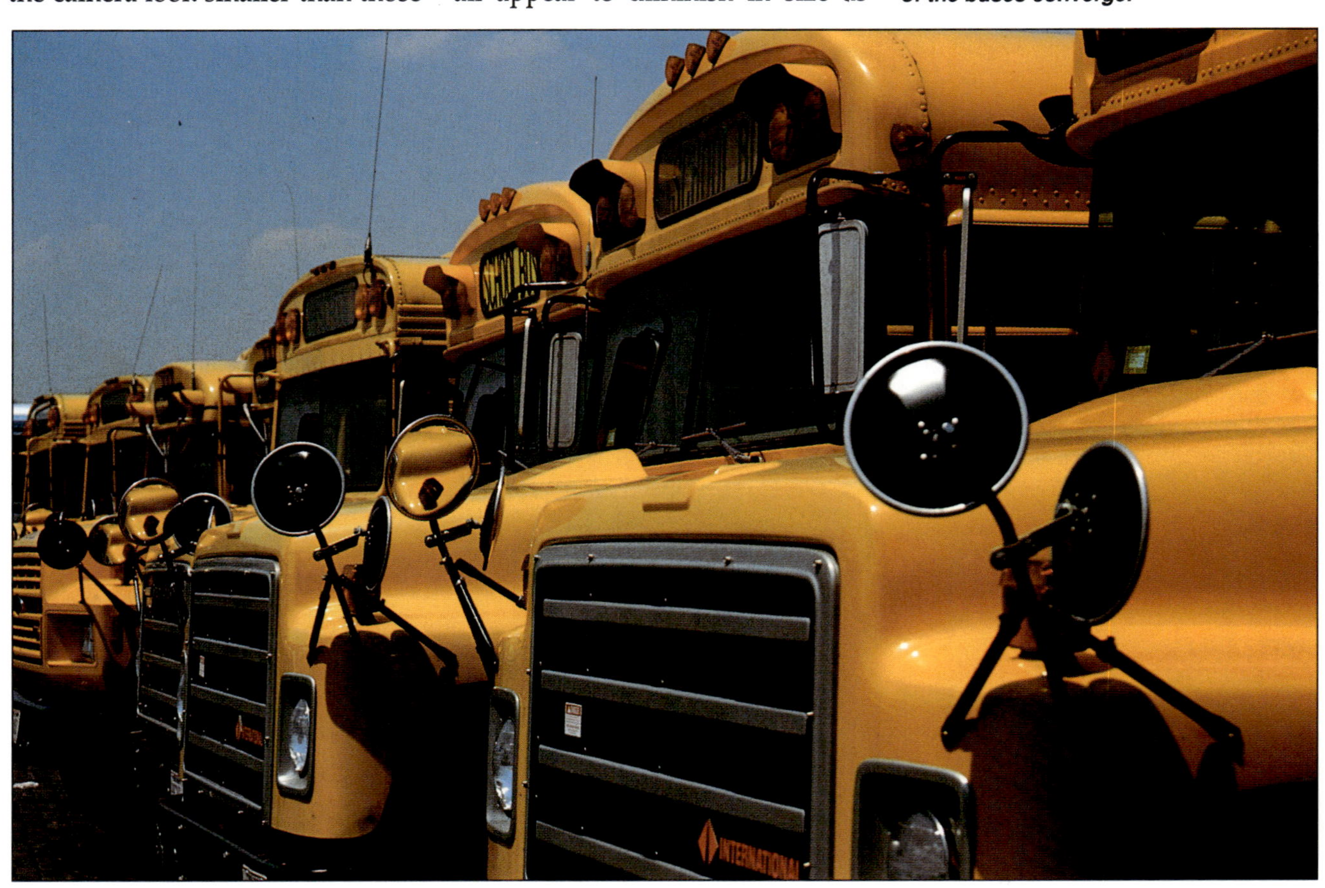

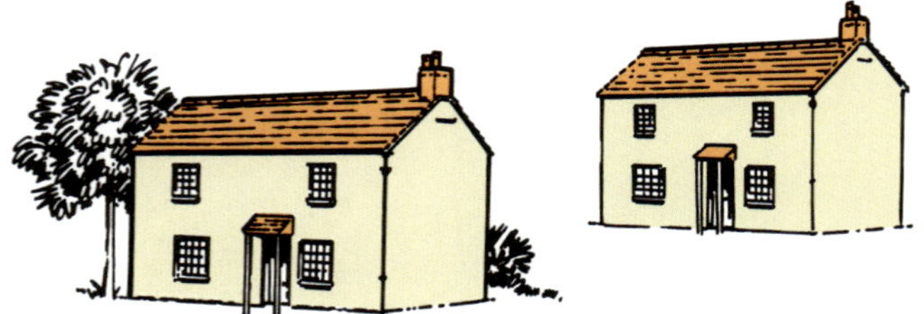

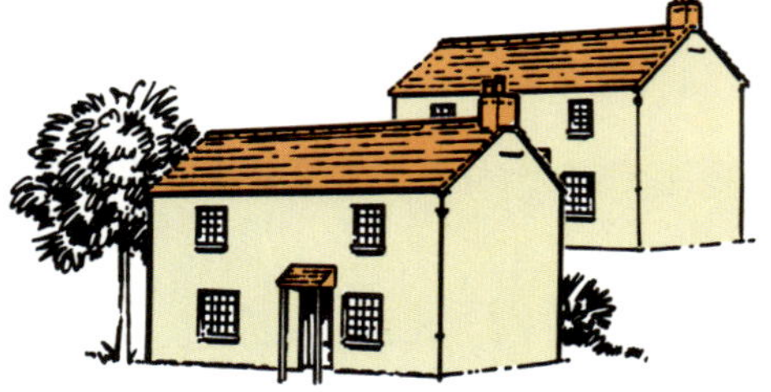

Overlapping forms
If one object in a picture partially obscures another you know that the partly hidden object is furthest away. Overlapping details in a photo provide clues to depth.

Imagine two houses positioned next to each other but on different planes (see diagram left). If you look at the two buildings so that they are apart (top picture), the sense of distance between them is minimal.

But if you change your viewpoint so that the houses overlap (bottom picture), the impression of depth is much greater. Equally, if the houses overlap too much so that one is directly behind the other, the sense of depth is lost again.

Overlapping objects are particularly useful for distant subjects where any difference in relative scale is slight.

The same is true when you are photographing objects using a telephoto lens. Because a telephoto tends to foreshorten distance, giving a flatter image, overlapping forms go some way to restoring a feeling of depth.

Selective focusing

If you look down a crowded street, the details of buildings and figures gradually become more indistinct the further away from you they are.

This reflects the limitations of human vision. If objects look blurred, your eyes persuade you that they are further away than ones that are in focus.

You can exaggerate this by using selective focusing in your photos. It is particularly good for close-up shots and subjects where the background is competing for attention.

For example, if you are taking a shot of a child in a playground and the background is too confusing, use a telephoto lens to limit your depth of field to the main subject, leaving the rest a blur.

The lack of detail in the background makes it seem to be further away than it actually is. As well as giving an illusion of depth, it helps the sharply focused subject stand out even more.

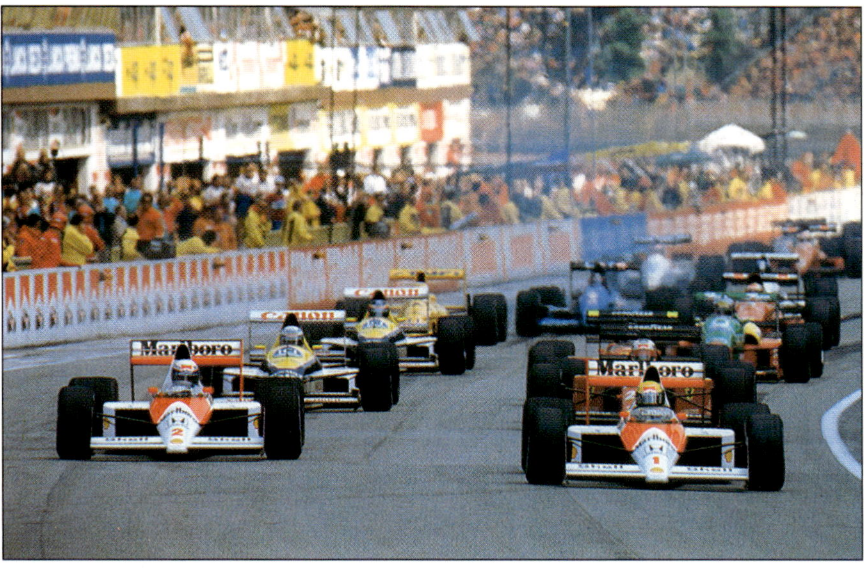

▲ OVERLAP
Overlapping and non-overlapping forms can be seen in the same picture here. On the right-hand side of the image the cars are directly behind each other, almost to a point where they cannot be seen, and there is hardly an impression of depth at all.

The cars on the left only partially obscure each other, so the feeling of distance between them is strong, even though a telephoto lens has been used.

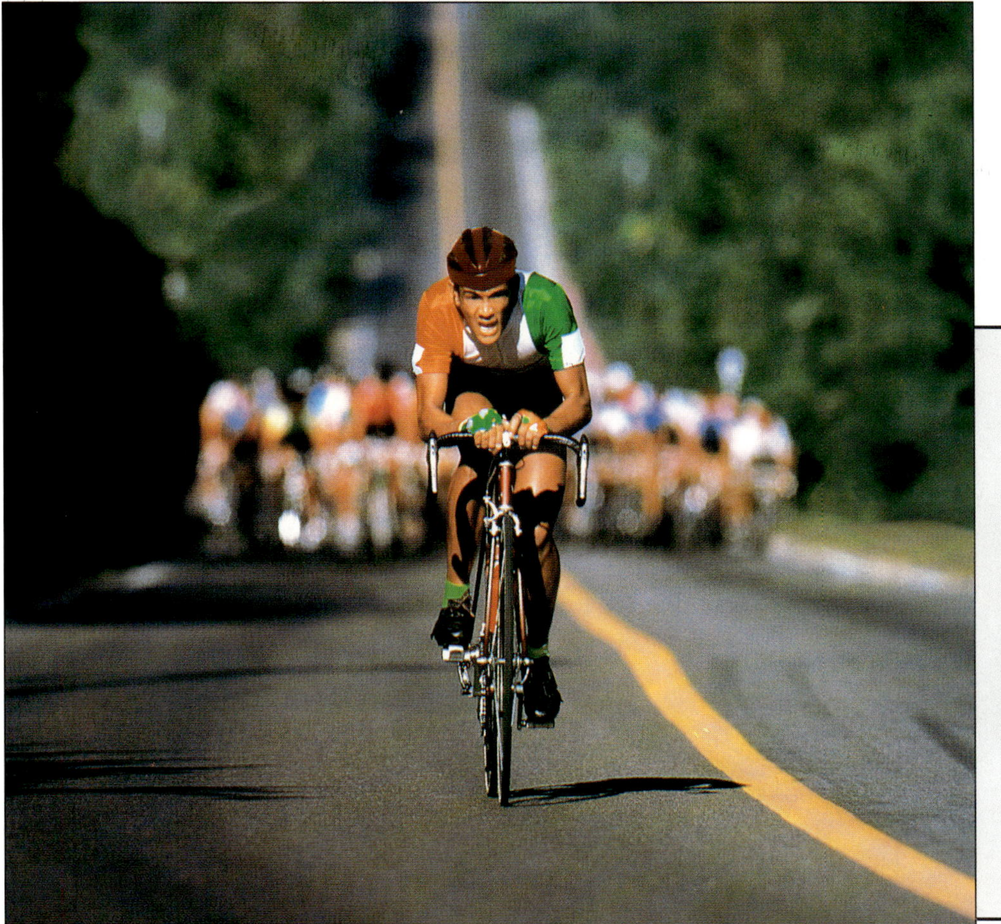

◀ LEADER OF THE PACK
With the pack thrown out of focus, the distance between it and the leading cyclist is exaggerated. The impression of depth is increased further by the yellow lead-in line drawing your eye into the picture.

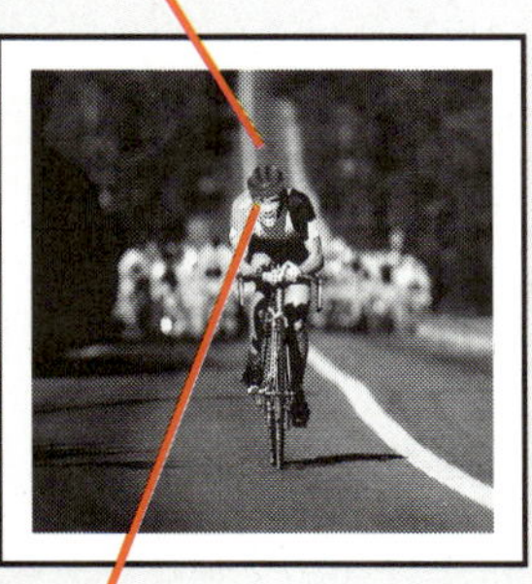

sense of depth increased by including stretch of road behind the pack

harsh sunlight brings out detail in cyclist, helping him to stand out from the blurred cyclists even more

Indicating scale

Relative scale and depth work best when the objects being compared have known sizes – obvious examples are people, cars or famous landmarks.

Imagine a scene where one person is standing in the foreground and another can be seen in the distance. Study the size of the two people. You know that if they were placed next to each other they would be about the same size. So the fact that one person is much smaller than the other immediately gives a strong impression of depth and scale.

▼ A SENSE OF SCALE
The cliffs in the background are belittled when you compare them to the lifebelt in the foreground. You know that the cliffs must be quite far away from you to look so small.

Mind games

Adelbert Ames, an American painter, devised a prop to show how your memory is conditioned to jump to conclusions when judging the relative size and scale of objects. This illusion is known as the Ames room and it consists of two men standing in an empty room, one in either of the far corners. The room seems normal, and yet one man appears to be twice the size of the other.

Even though you know that the two people in the picture must be of similar height, your brain is happier to accept what it sees, rather than imagine it is being tricked in any way (in fact, the rear wall has a sloping ceiling.)

However, you don't have to construct a whole room to create trick shots of your own. Take a look at the set up below right – the

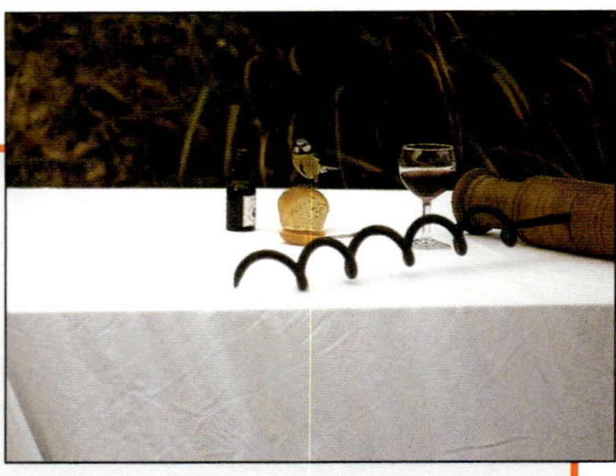

corkscrew seems to be twice the size of the loaf, wine bottle and wineglass. How can this be?

If you look at the top picture when the props are together you realize it is an optical illusion. The loaf and wine bottle are miniatures and the corkscrew is twice the size of a conventional one. Hunt around for your own miniature and oversized objects and see if you can create a similar effect to fool your viewers.

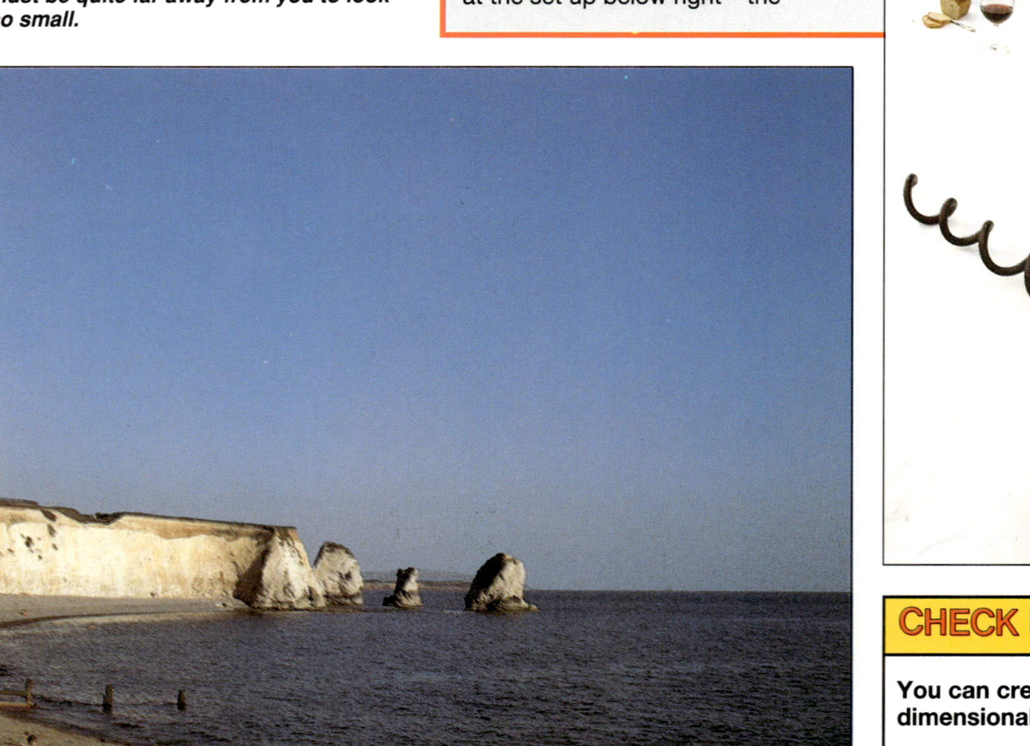

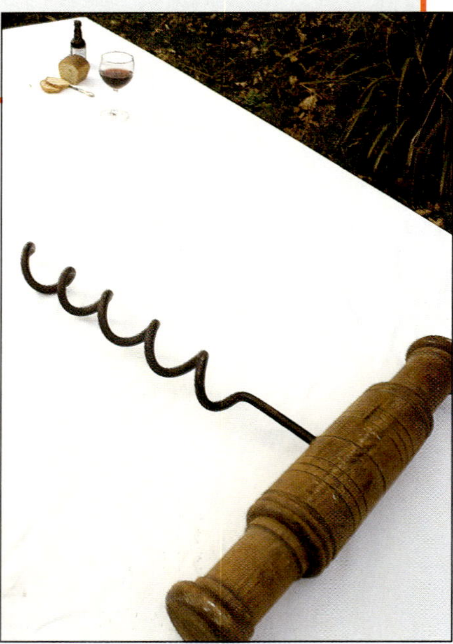

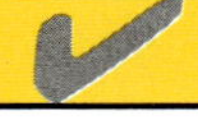

You can create a three dimensional effect by:

❏ **composing an image** so that there is interest in the fore, mid and background
❏ **diminishing perspective** – shapes appearing to get smaller as they recede into the distance
❏ **overlapping objects** – partially obscured shapes indicate distance
❏ **selective focusing** – out of focus background looks further away than it really is
❏ **scale** – known-sized objects in fore and background

Aerial perspective

Objects in the far distance appear hazier and lighter in tone than the same things viewed close to. This phenomenon is called aerial perspective, and by including it in your photos you immediately create a sense of depth.

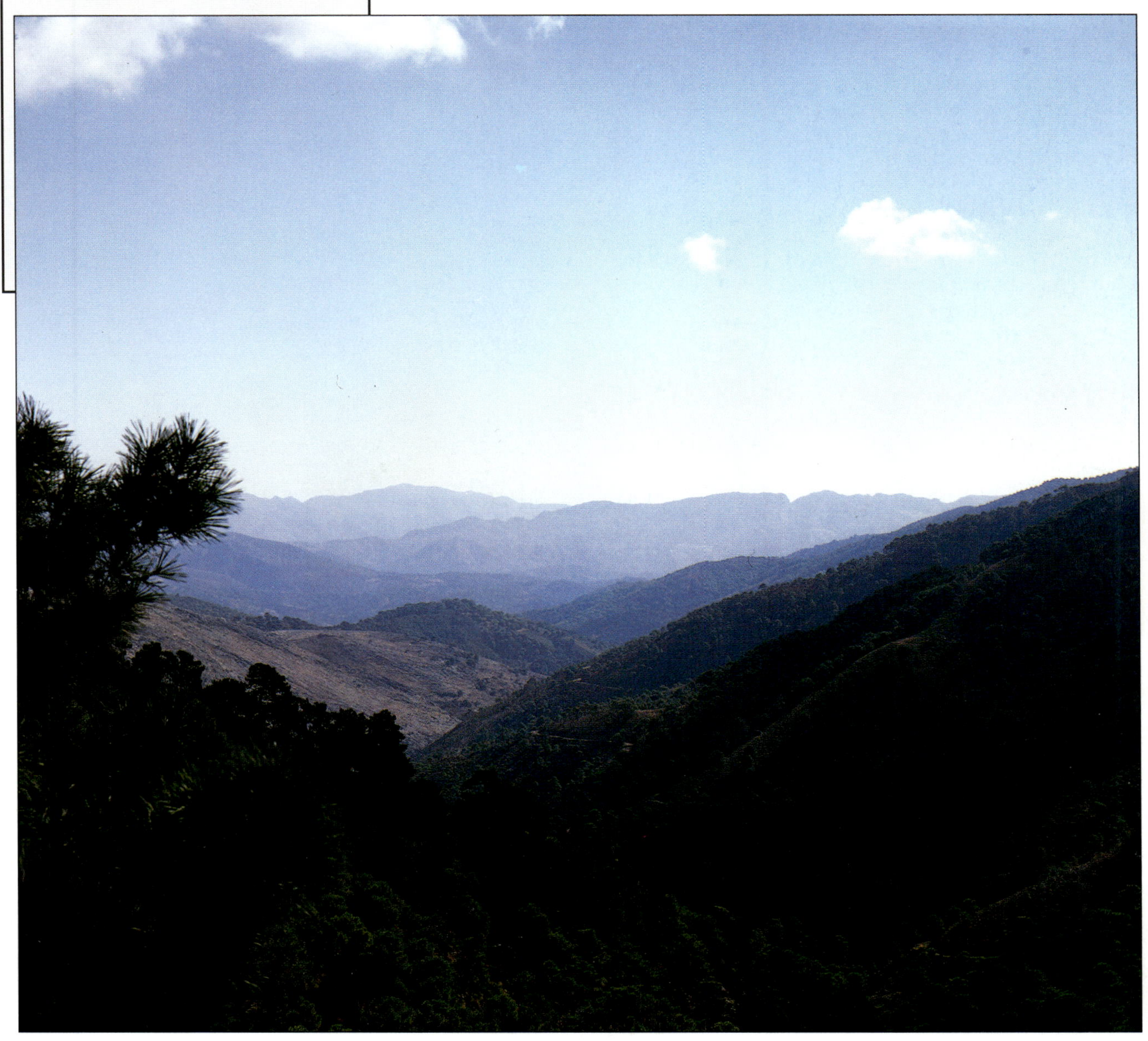

If the air were perfectly clear, it is reckoned that you could see for about 240 kilometres. But in reality, objects in the distance appear increasingly blurred. Why does this happen?

The air contains dust, pollutants and minute water particles which scatter UV (ultra-violet) and blue rays travelling through them for any distance. If these particles are dry, like smoke or dust, haze is produced. If they consist of water droplets, mist results.

Even scenes that look clear to you may seem hazy and blue in a picture because film is sensitive to UV light, while your eyes are not.

Aerial perspective affects your view of distant objects in three ways:
● It blurs the image so that the outlines cease to be sharp and fine details disappear.
● It lightens and narrows the tonal range so that colours appear paler and tonal changes less distinct.
● The atmosphere tends to absorb the warm side of the colour spectrum while reflecting the cool, so often any colours that are visible take on a bluish tinge.

▼ AERIAL VIEW
Aerial perspective is most apparent in pictures taken at high altitudes and over water because more UV radiation is present in the air.

How to enhance the effect

Aerial (atmospheric) perspective is a useful device for creating depth in landscape images, because you assume that indistinct objects are further away than ones that are in focus. There are several ways you can accentuate this:

● **Weather** If you take a photograph of mountains on a hazy day the feeling of depth is fairly strong. But if you take exactly the same shot in mist, the aerial perspective becomes so pronounced that the landscape appears to be made up of several distinct planes.

● **Time of day** Try shooting your photos just before sunset when atmospheric haze is at its greatest. The low angle of the sun means that light must pass through more of the atmosphere, so more rays become scattered.

● **Filters** Use a pale blue or graduating filter (dark at the bottom and light at the top) in order to emphasize the changes in tone of receding objects.

● **Viewpoint** Shooting towards the light amplifies the effects of aerial perspective by forming a series of silhouettes. These range from black through increasingly paler shades of grey as they recede from the camera, creating a strong feeling of depth.

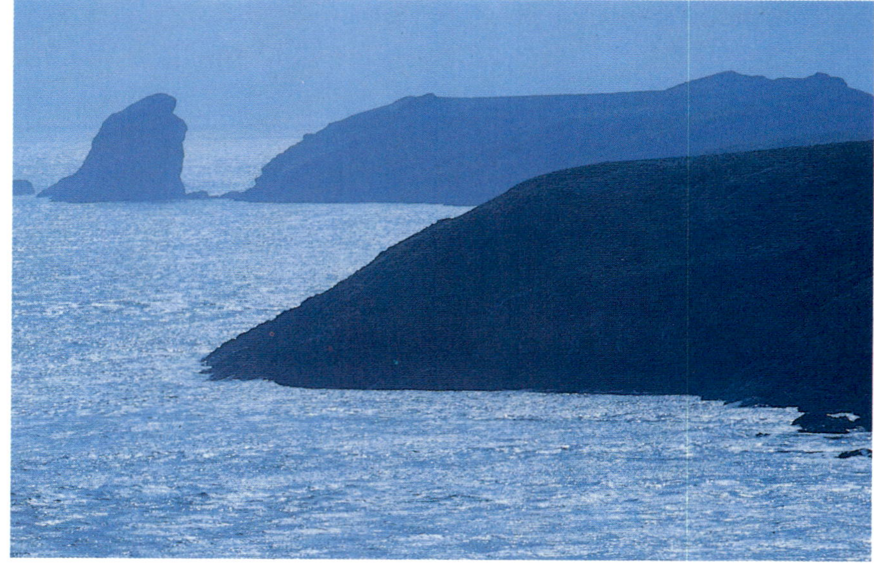

▲ MOODY BLUES
The photographer used a blue filter to exaggerate the difference in tone between the two headlands. By shooting towards the light he has reduced the scene to an almost monochromatic study.

▼ SUNSET TIMES
Sunset is an ideal time for taking advantage of aerial perspective because haze is particularly evident at this time of day. Shooting towards the sun enhances the impression by creating silhouettes. But remember not to stare directly into the sun or you could damage your eyes.

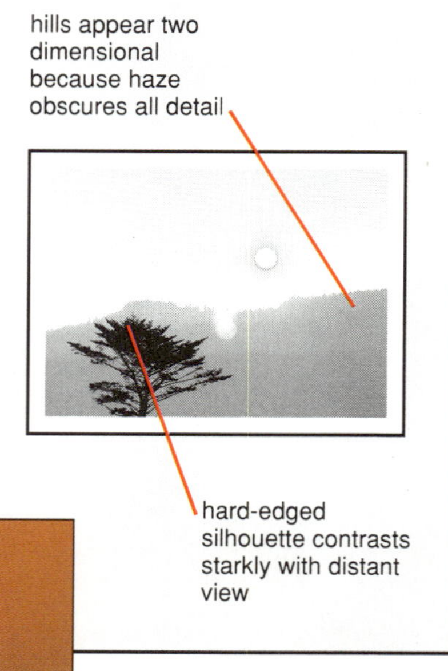

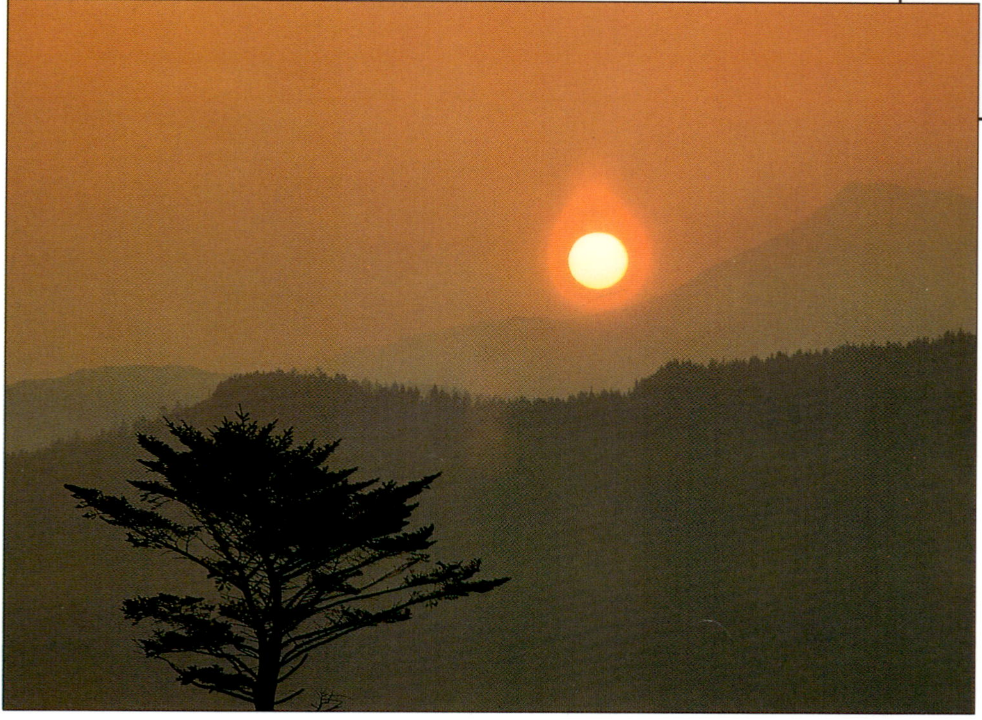

▶ STORMY WEATHER
Leaden skies (and indeed all types of cloud) diffuse light well, blurring distant objects in the process and creating a very moody image. The photographer has made sure the foreground elements are very sharp to emphasize the feeling of depth.

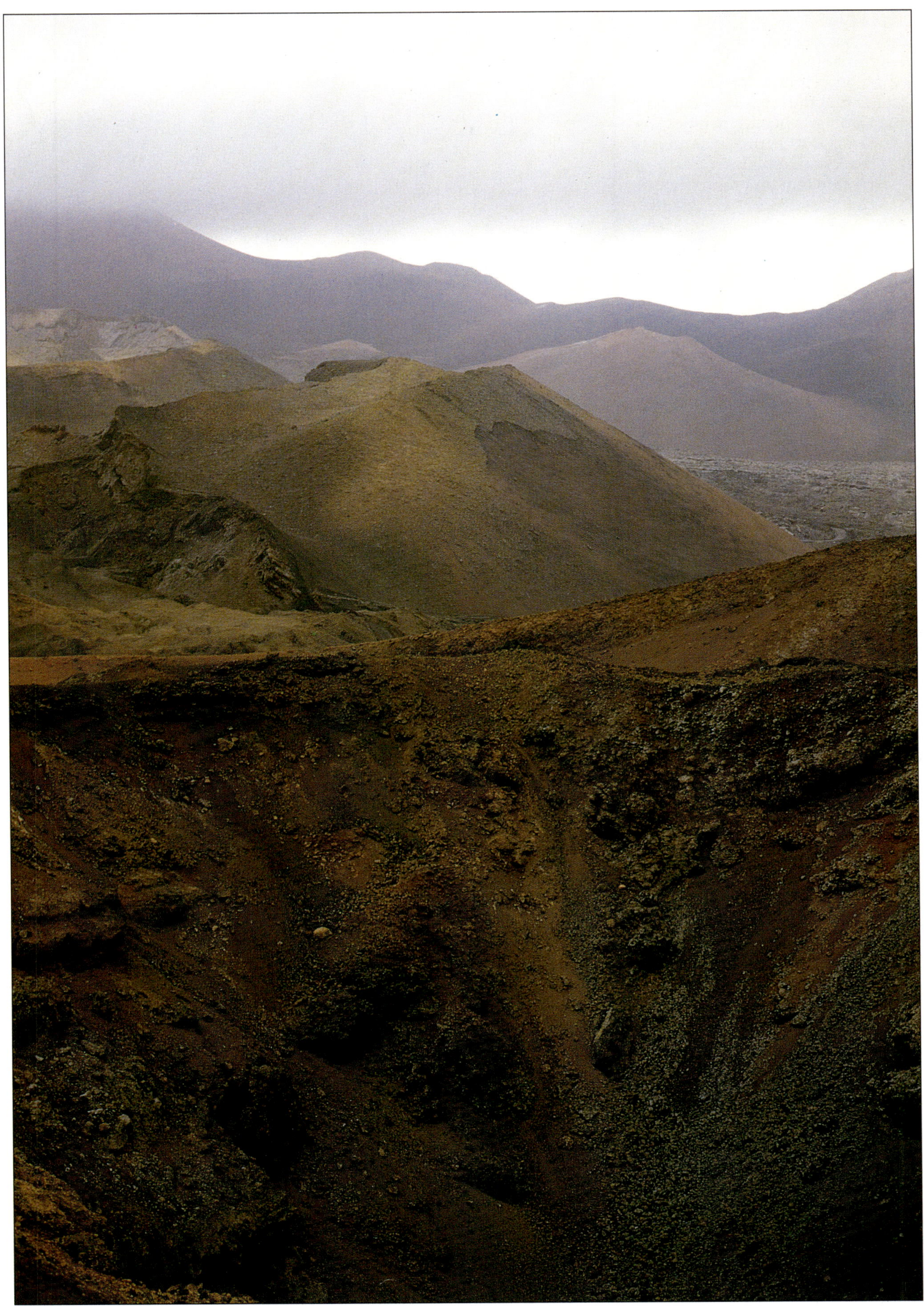

Cityscapes

Aerial perspective is not confined to mountainous scenes – you can see its effect in urban areas too. Dust and pollution can create enormous amounts of haze in cities, and you can use it to produce moody, almost monochromatic shots.

Take care that you reproduce the changing tones accurately. Measure the exposure for the mid-distance buildings of a scene, so that pale details in the background and dark ones in the foreground are reproduced accurately.

CHECK IT!

Exaggerate aerial perspective by:
❑ taking photos at sunrise or sunset when haze is more evident
❑ shooting in misty or stormy conditions
❑ using a pale blue or graduating filter
❑ shooting towards the light

▼ TONES ARE A'CHANGING
Low sidelighting and urban smog have been combined to give a series of graduating shades with detail in all but the brightest highlights.

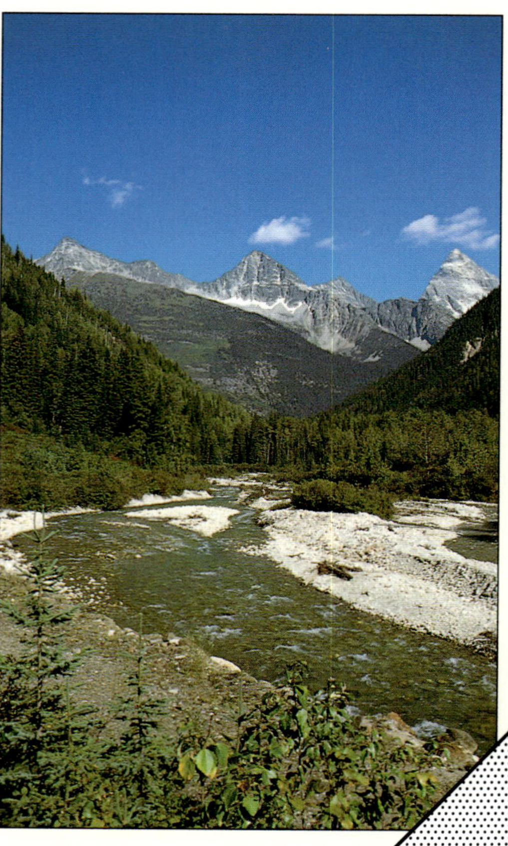

Tip

Minimizing haze

Although aerial perspective is a useful device, there are many times when a crystal clear image is called for and you need to cut out haze. In black and white photography this is easy – just use a red filter.

Haze is harder to get rid of in colour shots. (Using a red filter on colour film turns the whole image red.) When haze is slight you can use a skylight or UV filter to absorb some of the ultra-violet light.

On a sunny day, as in this example, you can use a polarizing filter to deepen a blue sky, making the picture appear well defined near the horizon.

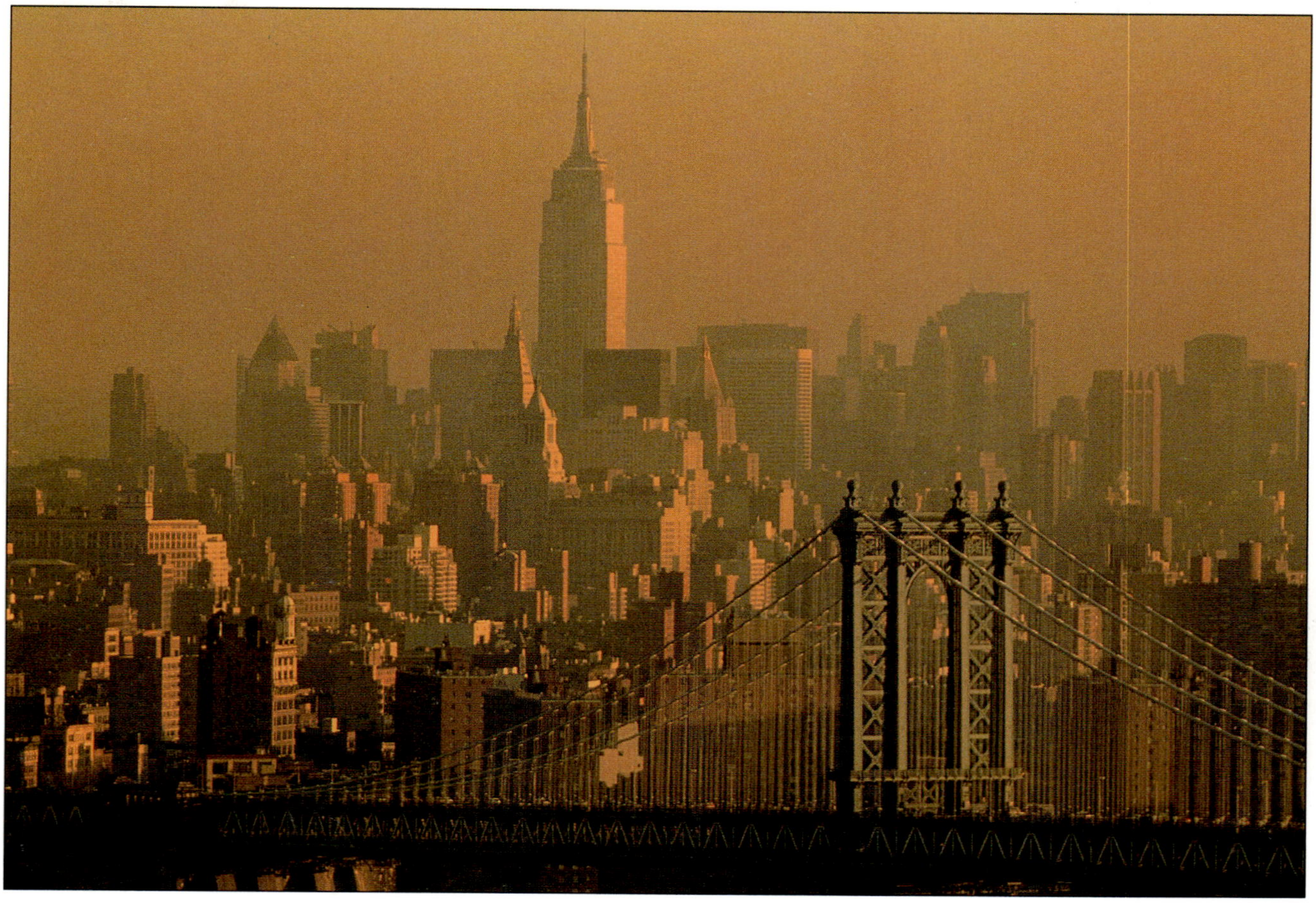

Seeking out shape and form

Often a photograph is immediately attractive because it conveys a distinctive shape, form, texture or pattern. All these elements help you to identify what you're seeing, adding realism to a flat, two dimensional image.

In everyday life you tend to take the objects around you for granted, accepting them for what they are or what they do. But what qualities do you notice when you take a really close look at an object?

Try studying a bowl of fruit and jot down a list of the shape, form, texture and markings of the different items. Then decide which is the dominant feature in each case – it may be the pitted surface of an orange, the elongated shape of a banana, or the pattern created by a bunch of grapes.

These four visual qualities have a combined effect on the appearance of an object. But you can also create interesting compositions by stressing just one of these elements and suppressing all the others.

In the next few pages, we look at ways of capturing and emphasizing shape, form and texture, thinking about viewpoint, focal length and lighting.

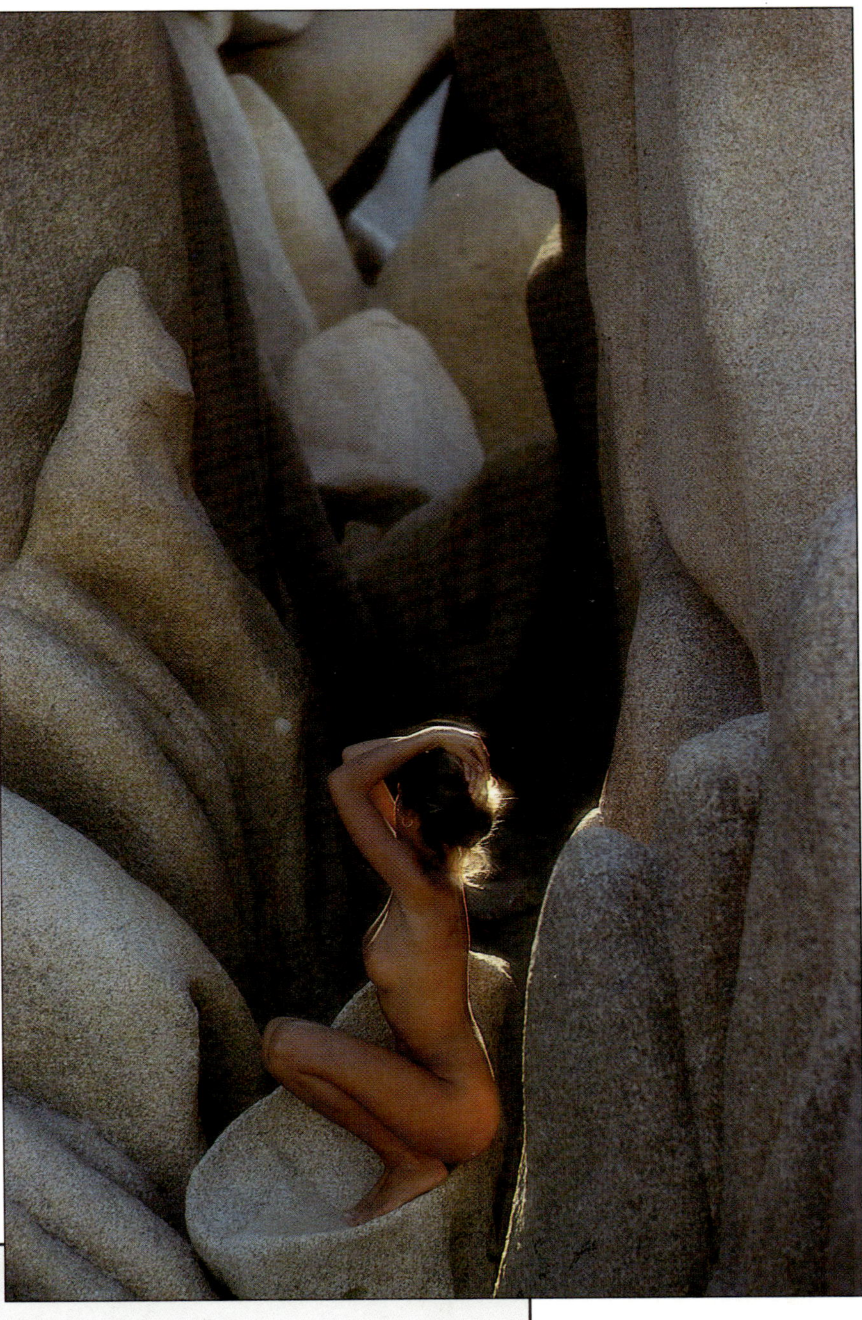

IDEAL COMBINATION
Shape, form, texture and pattern can either be used on their own to create a picture, or they can be combined, as in this example. Here, the woman's smooth contours echo those of the repeated rocks behind, and rimlighting helps to separate her shape from the similar toned background.

FORM
If you want to make your subject look realistic you need to suggest its three dimensional form. In this picture the contours of the woman and the rocks are made apparent by the changes in tone across them.

SHAPE
A bold, two dimensional outline is the simplest way of revealing the identity of an object. Here, rimlighting accentuates the shape of the woman and the nearby rock.

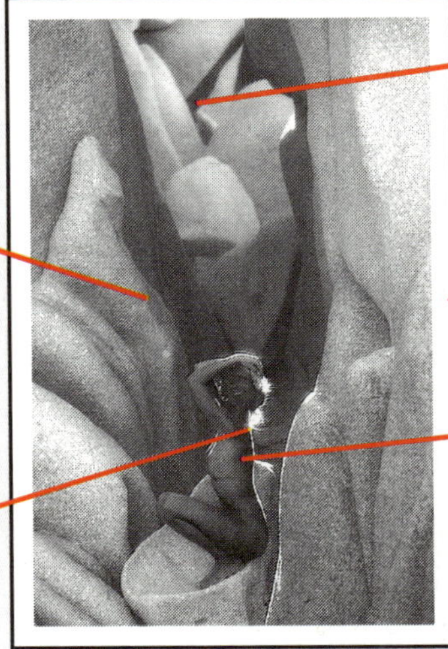

PATTERN
When objects are repeated in an image a pattern is formed. You can make pattern the subject of an image or you can use it to create an interesting background, as in this case.

TEXTURE
Another way of adding realism to photos is to convey how an object would feel to touch. In this example the smoothness of the model's skin and her background are strongly felt.

Looking and seeing

By learning how to identify the different aspects of an object, you can determine which element(s) you want to bring out in a photograph: **Shape** is the two-dimensional outline of an object or its representation in an image. To accentuate shape you need to isolate a subject from its background so that the outline stands out clearly. Think of a yellow balloon against a deep, blue sky or a silhouette of a person. **Form** gives the viewer a great deal more information about a subject because its three-dimensional volume is also apparent. Imagine the contours of the human body or the solidity of a huge boulder.

Texture is the visible surface quality of an object. It adds character to a shot by reminding you how an object feels to touch. Picture the shiny surface of a new car or the roughness of a rusty metal pipe.

Pattern is the repetition of objects, shapes or colours in an ordered or random manner. Recurring shapes, textures and forms all make successful patterns – think of a patchwork of fields, ripples on water, a stack of chimney pots or a row of soldiers on parade – some naturally occurring, others manmade.

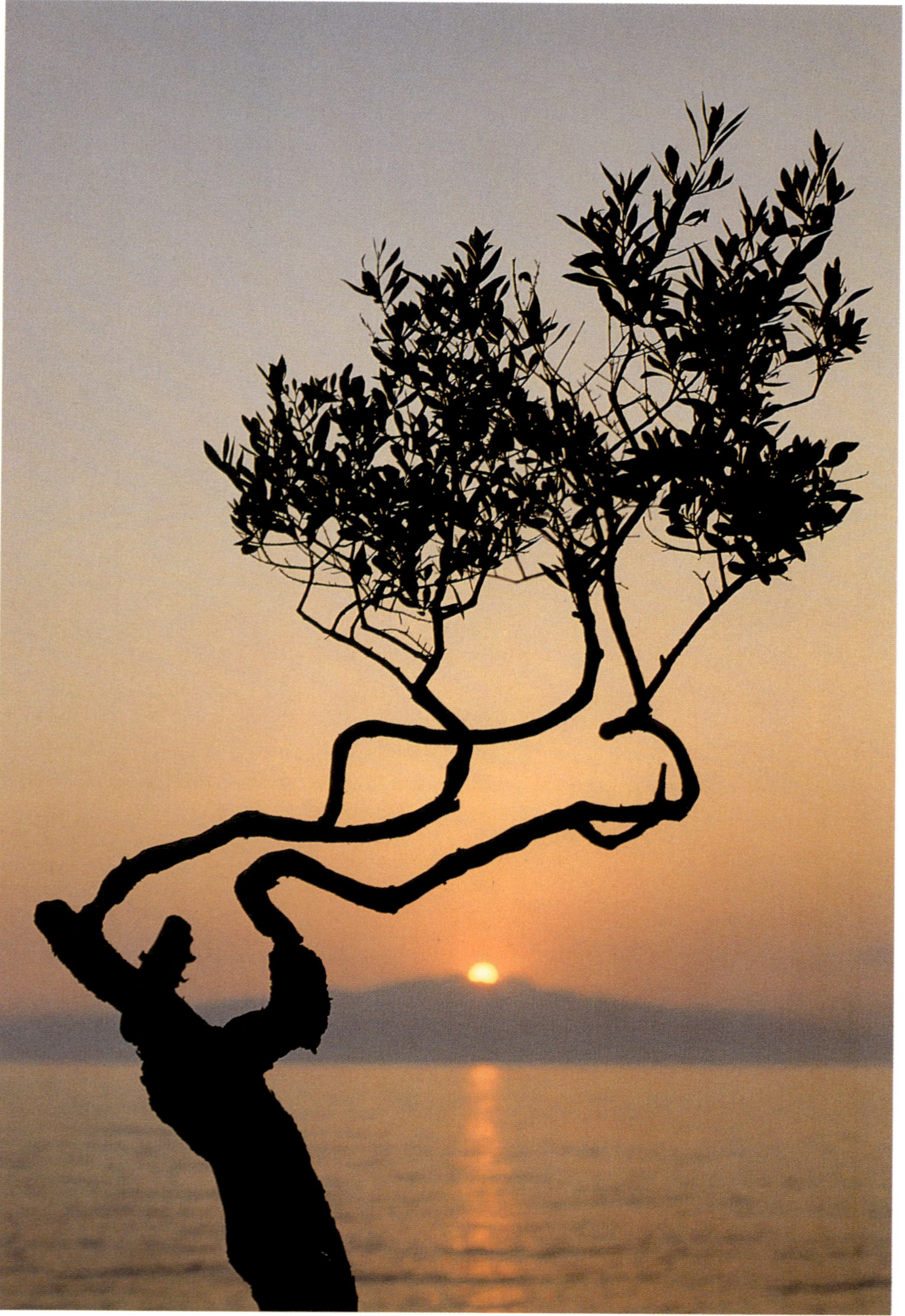

◄ **EMPHASIZING SHAPE**
A silhouette is the simplest form that an image can take. Because the resulting image is graphic and two dimensional, the success of this picture relies on the interesting tracery of the tree's branches and foliage.

► **DISCOVERING PATTERN**
Woodlands are great places for seeking out patterns, whether you shoot an overall view, one particular tree or the veins of a leaf. Here, the bold, vertical lines of the tree trunks draw your eye up and down so that every centimetre of the image is explored.

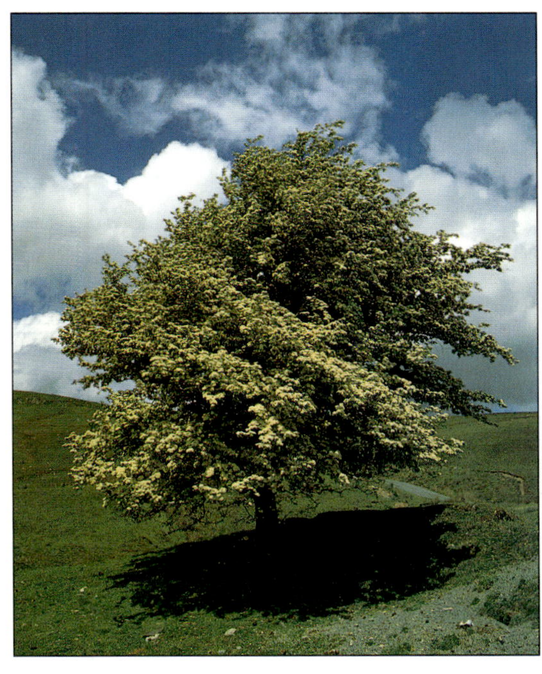

◄ REVEALING FORM
Lighting is very important when it comes to revealing an object's form. Here, the tree's volume is made apparent by the tonal changes in the foliage and by the shadow cast on the ground.

► CONVEYING TEXTURE
The rough surface of the bark has been captured so realistically on film that you know exactly how it would feel if you could run your hand over it.

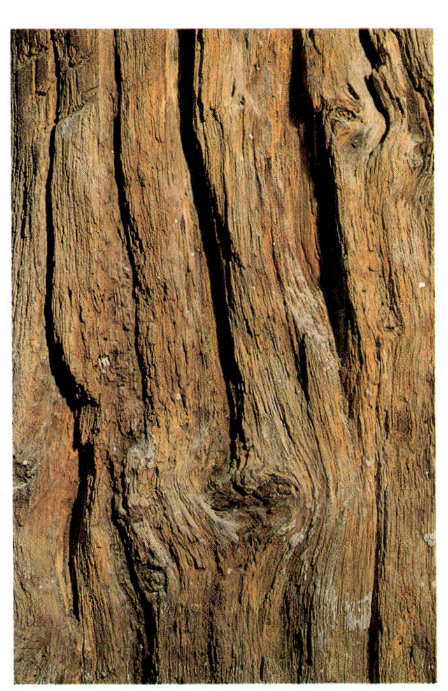

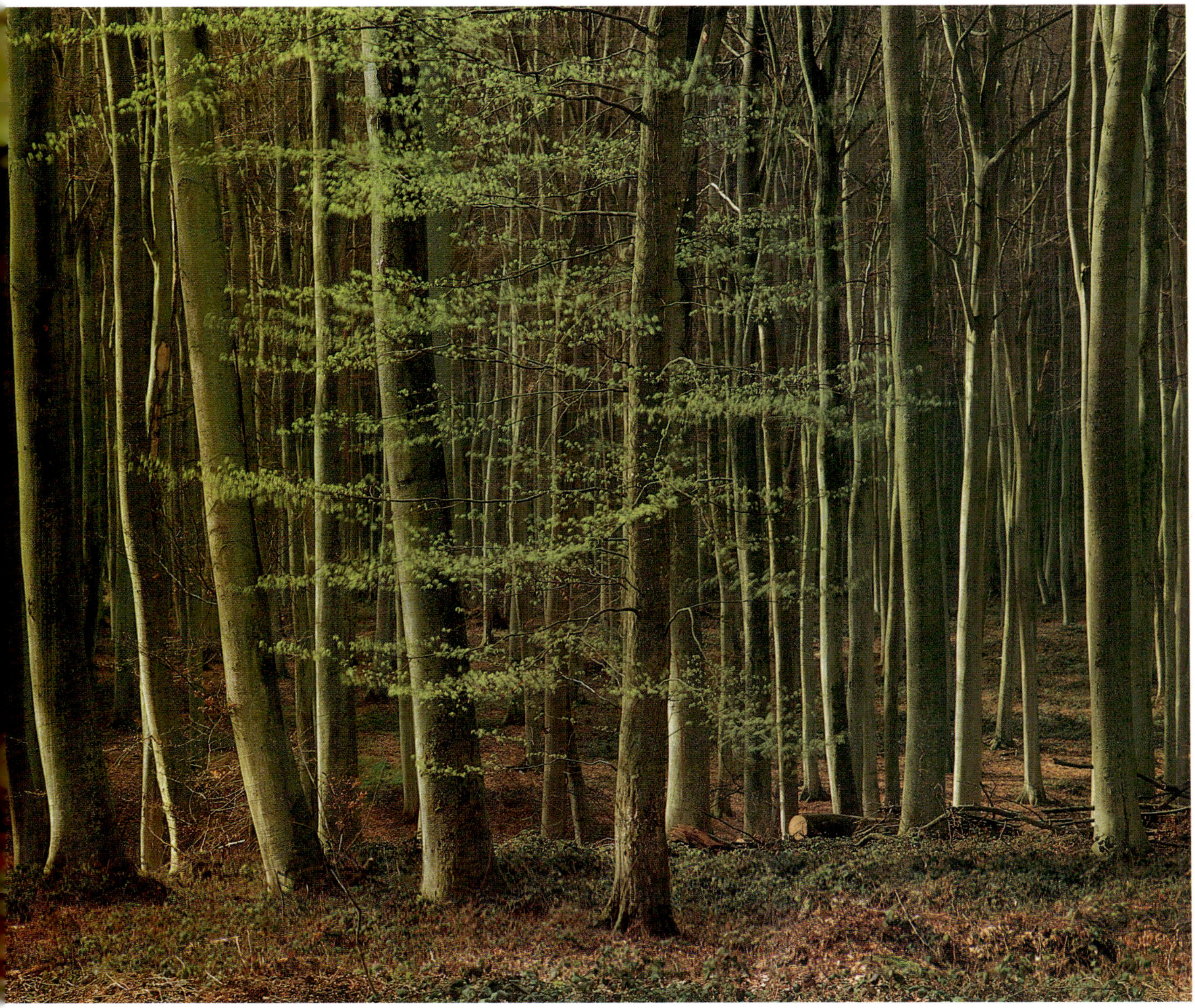

Emphasizing shape

Shape is the simplest and most important means of identifying an object. If you look at a photograph of a tree in which only its outline is shown, you immediately recognize what it is. You may also be able to tell what type of tree it is and in which season the shot was taken.

Once you have decided that shape is going to be the dominating aspect of your picture, you need to isolate your subject from its surroundings so that its outline is clear. There are several ways of doing this.

Silhouettes

One of the most dramatic ways to reveal shape is by placing your subject in silhouette. A true silhouette eliminates the form, colour and texture of an object, leaving the subject to communicate itself to the viewer by means of shape alone.

Silhouettes have an eyecatching simplicity. To make sure they have as much impact as possible, choose a light background and pick a simple, bold shape.

Colour contrast

A plain, contrasting background can make the shape of your subject look well defined. For example, a red sail against a blue sky is far more striking than a blue sail would be.

If your subject is movable or you can alter your viewpoint, choose your own background to make the most of a good outline.

Selective focusing

Backgrounds can contrast not only in colour, but also in degree of sharpness. A crisply focused subject stands out well against a blurred background.

Selective focusing is especially useful when you can't change your viewpoint to find an uncluttered background.

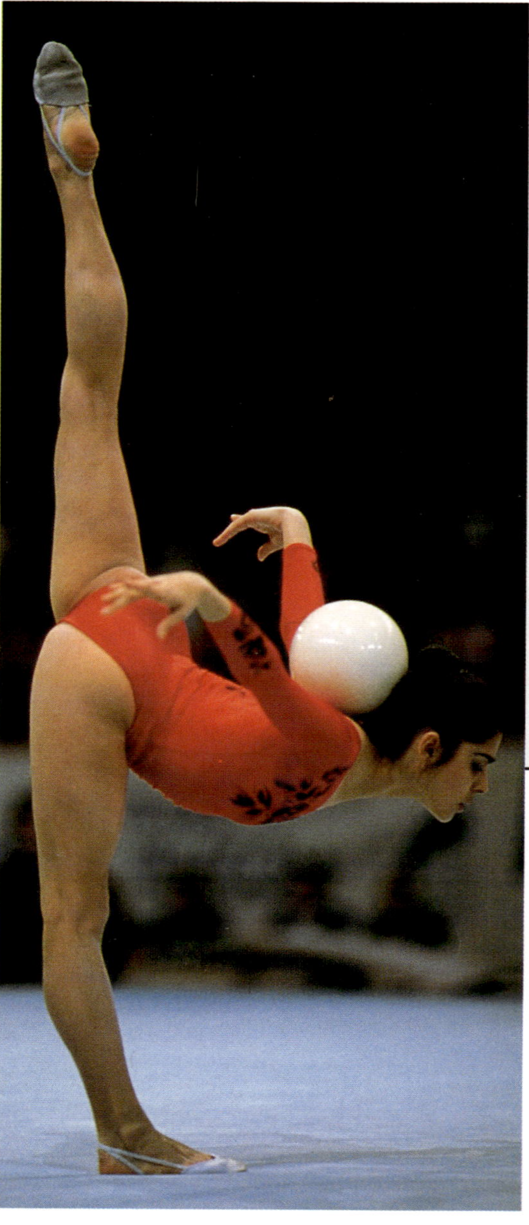

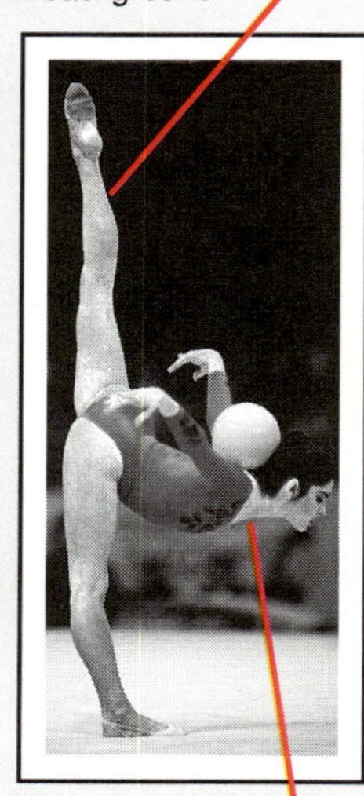

◄ **STRIKING A POSE**
Selective focusing helps to lift the gymnast's shape out of a confusing background. However, enough detail is left visible to place the subject in context.

► **MINER DETAIL**
Silhouettes always emphasize shape. Even though only the outline of the pit head is evident, its shape alone provides the viewer with enough information.

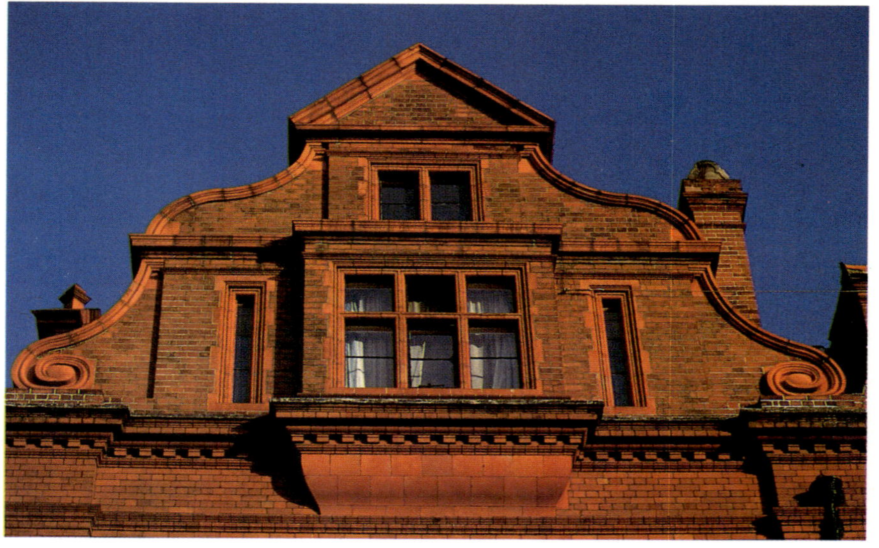

► **BOLD AND BRIGHT**
A plain, blue background helps to define the colour and outline of the rooftop. The photographer increased the colour contrast by using a polarizing filter to deepen the blue of the sky.

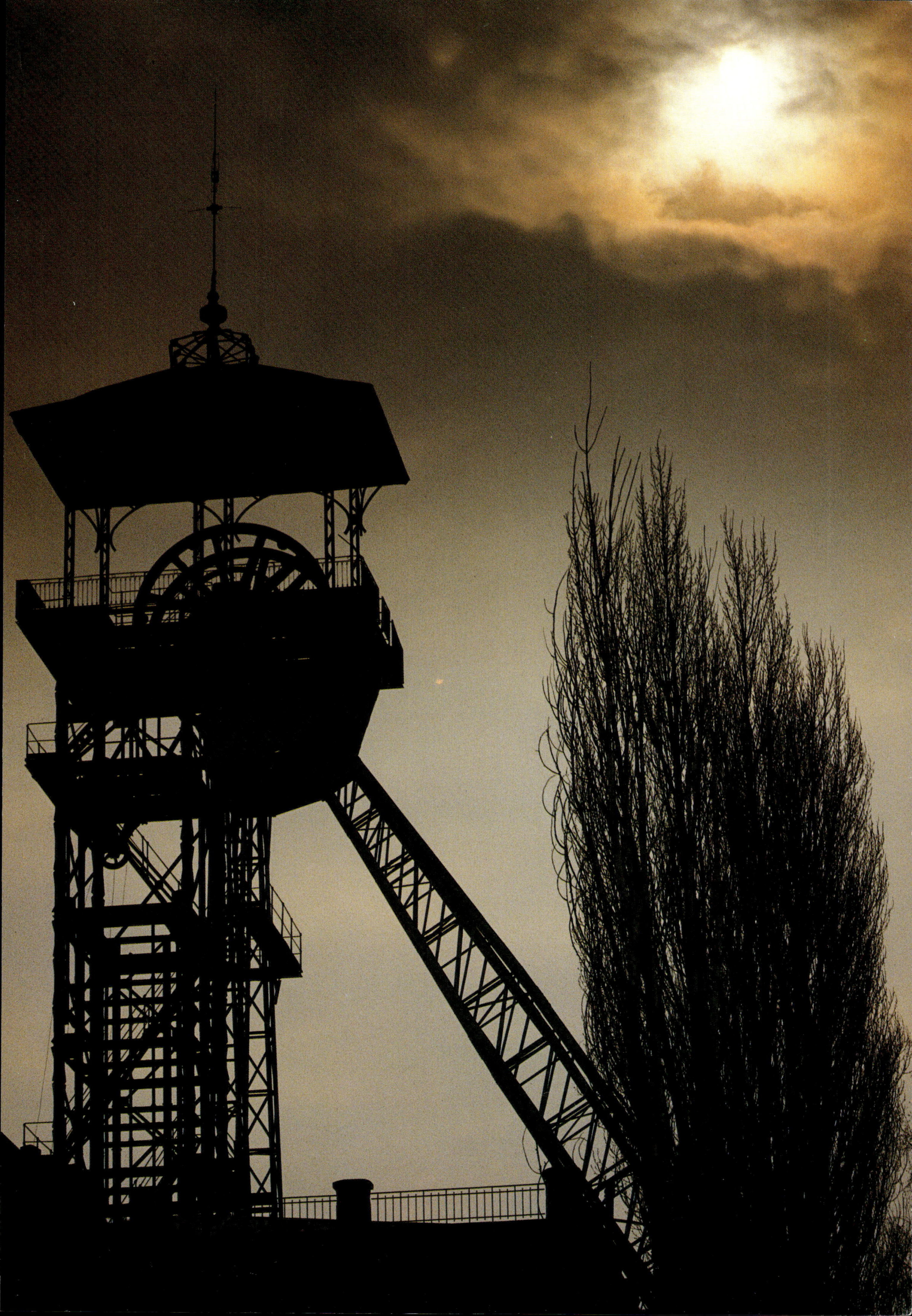

Rimlighting

When the light source is mostly behind your subject, but also higher or to one side of it, a narrow strip of light picks out the top and side edges of the object. Called rimlighting, this technique reveals some detail but the main effect is to stress overall shape.

Rimlighting is particularly effective if you want to bring out the shape of a dark subject against a dark background. For example, if you photograph a black cat or dog indoors with daylight coming through a high window behind, almost its entire outline is ringed with light.

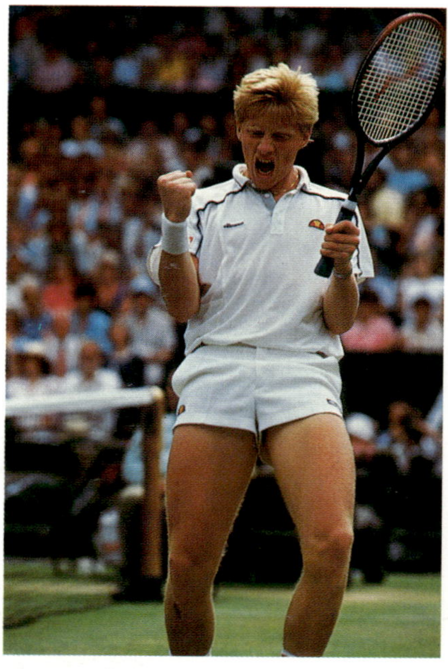

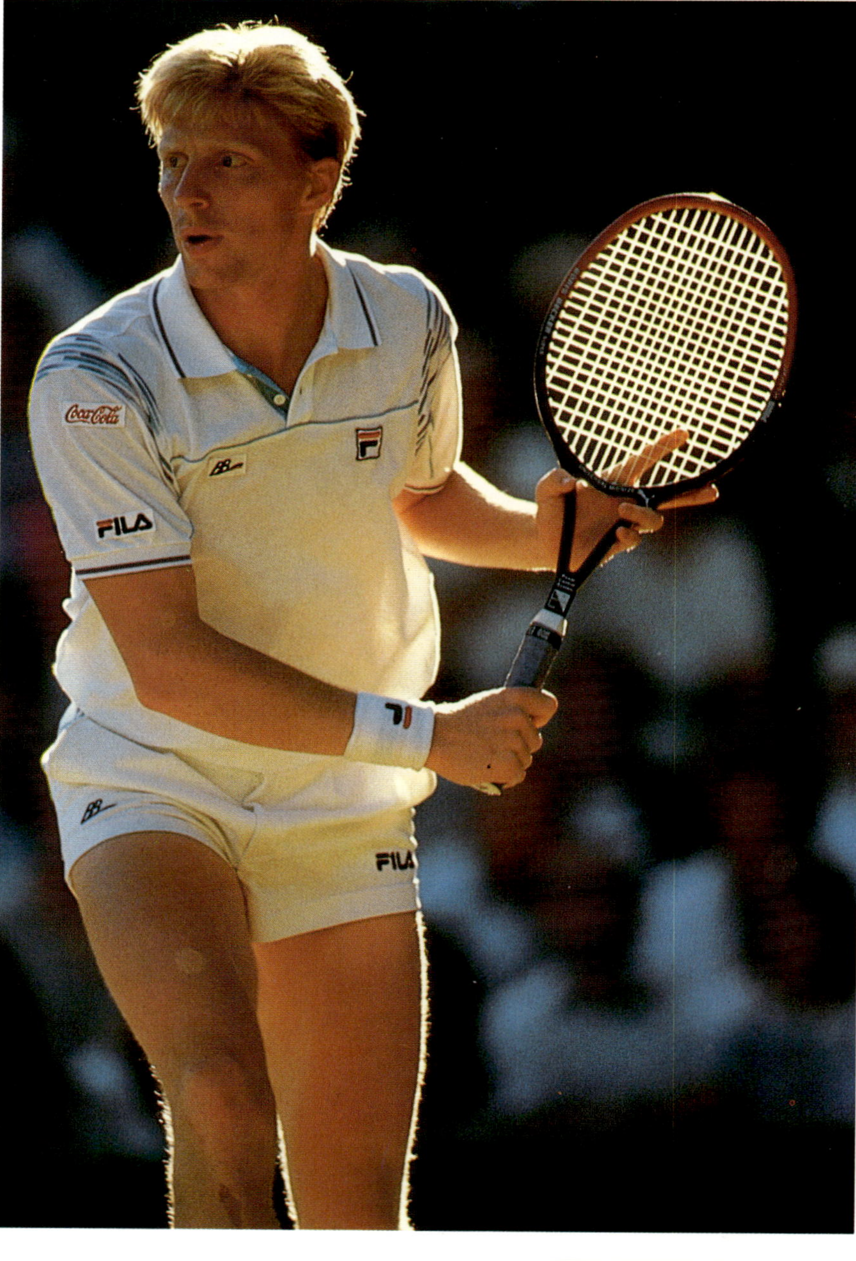

▲ HALO OF LIGHT
With minimal highlights (above left), the tennis player doesn't stand out clearly from the background. But rimlighting (above right) separates him from the crowd. A narrow band of sunlight rings the player's body with light, highlighting his hair in particular.

Abstract design

Tip

Simple shapes can make pleasing, abstract pictures. By moving in close you may be able to conceal your subject's identity and create an interesting, graphic design.

Placing contrasting shapes side by side can be effective in abstract images too. Contrast is one way to make sure each shape gets equal attention. Use bold colours to add further impact.

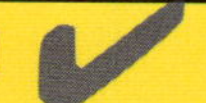

You can separate your subject from its background by:

❑ placing your subject in silhouette so that form is lost
❑ selective focusing (creating a blurred background)
❑ using a plain, contrasting colour for the background
❑ rimlighting (backlighting) your subject so that its edges are ringed with light

Revealing form

Form is the volume of a subject – its contours and roundness; and although you cannot reproduce a third dimension on a two dimensional print or slide, there are several ways you can suggest it.

An object's form is harder to convey in a photo than its shape, because you have to imply its depth and solidity as well as its outline. Viewpoint and lighting, which in turn affect the position and shape of shadows, are the keys to revealing your subject's volume.

For instance, a hilly landscape looks flat and dull when the sun is directly overhead because no shadows are cast. But when clouds pass over the sun, their shadows bring out the form of the hills.

You can also use shadows to make objects appear solid even though they are not. Think of the graduations of tone in a cloud, the momentary depth seen in a wind blown flag or the crest of a wave just before it breaks.

Memory can play an important part in your perception of form too. If you look at an image of a face where one half is lit and the other is in deep shadow, you still accept the face as being complete and three dimensional.

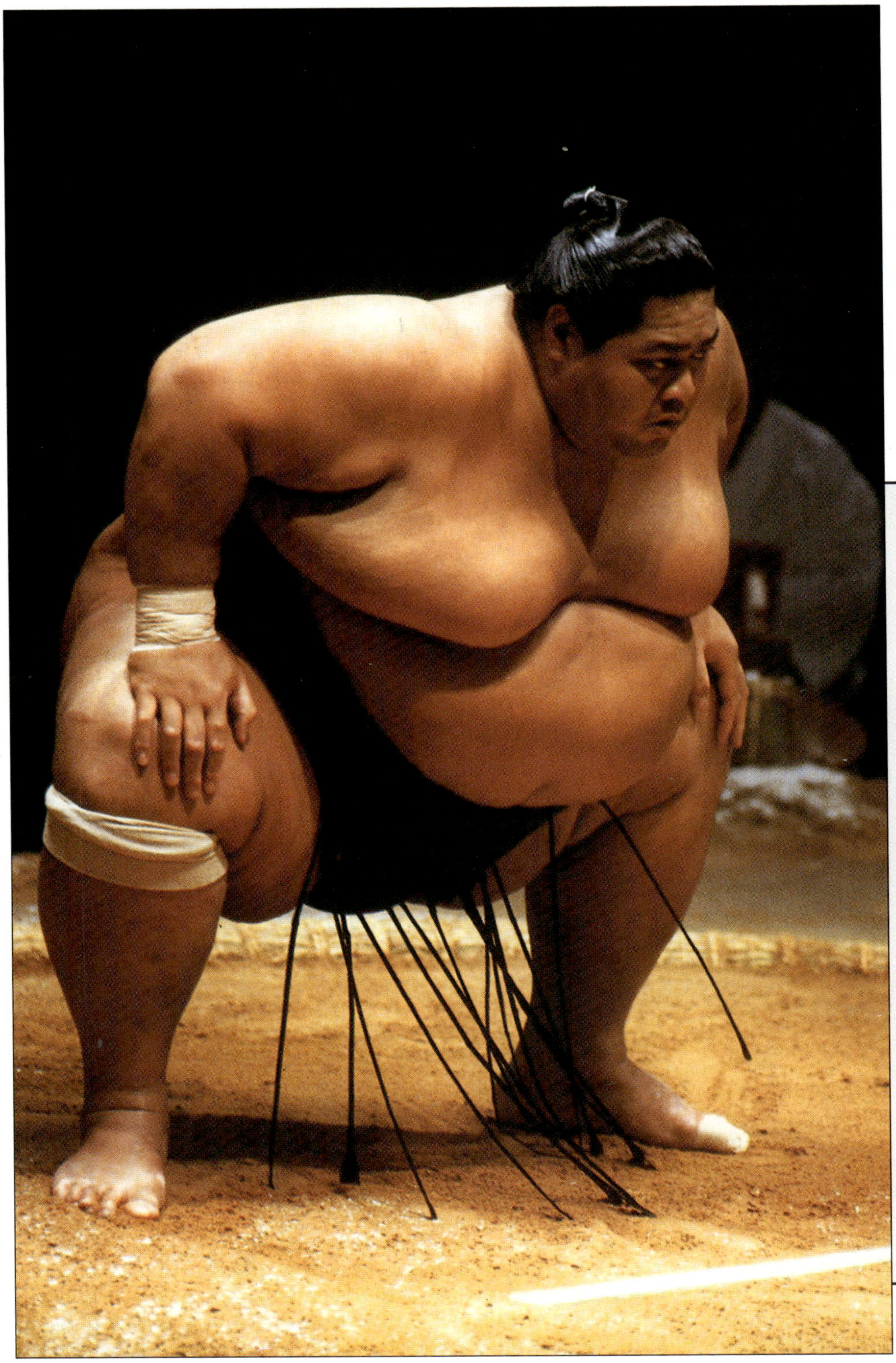

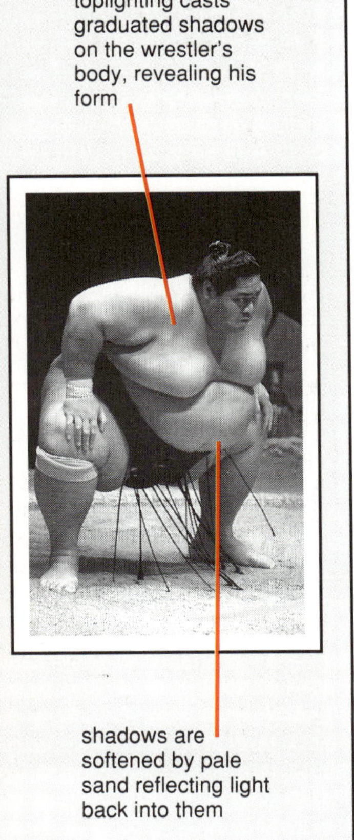

Effective lighting

To reveal the form of an object you need to be able to control the amount of light and shade falling on to it. This is because the degree of shading and the softness of the shadow's edge are the most important factors for showing volume effectively.

In order to achieve the desired effect you need to consider the direction, strength and quality of the light you are going to use.

Direction of light You can increase the apparent form of an object by altering the position of your light source to get the right balance of light and shade.

Although frontlighting is ideal for showing shape and detail, it reveals little form because no shadows are visible. Backlighting, on the other hand, produces too much shadow.

Sidelighting is the ideal compromise because it produces an equal mix of light and shade. This degree of shading from side to side across the image gives an impression of depth.

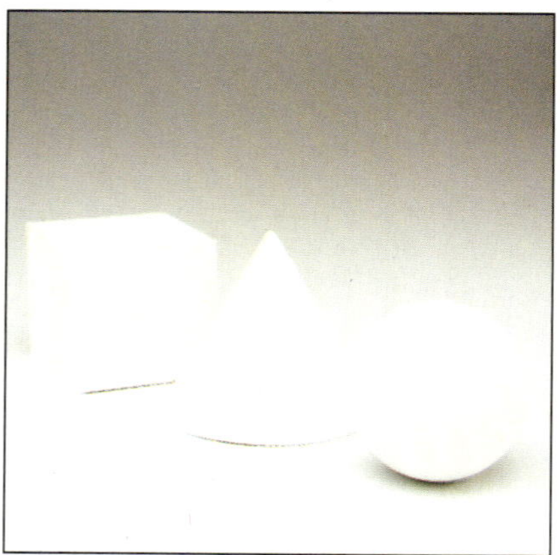

◀ FRONTLIGHTING
The shapes of the three objects are evident with frontlighting, but their form is hidden. This is because of the lack of shadows. Note how the cube looks particularly flat because all three planes are the same tone.

▶ SIDELIGHTING
Shadows are cast on to the objects with sidelighting, which emphasize their form well. The cube looks solid because each of the three planes is a different tone.

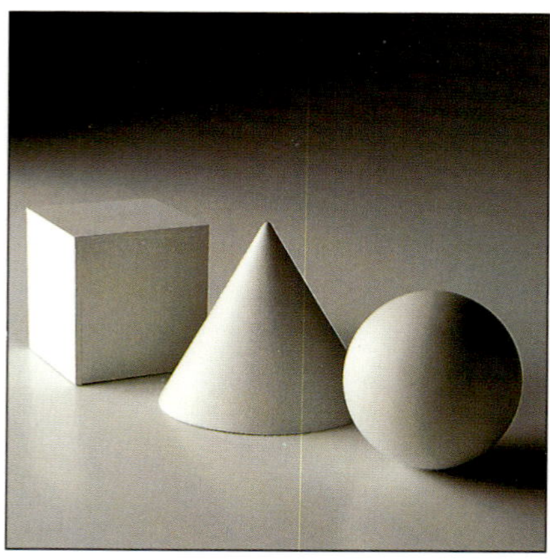

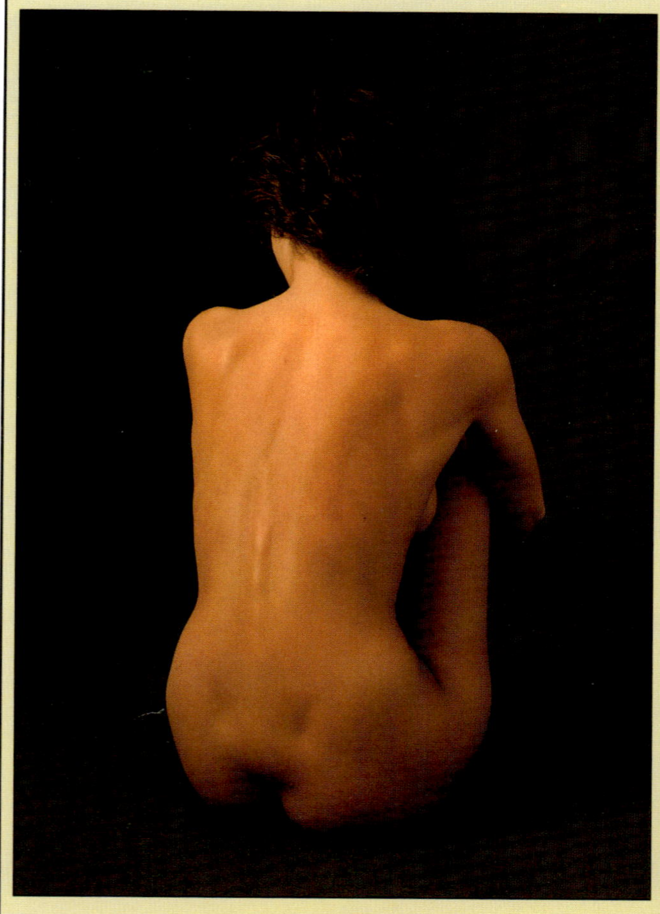

DIFFUSED FRONTLIGHTING

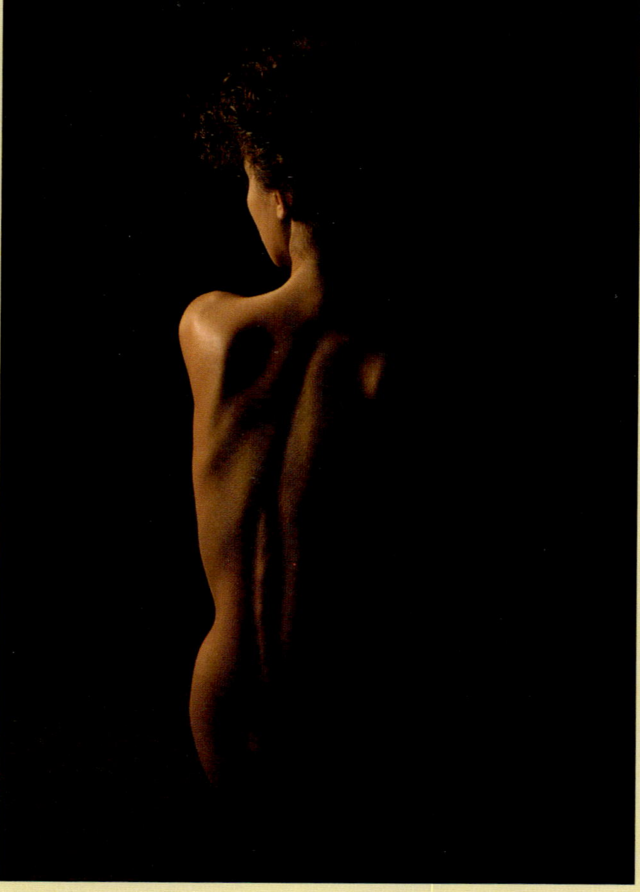

HARD SIDELIGHTING

Points of view

Don't forget that your choice of viewpoint can help you to convey the form of an object. For example, if you photograph a cube head on so that only one surface is facing the camera, the resulting image is flat and two dimensional.

However, if you turn the cube round so that two surfaces are visible to the camera you achieve a three dimensional effect.

If you then raise your viewpoint so that the top surface can also be seen, the feeling of depth is further heightened. The more surfaces you make visible, the greater the feeling of depth. This 3-D effect is increased by using sidelighting.

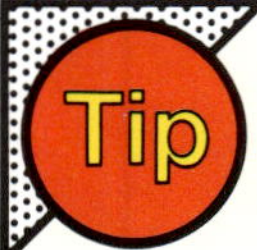

Finding the right light

For this series of images the photographer altered the quality and direction of the light source to see how it changed the way the model's form was recorded.

◄ CONCEALING FORM
Diffused frontlighting (far left) defines the model's shape very well, but with little shadow her form is not very evident.

◄ CONCEALING FORM
Hard sidelighting (left) emphasizes the shape of the girl's left side well. But the light is harsh and her right side is totally lost in shadow.

► REVEALING FORM
Diffused sidelighting (right) throws soft shadows on to the girl's back. The subtle graduation of tones reveals her form perfectly.

Strength of contrast refers to how hard (dark) or soft (light) the shadows appear in an image. Hard, directional lighting throws dark shadows, and although dramatic images are produced, detail and form are lost.

You can soften harsh shadows by placing a piece of white card or a sheet opposite your light source. This reflects light back into the shaded areas and some detail is restored.

Quality of light Diffused sidelighting provides more information about an object than direct lighting because the area of light produced is larger and the shadows are soft.

You can diffuse lamplight easily by shining it through translucent material, such as an ordinary stocking. Natural light can be scattered too. For example, if you place tracing paper over a window harsh sunlight is softened.

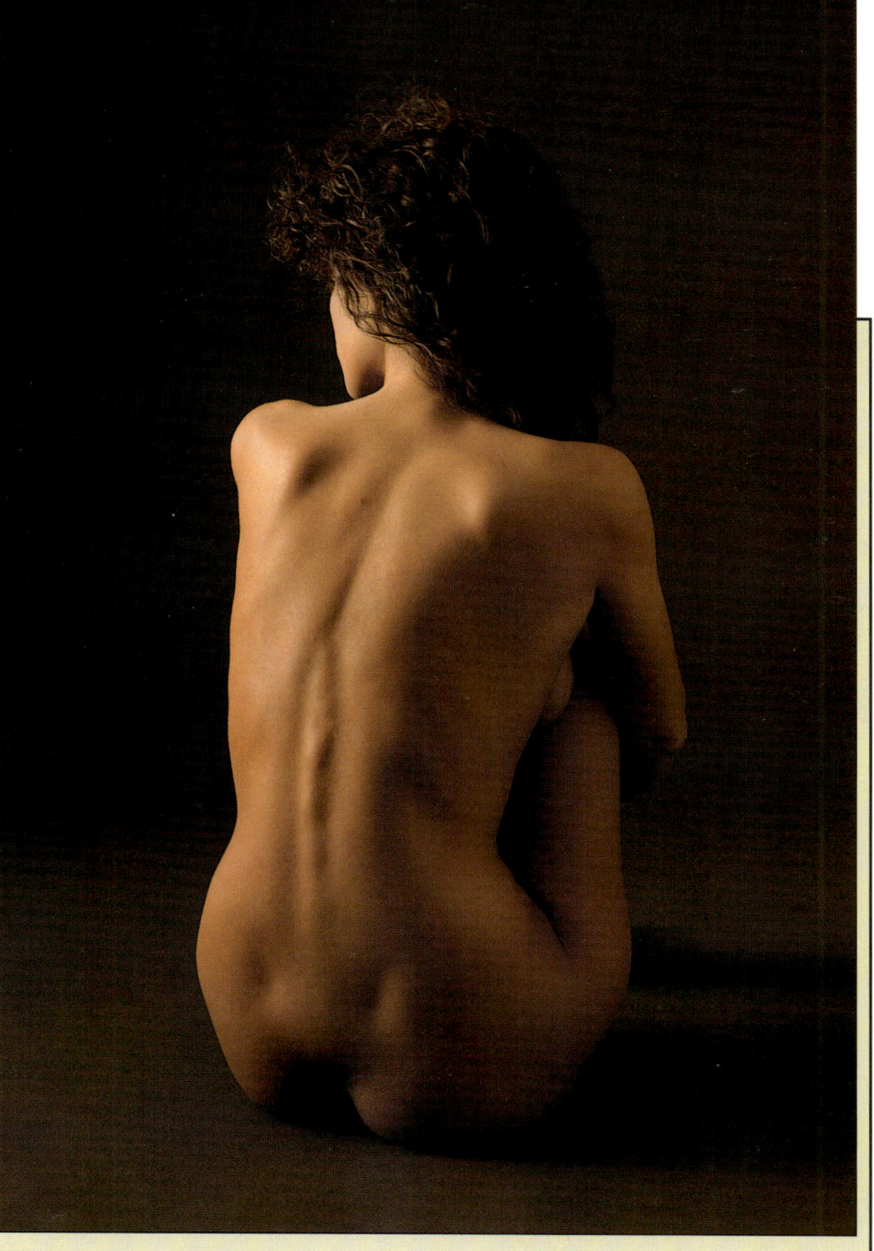

DIFFUSED SIDELIGHTING

Highlighting form

In the case of shiny objects such as polished bronze, chrome and glass, you can use highlights to suggest form. Most surfaces scatter some light, but shiny ones reflect light in one direction only, causing highlights.

For example, if you photograph a shiny car in dull, overcast weather hardly any highlights are produced: instead the car looks dull and flat. In brilliant sunlight, though, the reflections are much more intense, clearly revealing the curves of the glossy car.

Using pattern

Stripes of shadow and light cast by the sun shining through Venetian blinds can lend a sense of volume to a figure. Even though parts of the object are in darkness, enough information is shown for your brain to fill in the lost details.

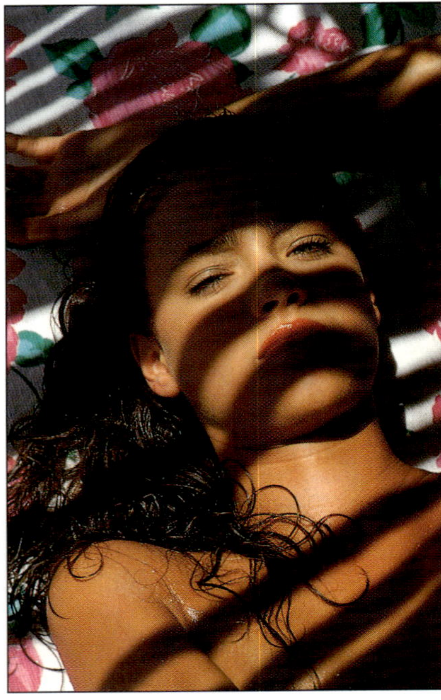

▶ **TWO HALVES MAKE A WHOLE**
Sunlight shining through blinds has placed half the girl in light and half in darkness. However, her form is clearly shown by the way the edges of the shadows dip and rise as they follow the girl's contours.

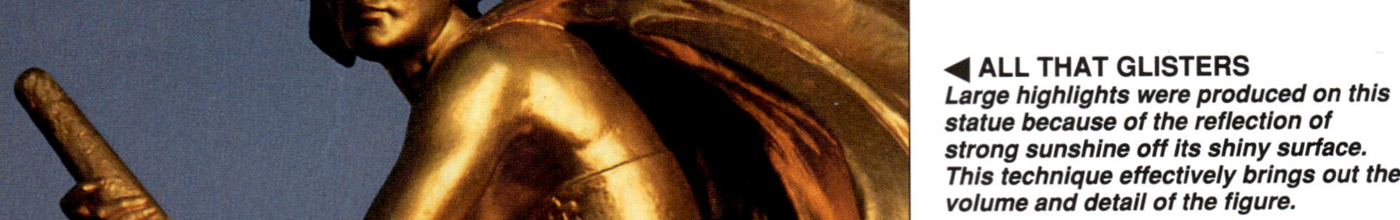

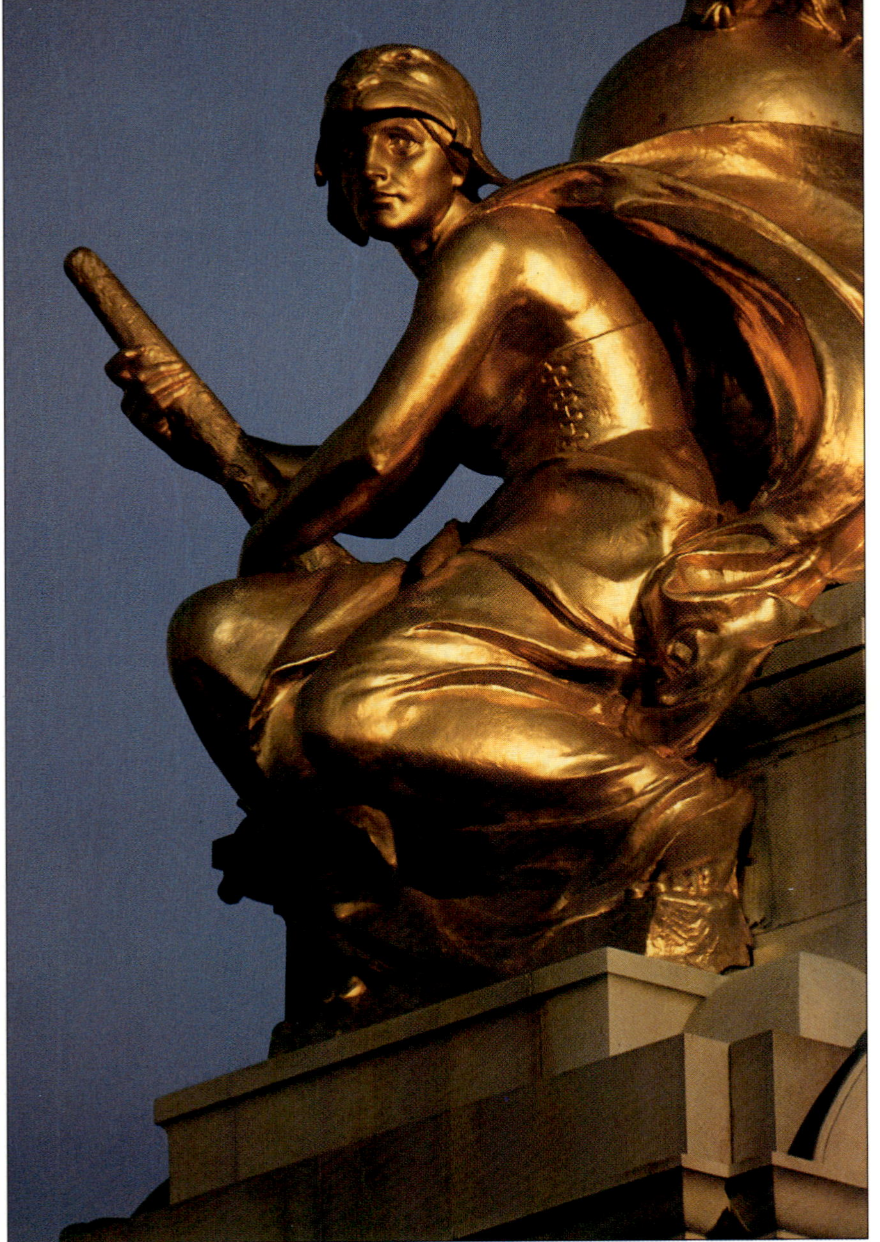

◀ **ALL THAT GLISTERS**
Large highlights were produced on this statue because of the reflection of strong sunshine off its shiny surface. This technique effectively brings out the volume and detail of the figure.

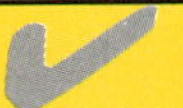

How to reveal form:

❏ use sidelighting to create a range of graduating tones
❏ use diffused light – place translucent material over your light source
❏ turn your subject so that as many surfaces are facing the camera as possible
❏ soften the shadows by reflecting light into them with a piece of white card or a sheet
❏ produce highlights on reflective surfaces by photographing them in hard, directional light

Conveying texture

Whether rough, smooth, hard or soft, texture helps to add realism and character to your photographs. But as well as enhancing an image, texture can make an interesting subject in its own right.

While the structure of an object is its form, the material from which it's made contributes to its texture. When photographed well, texture reminds you how an object would feel to touch.

You can see some of the best examples in photographs of food where items have to look good enough to eat. Think of the tight, smooth skin of an apple or a crusty loaf of bread.

Most people are used to noticing textures on a small scale, such as the roughness of a rusty pipe or the smoothness of a pebble. But try looking for texture on a larger scale too – the surface of the sea or the rugged appearance of a mountain, for instance.

Your choice of lighting and viewpoint are very important for conveying texture. But the success of your picture also depends on accurate focusing and a very steady hand or tripod, so that the image you produce is pin sharp.

▶ **AROUND THE RUGGED ROCKS**
Late afternoon sunlight picks out the rough surfaces of both the rocks and the sea. Even though dense shadows are formed, you assume that the texture of the rocks is uniform.

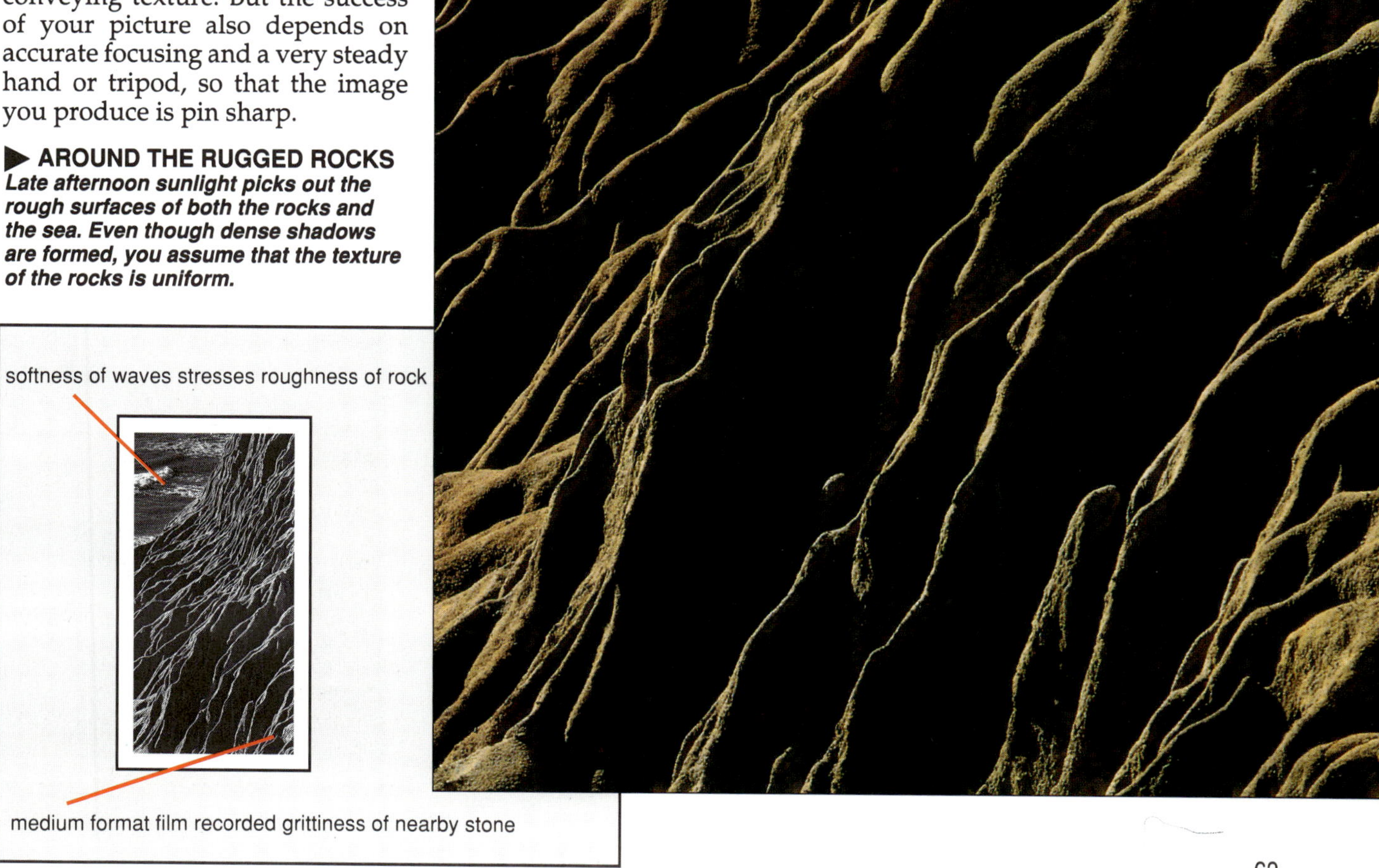

Angle of light

Texture is best revealed by angled lighting from the side, top or rear. Frontlighting shows off detail but conceals texture because no shadows are thrown.

For example, take a look at a south facing wall on a sunny day. Notice how the texture stands out when the sun strikes the wall at an angle in the morning, and how it vanishes when the sun moves round to shine fully on it at midday.

Sidelighting is the most popular way of revealing texture, but light from behind or above your subject can be effective too. For instance, the texture of animal fur is often best displayed using backlighting because it helps to separate your subject from its background. But avoid using toplighting for people because it casts unsightly shadows under the nose and eyes.

▼ VIEWPOINT AND TEXTURE
Fine textures benefit from a close look, but when your subject has a richly textured surface, even a quite distant camera position will reveal every wrinkle.

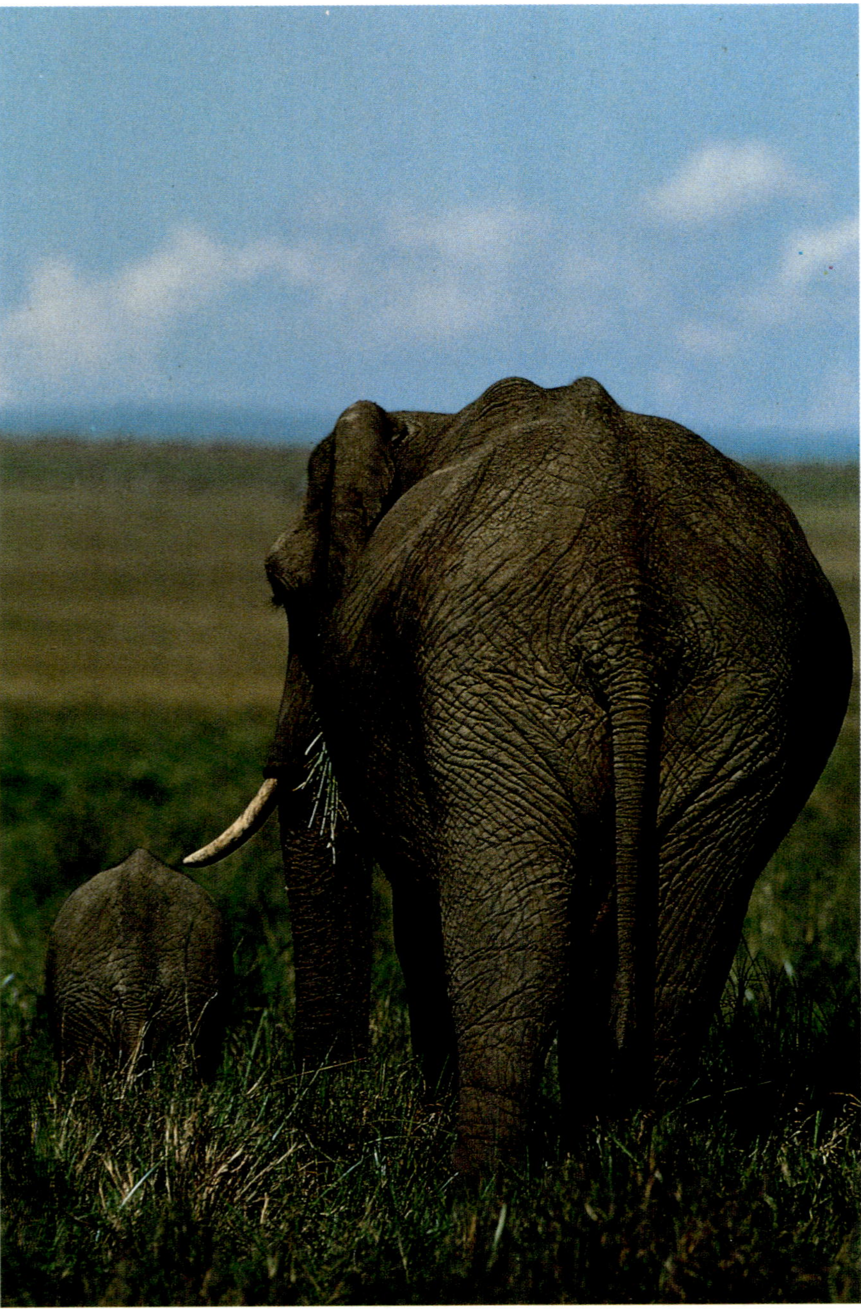

A sense of scale

Instead of just playing a supporting role, you can make texture the subject of your image, and moving in close is often the best way to achieve this. For example, a brick looks rough when seen close up, but viewed as part of a building it looks smooth.

Even smooth surfaces can reveal a vivid texture when photographed near to. Imagine the tiny indents on the surface of an orange or the fine weave of silk.

But choose your viewpoint carefully – too close and the texture may be so coarse as to look unrealistic, too far away and the object may look too smooth.

▼ FEELING ROPY
By shooting the image from a close viewpoint the photographer has isolated the fibrous detail of the rope. You can tell what the rope feels like just by looking at the picture.

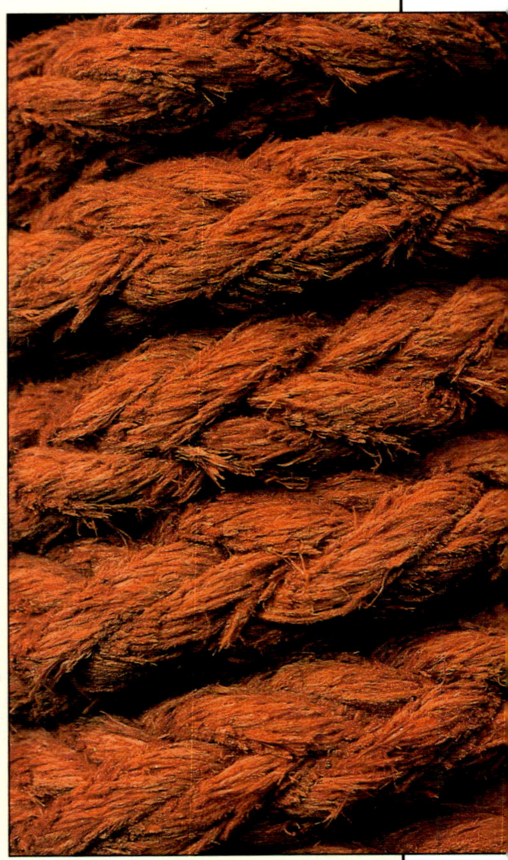

Emphasizing the effect

To accentuate texture you need to increase the contrast of the lighting, either by directing it from a sharper angle or by changing camera position. For flat surfaces such as water, cobblestones or wooden floorboards, raking (low angled) light produces the most dramatic images.

Shooting towards a low sun is ideal for this forceful effect. However, don't point your camera directly at the sun – position it so that its angle to the surface is the same as that of the sun.

While light can easily be skimmed over a flat surface, curved objects are only partly illuminated. But even though some of the object is in shadow, you tend to accept that the texture is the same over its entire surface.

▶ **SKIMMING THE SURFACE**
Low angled light, almost parallel to the surface, grazes the cobbles, revealing their smooth, slippery surface. The dense shadows help to emphasize the highlighted parts even more.

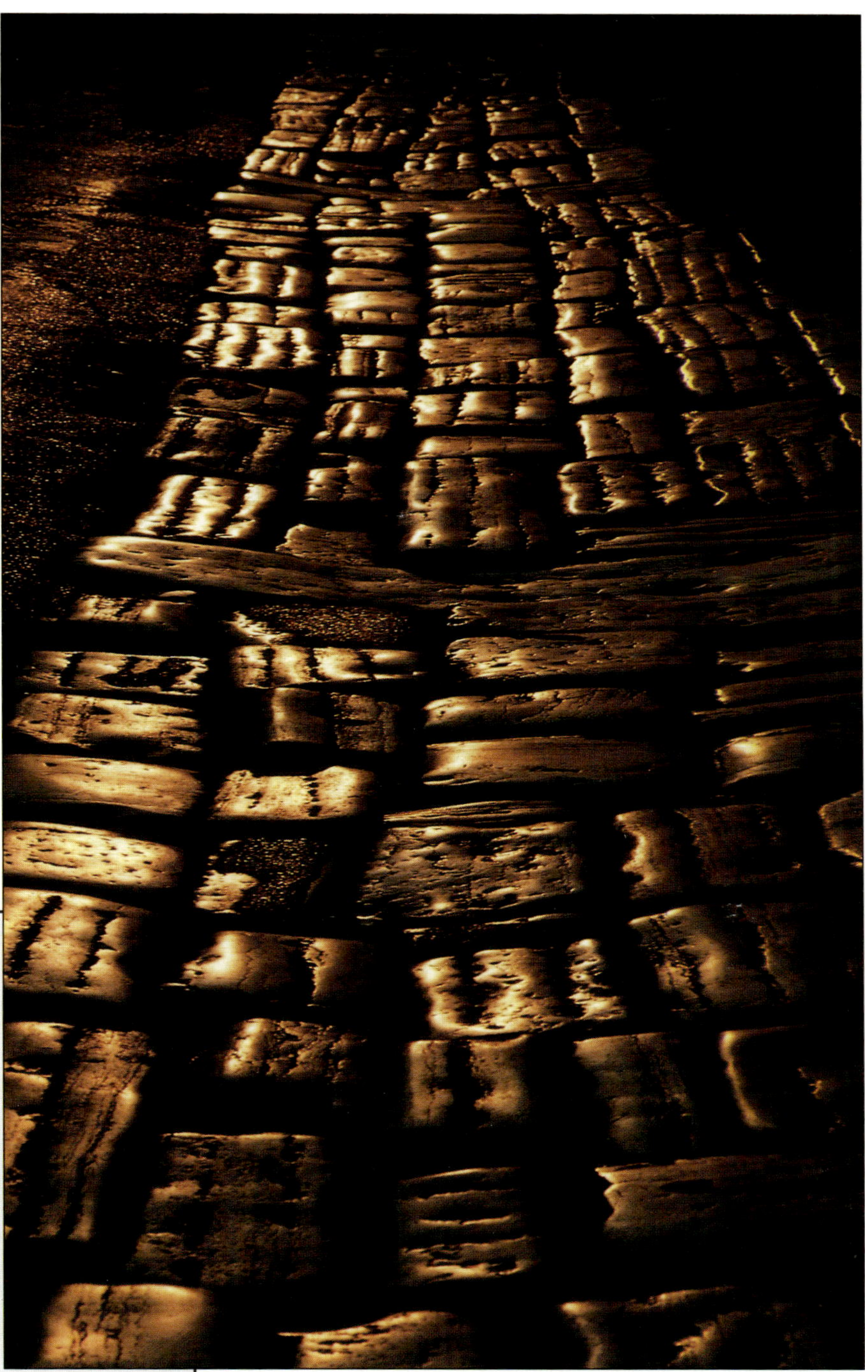

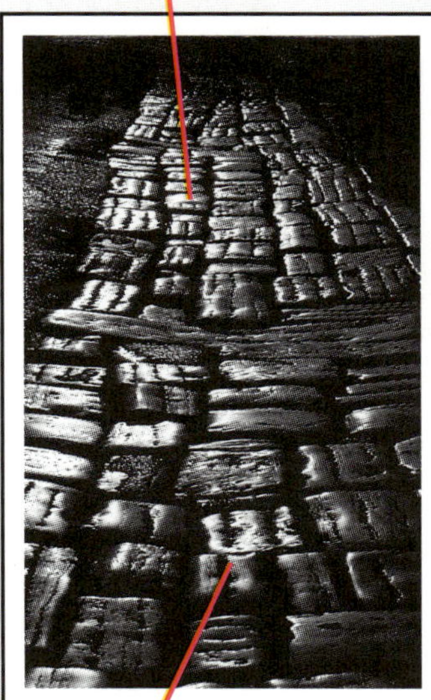

Accentuating texture

Tip

Exposure can quite often be used to accentuate texture, particularly if you use lighting with a reasonably high contrast range. A degree of underexposure often increases the textural quality of a subject. Skin tones in a portrait, for example, will have a stronger texture when they appear darker than usual. If on the other hand you want to minimize skin texture, slightly overexposing the shot, or using a soft focus filter usually works.

Quality of light

When you want to reveal texture you must also consider the quality of light you are going to use. This depends on the type of surface you are photographing.

For subjects which already have a pronounced texture such as bark or a wrinkly face, diffused lighting is enough to bring it out. It throws soft shadows, so little detail is lost in the hollows. If only hard light is available use tissue paper or a stocking over the light to soften it indoors, or wait for a cloud to pass over the sun outdoors.

However, for subtle textures such as silk or fur you need to use hard lighting to create strong highlights and shadows. Look for direct sun outdoors or use a strong, bare light bulb indoors.

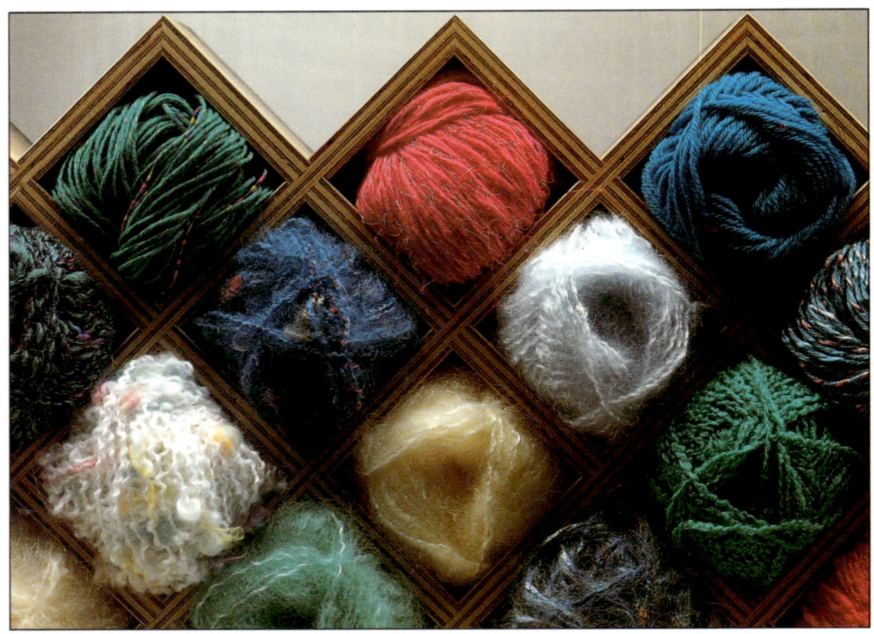

▲ A TOUCHY SUBJECT
Fairly hard, angled lighting was used to bring out the textures of these colourful balls of wool, reminding you how they would feel to touch. As a general rule, the finer the texture the harder the lighting needs to be.

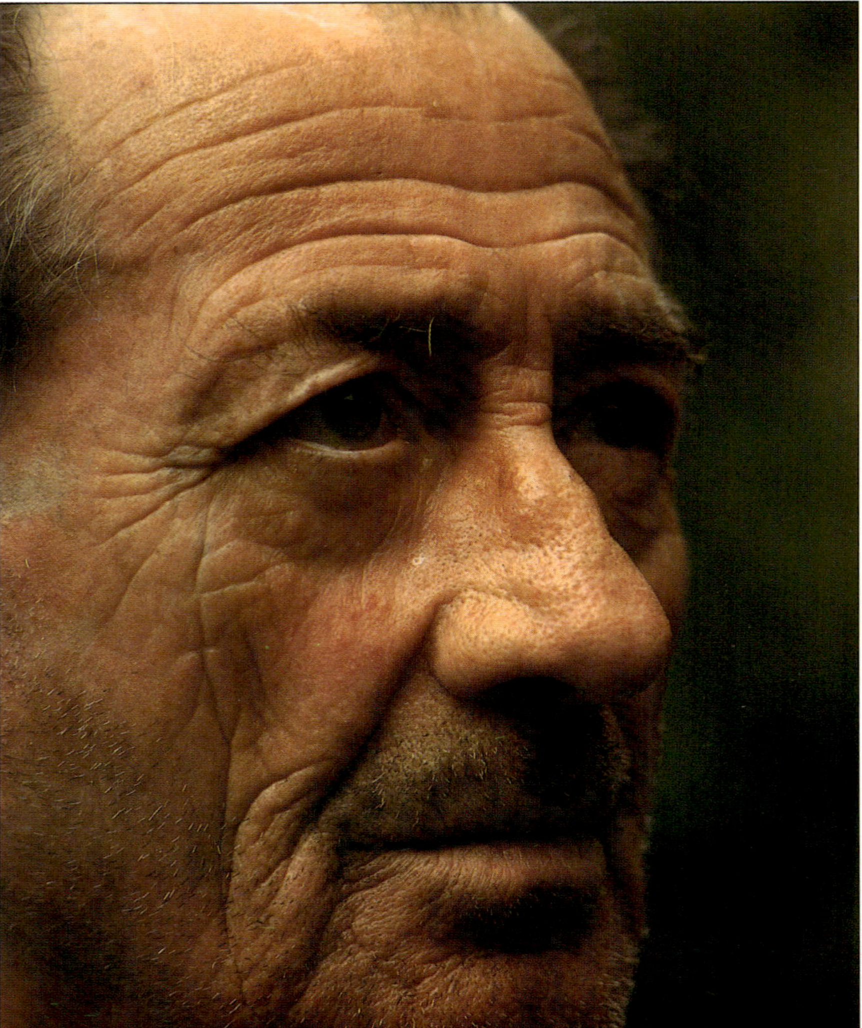

◀ LIGHT RELIEF
The wrinkled texture of the man's face gives this portrait a strong, gritty character. Diffused light illuminates his face fairly evenly and creates soft shadows so that as little of the texture and detail as possible are lost.

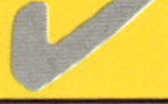

CHECK IT!

Here are a few reminders:

❏ angled light from the side, top or back reveals texture – frontlighting conceals it

❏ the subtler the texture the harder the lighting needs to be

❏ rough textures are obvious in any light, but diffused lighting is preferable because it creates soft shadows

❏ a close viewpoint can often help you to convey texture

Seeing in colour

Colour is often the first thing to grab your attention in a photo – and can leave the most lasting impression. With a little knowledge of how to mix colours in your photos, you've got the recipe for success. Start by understanding why different colour combinations have different effects.

Successful composition in colour requires a clear awareness of colour and how to use it. On the next few pages we look at colours which contrast, harmonize or create a sense of warmth or coolness.

The combinations of colours in a photo can greatly influence the picture's effect. Some are striking while others are easy on the eye, creating a soft, tranquil feel. For example, yellow and blue look bright and cheerful together, while blue and green are calming. Why does this happen?

The colour wheel

If you take all the colours of the rainbow and put them in a circle you end up with a device called a colour wheel.

By studying the wheel you can see how colours react together. Take red as an example. Look at where it is in relation to other colours on the wheel. It's in a band of colours that all give off a warm glow and blend pleasingly with each other. And although it stands out, imagine it next to its opposite, blue-green – the contrast would make the red even more vibrant.

Colours may contrast or harmonize, depending on where they are positioned on the colour wheel. Recognizing the effect of different colour combinations enables you to have greater control over the mood of a photo. For example, the golden hues of a sunset give a sense of warmth; green fields shot against a blue sky evoke a sense of calm.

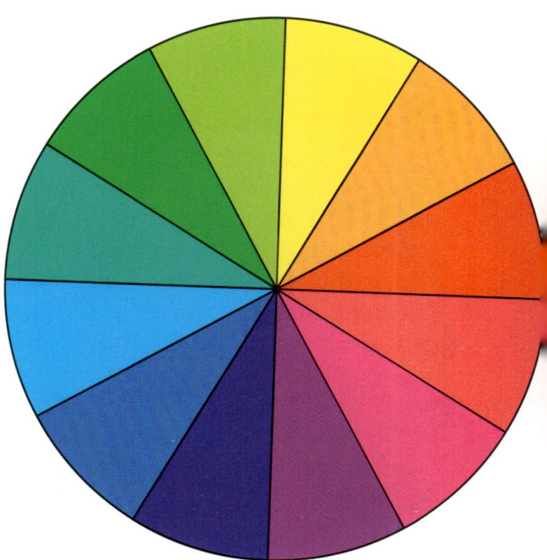

▲ THE COLOUR WHEEL
This circle of colour helps you see how colours react to each other. Remember that it's an idea, not a scientific tool, so use it as a guide. Colours you see and photograph rarely have the rainbow purity of the spectrum.

▶ BOLD AND BRIGHT
Without shadows and highlights to weaken the impact, these naturally bright colours look exceptionally strong and become the main interest of the picture.

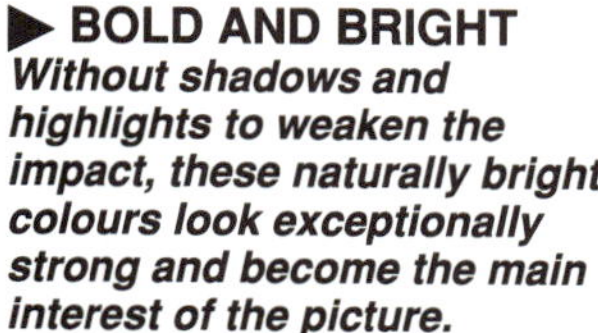

blue of reflective sunglasses repeats blue of background and model's eyes

warm orange contrasts with cool blues

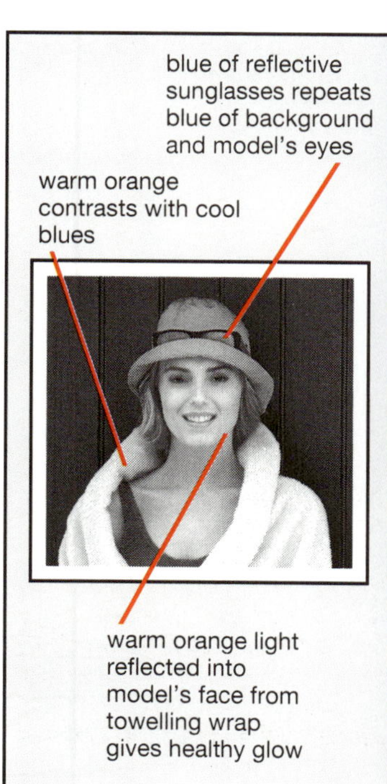

warm orange light reflected into model's face from towelling wrap gives healthy glow

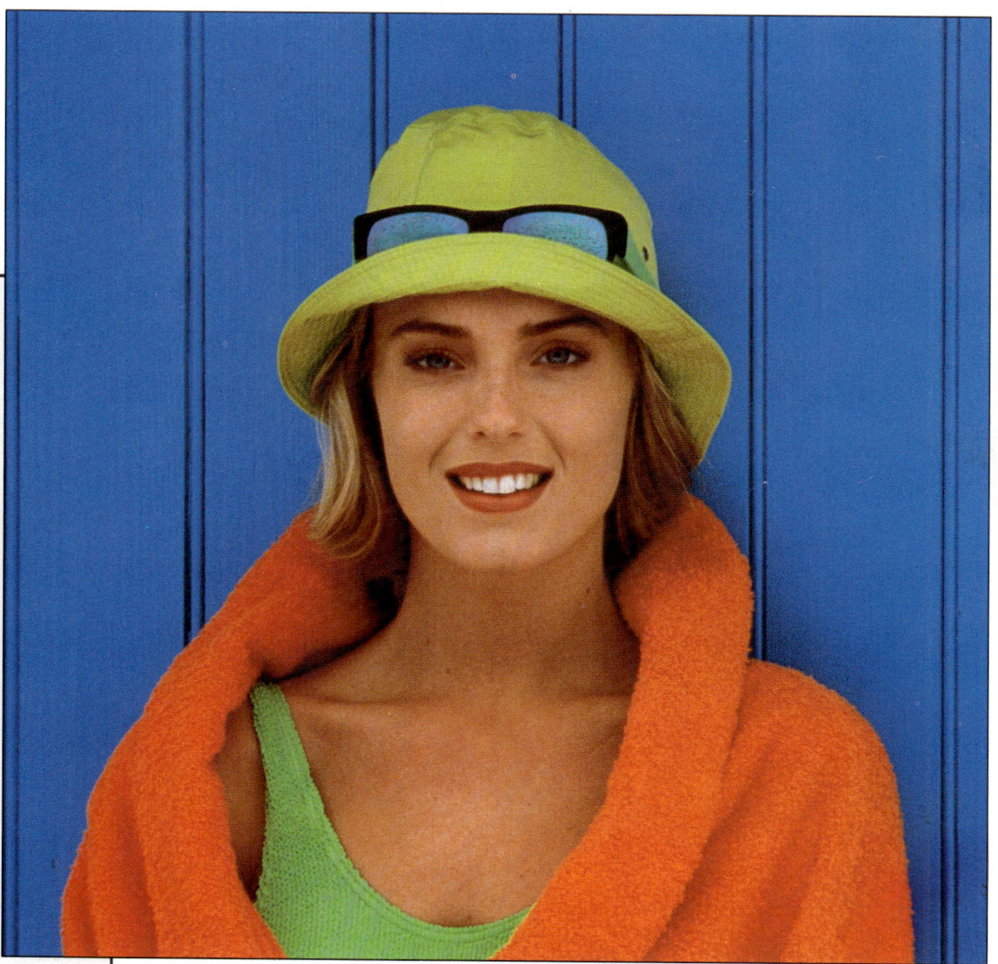

How colours look together

When composing, think about the colours you are including as well as how you arrange elements in the frame and light them. Even in a scene such as a landscape, which you can't change, you can frame different areas to include colours that are similar and soothing, or a patch of colour that stands out because it's so different from all of the others.

Contrasting colours appear opposite each other on the colour wheel. Red is opposite cyan (a blue-green colour) on the wheel. These colours are not similar but mix dynamically.

Harmonizing colours are next to each other on the colour wheel. They might be a mixture of green and yellow or purple and blue but they still harmonize if they are close to each other. For example, red is next to orange on one side of the colour wheel. These two colours go well together.

Warm colours Colours which are close to each other on the red side of the wheel are described as warm. They tend to create a feeling of heat and passion, because in nature they are the colours of the sun and fire.

Cool colours On the opposite side of the colour wheel to the warm reds are the blues. Blues tend to have a cool feeling – think of the sea, and the saying 'blue with cold'.

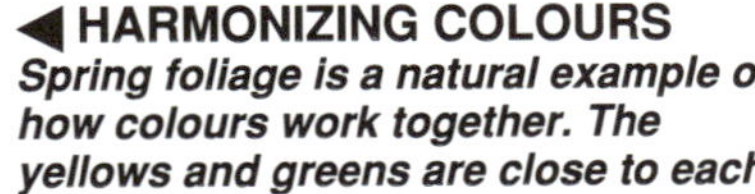

◀ HARMONIZING COLOURS
Spring foliage is a natural example of how colours work together. The yellows and greens are close to each other on the colour wheel. Colours harmonize with their neighbours.

▼ ▶ CONTRASTING COLOURS
This pretty combination of yellow and lilac contrasts because these colours are opposite each other on the wheel. Each enhances the other. Opposite colours always contrast.

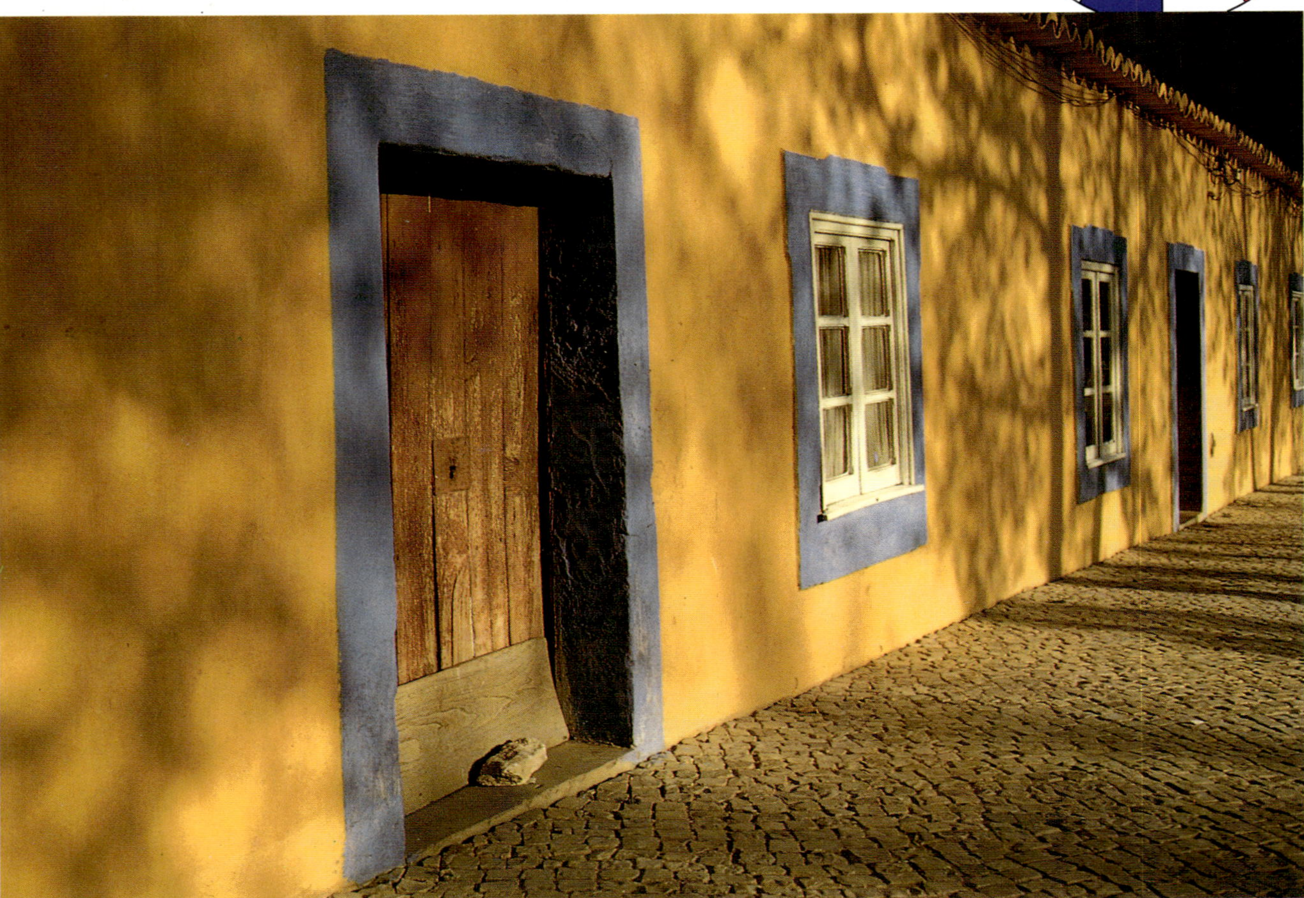

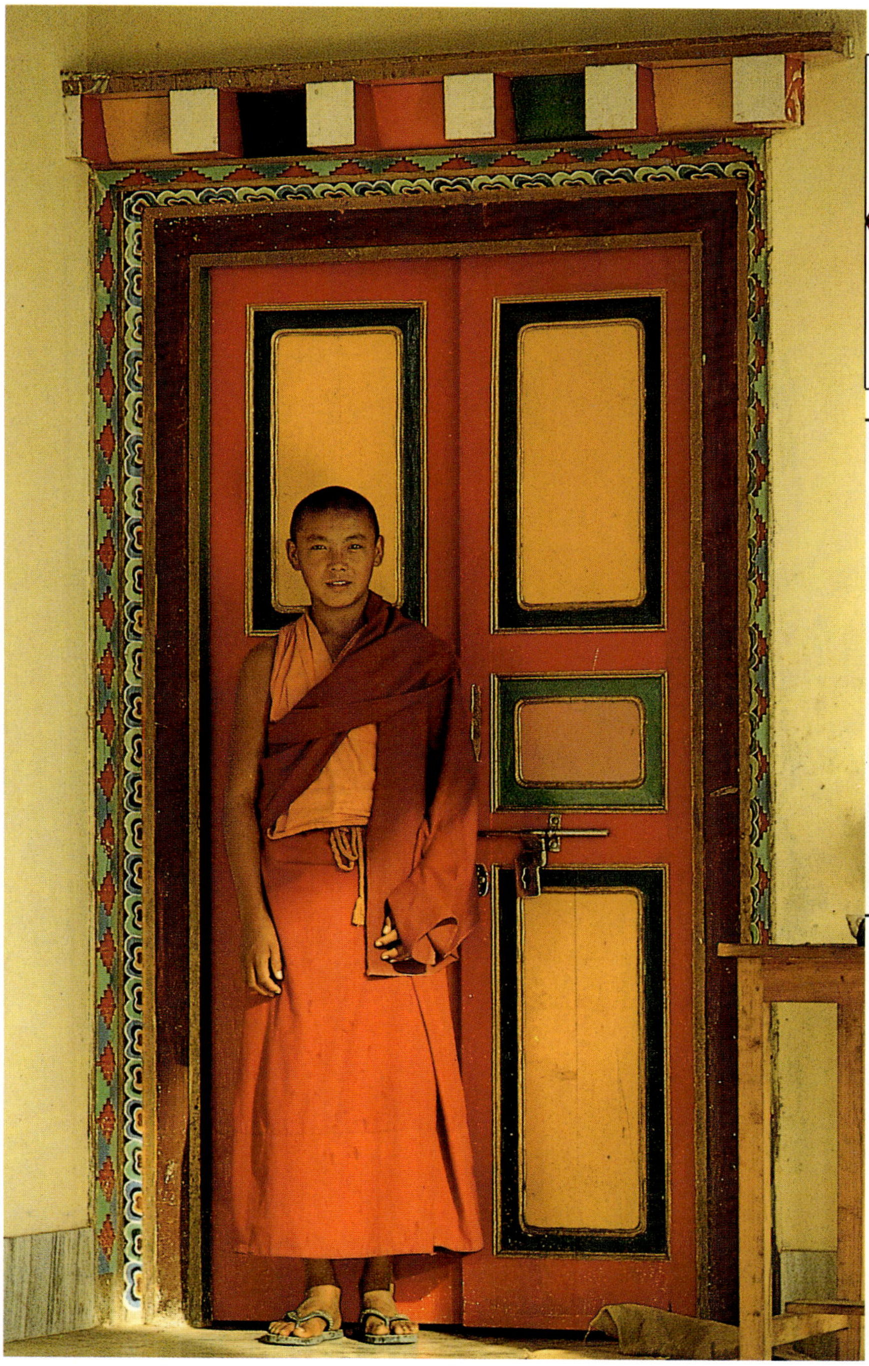

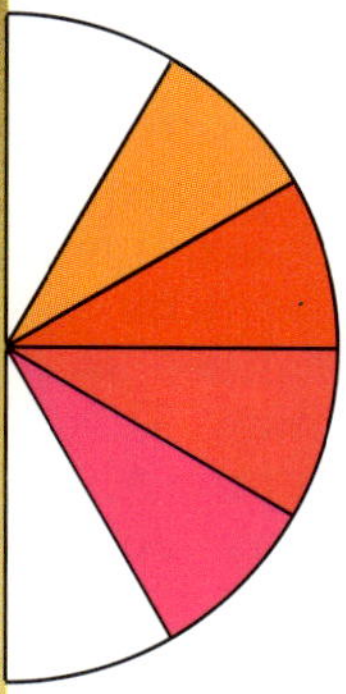

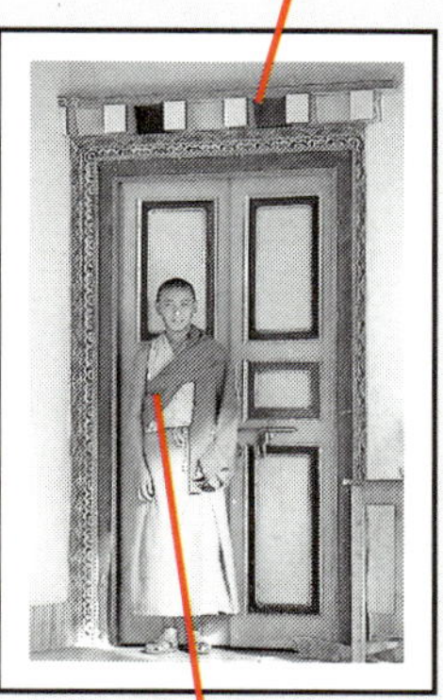

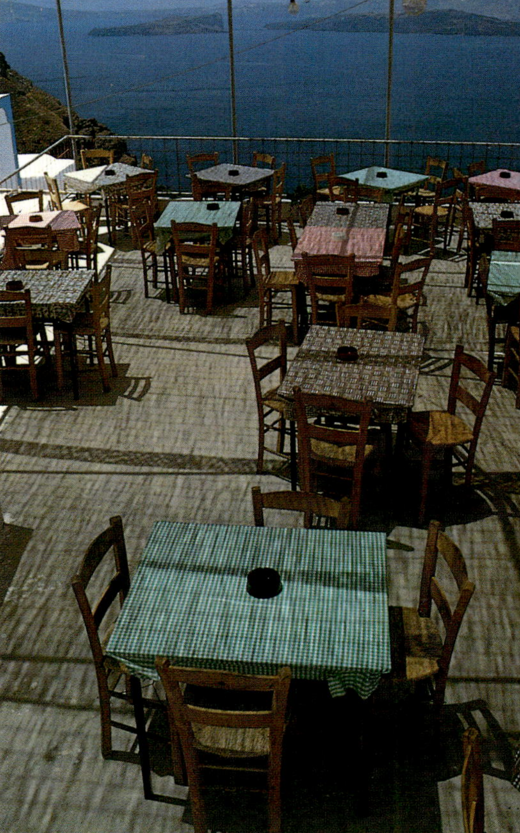

Looking at colour

Tip

Learn to look at colours even when you don't have your camera with you, so that you increase your ability to notice how they work together.

Ask yourself these questions –
❏ Do the colours go together satisfactorily?
❏ If so, is it because the contrast attracts the eye or because they blend well?
❏ Are they warm or cool colours?

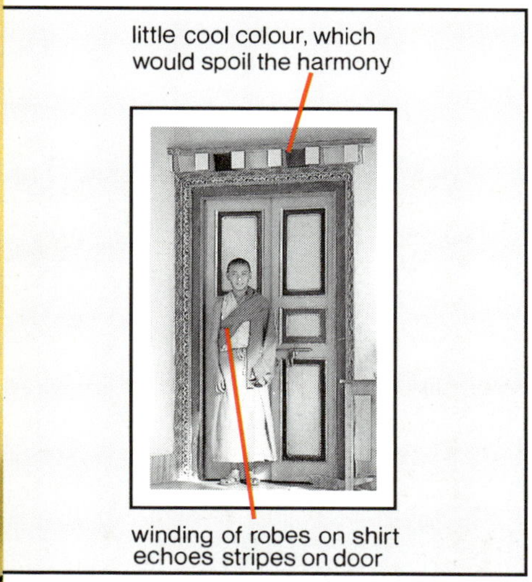

▶ **COOL COLOURS**
The colours in this picture are at the blue end of the wheel, so you feel cool, as if you were sitting there in the shade. The colours of the tables and chairs are pastels, which add to the sense of respite from the relentless heat beyond. Any colour on the blue side looks cool – the opposite to the passionate reds.

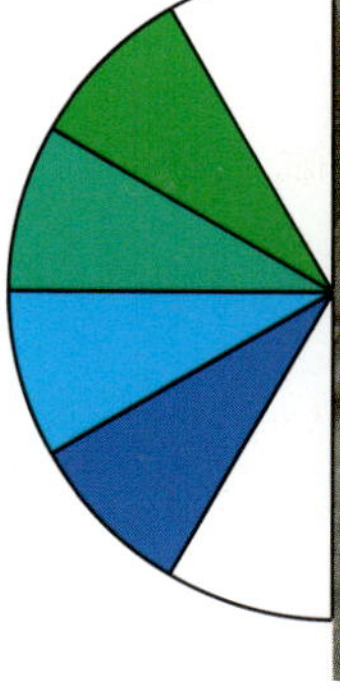

Accent colour

You may find an interesting subject to photograph but have a problem with seeing something specific to make the focal point in the picture. A small splash of colour called an accent is often the solution. This attracts the eye and, if it is properly placed, draws the viewer into looking at the rest of the picture.

Good composition is vital when using an accent colour. Carefully choose your viewpoint and frame to make the most of it – try to place it on a point where the imaginary third lines cross.

Strong colours are particularly useful for colour accents, because they stand out well against neutral colours in the background and help to give the picture depth and scale.

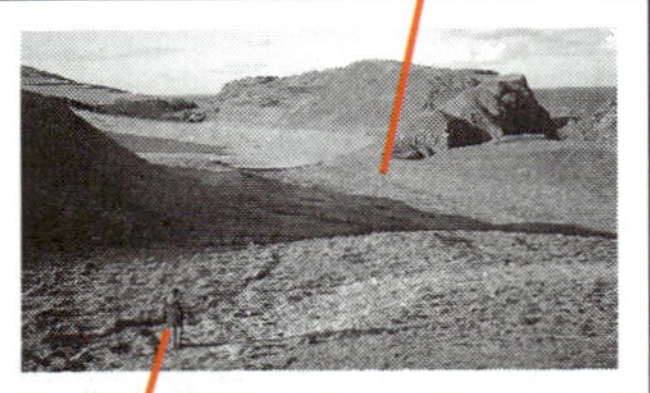

unrelieved by the figure, blue sea and green turf would look uninteresting

red coat is small enough to catch the eye, but not big enough to dominate

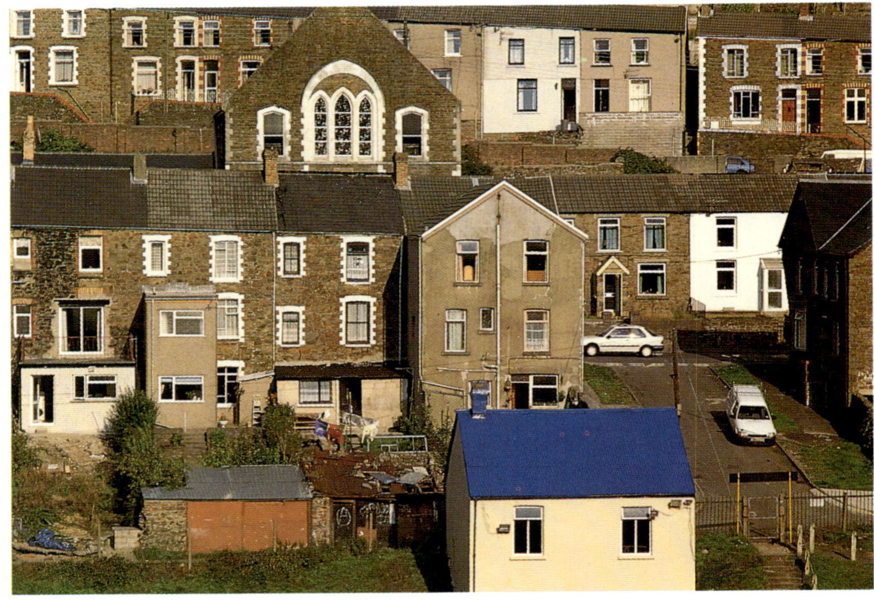

▲ ADDING INTEREST
The deep blue colour of the roof of the building comes as a surprise against the rather dull, uniformly weak colours of the other buildings. It adds a splash of colour and interest to the picture.

▼ CREATING A FOCUS
Finding a point of focus is particularly effective when photographing a landscape. The bright red of the girl's jacket is the strongest colour in the picture and stands out against the contrasting green and blue. It attracts the eye and is well placed to add depth and scale.

Using colours well means developing an awareness of how:

❏ colours opposite each other on the wheel contrast.
❏ colours next to each other on the wheel harmonize.
❏ colours on the blue side of the wheel create a cool mood.
❏ colours on the red side of the wheel create a warm mood.

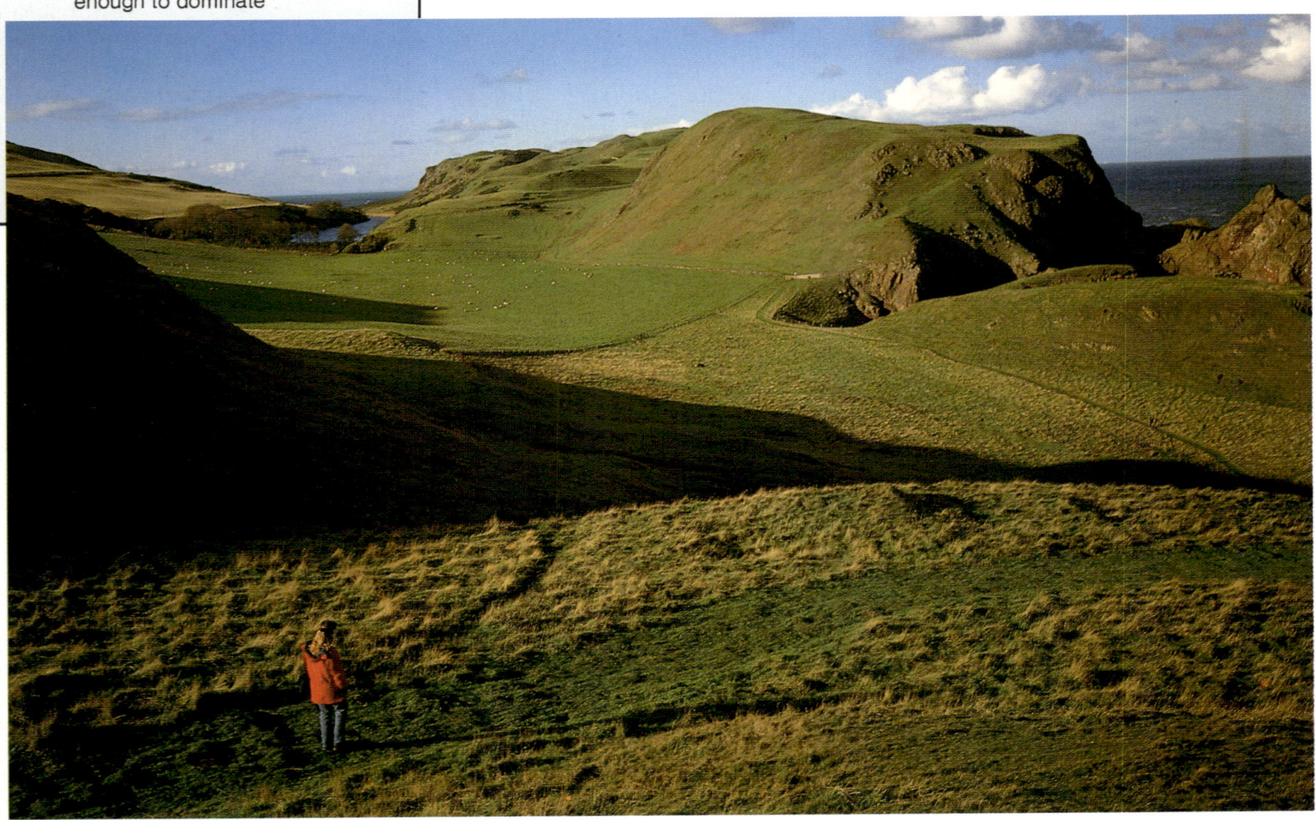

Making more of colour

Coloured objects do not necessarily have to be very interesting to make a good photograph. There are times when it is the colour, and not the subject, which captures your imagination.

When the colour makes a greater impact on you than the object itself – for example, a pile of red apples on a market stall – you have to decide how to compose the picture. The colour rather than the apples is the subject, so how can you make the most of it?

In such cases, it's often best to go for a close-up and fill the frame. The success of your picture will, however, depend on two key factors: how saturated (pure) the colour is and what colours you choose to include. As a general rule, the fewer colours you use the more dramatic the effect.

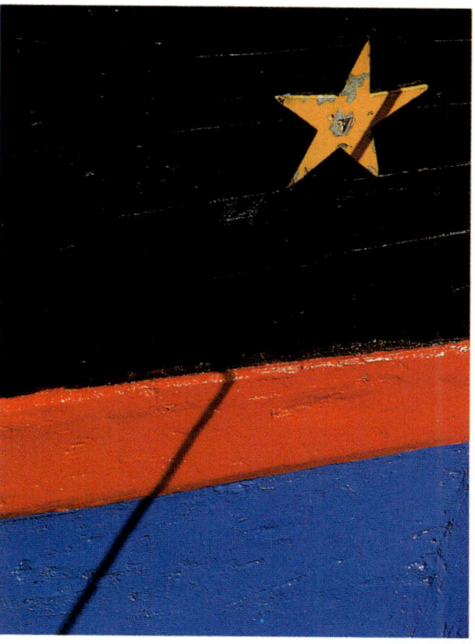

▲ CLOSING IN
By closing in on just a small area, the side of this fishing boat becomes an abstract pattern of rich colours. Like the pattern on a flag, this simple mix of contrasting colours stands out clearly.

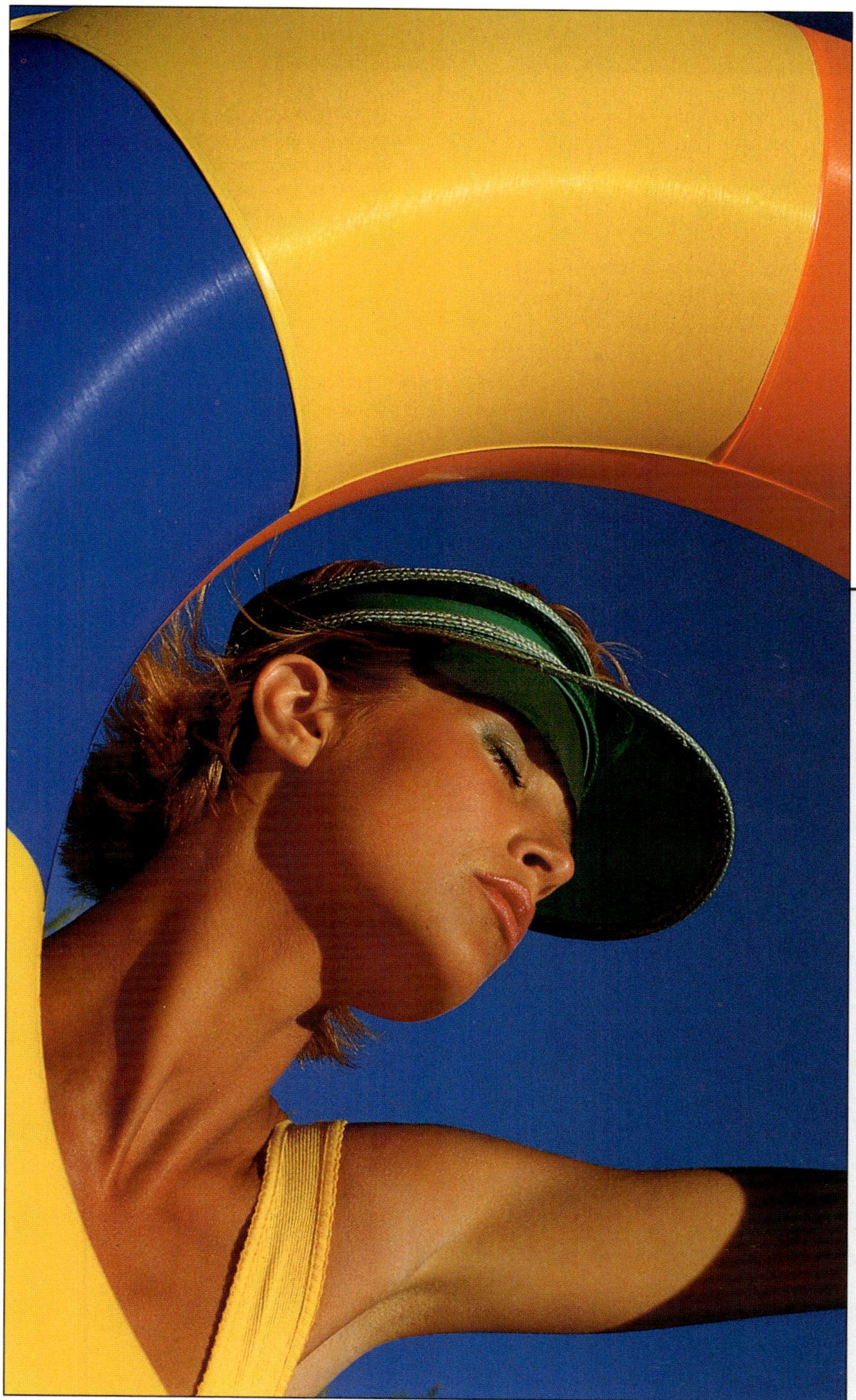

◄ CHOOSING A VIEWPOINT
Pointing the camera upwards, the photographer uses the ring to give a circular frame to the brilliant blue sky. This backdrop keeps the picture as simple as possible and stops a striking colour combination becoming a muddle.

blues of sky and ring match each other – one picture element ties in with another

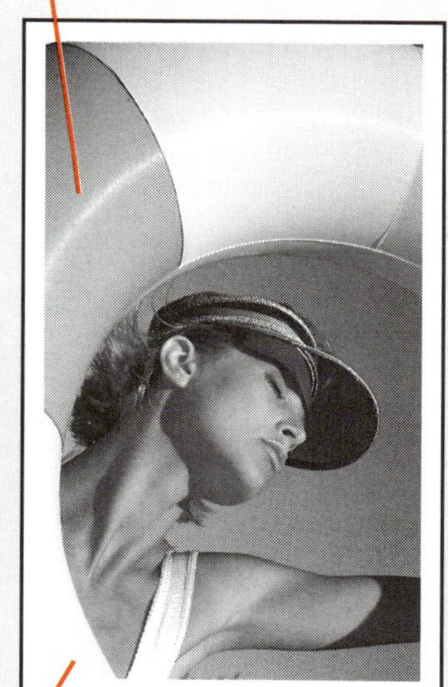

limited use of colour strengthens picture – girl's yellow top blends with yellow on ring

What is saturation?

The saturation of a colour means how strong or weak it looks. A fully saturated colour is the strongest possible, achieved in perfect light conditions.

Colours look most saturated in soft, diffused light. This has weaker highlights and shadows compared to the light on a sunny day.

A colour becomes desaturated when bright light makes it a weaker tint. This is the same as the effect of overexposure. Equally, if you add shadow the colour becomes darker and desaturated. This looks the same as an underexposed picture.

How to strengthen colour

Apart from saturation, there are several ways to strengthen colour.
❏ Some colours attract your eye more than others in a photograph. Warm colours, particularly red, demand attention – so try to include these. Cool colours, like blue, do not – they tend to fade into the background.
❏ Make sure that your subject is framed by a neutral or dark background. The subject will show up more clearly because of the absence of rival colour behind it.
❏ If you take a picture just after it has been raining the colours often look stronger. Rain takes some of the dust out of the atmosphere, so afterwards the light is clearer and

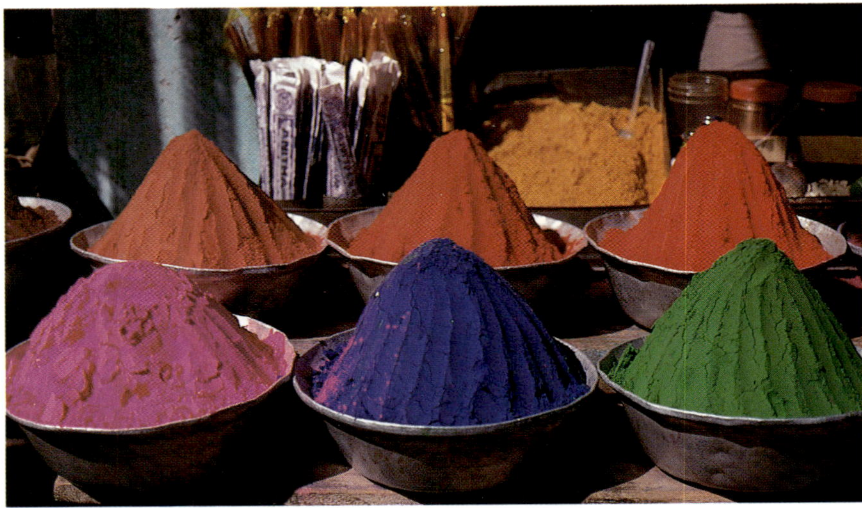

▲ CLASHING COLOURS
This gaudy array of colours makes an irresistible picture. It is often best to use only one or two colours but in this case it is the riotous mixture that makes the shot.

raises the contrast between colours.
❏ If you are using slide film, under-exposing the film by half a stop strengthens colour. With print film half a stop of *over*exposure can have a similar (though less pronounced) effect.

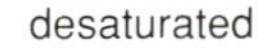

▲ LOOKING AT SATURATION
The band in the middle is fully saturated, pure colour. The area on one side is desaturated because light has been added. At the other end the colour becomes desaturated with shadow. The same applies to any colour – pure colour is strong; light and shade weaken it.

Whatever the composition, when you concentrate on colour you should aim for maximum saturation.

▶ JUMPING OUT
With a careful choice of background, colours jump out at you. Here the dull, neutral background puts the focus on the brightly coloured clothes the boy is wearing. The rainwear also has a shiny finish, which reflects more light making colours seem brighter.

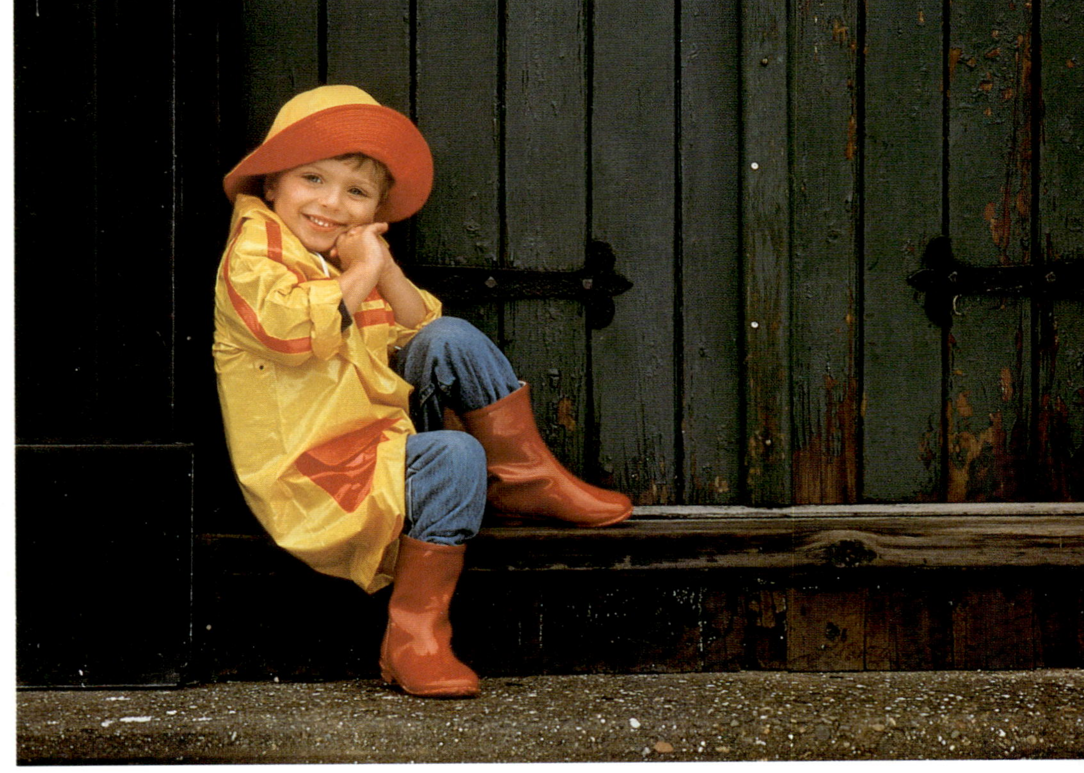

◀ **RICH COLOURS**
The weather affects the colour saturation of a picture. This shot was taken on an overcast day so the light is diffused and the colours look true to life. Notice how much more forceful the red is than the blue.

▼ **NATURAL COLOURS**
Nature provides some wonderful subjects for colour photography. Saturated colour doesn't always have to be bright – here there are no strong highlights or shadows and this brings out the rich colours of the leaves.

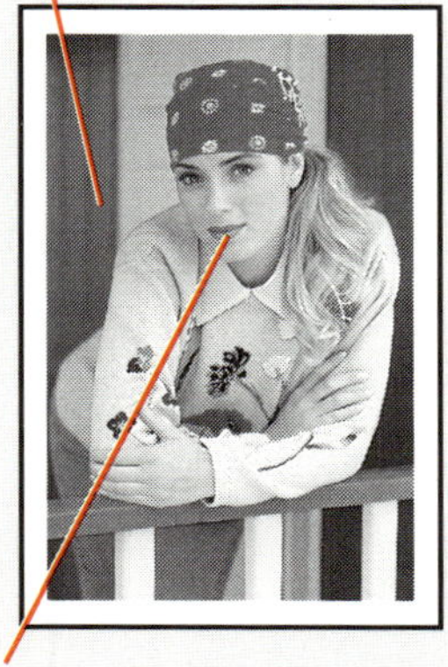

few shadows or highlights because of diffused light so colours are even in intensity

scarf and mouth are most striking because red jumps forward

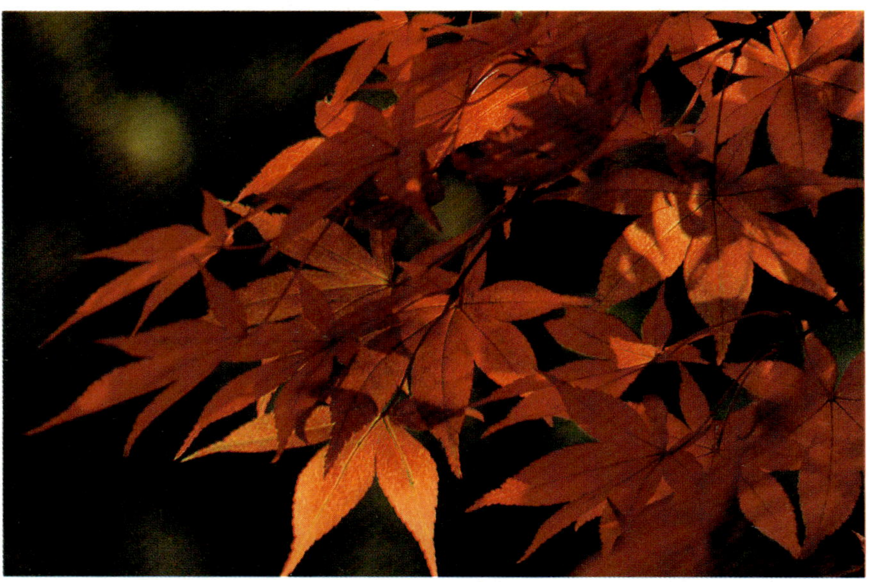

Using one colour

The fewer colours you use, the more they need to dominate the picture. When you get down to one colour, fill the frame – whether you're closing in or taking a wide view.

If you have a lot of strong colours in a picture, they tend to compete for attention. This can be effective if a chaotic image is what you want. But by using just one or two hues you can achieve a starker, more dramatic image.

Filters

To make colours look stronger you can alter them artificially by using colour correction filters. If you use a filter that is the same colour as the subject this makes the colour seem even richer.

For example, a yellow filter will exaggerate the stunning colours of a golden sunset and make them look more vivid.

However, bear in mind that a filter affects all colours equally. This can be a problem if the picture includes more than one main colour. For example, a yellow filter may bring out the yellow and gold but it will dull all other colours and decrease contrast.

To strengthen colours you can:
❑ go in close to the subject and fill the frame with colour.

❑ underexpose slide film by about half a stop.

❑ eliminate glare by using a polarizing filter.

❑ frame strong colours against neutral or dark ones.

❑ look for weather conditions that will improve saturation.

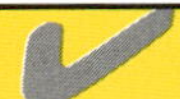

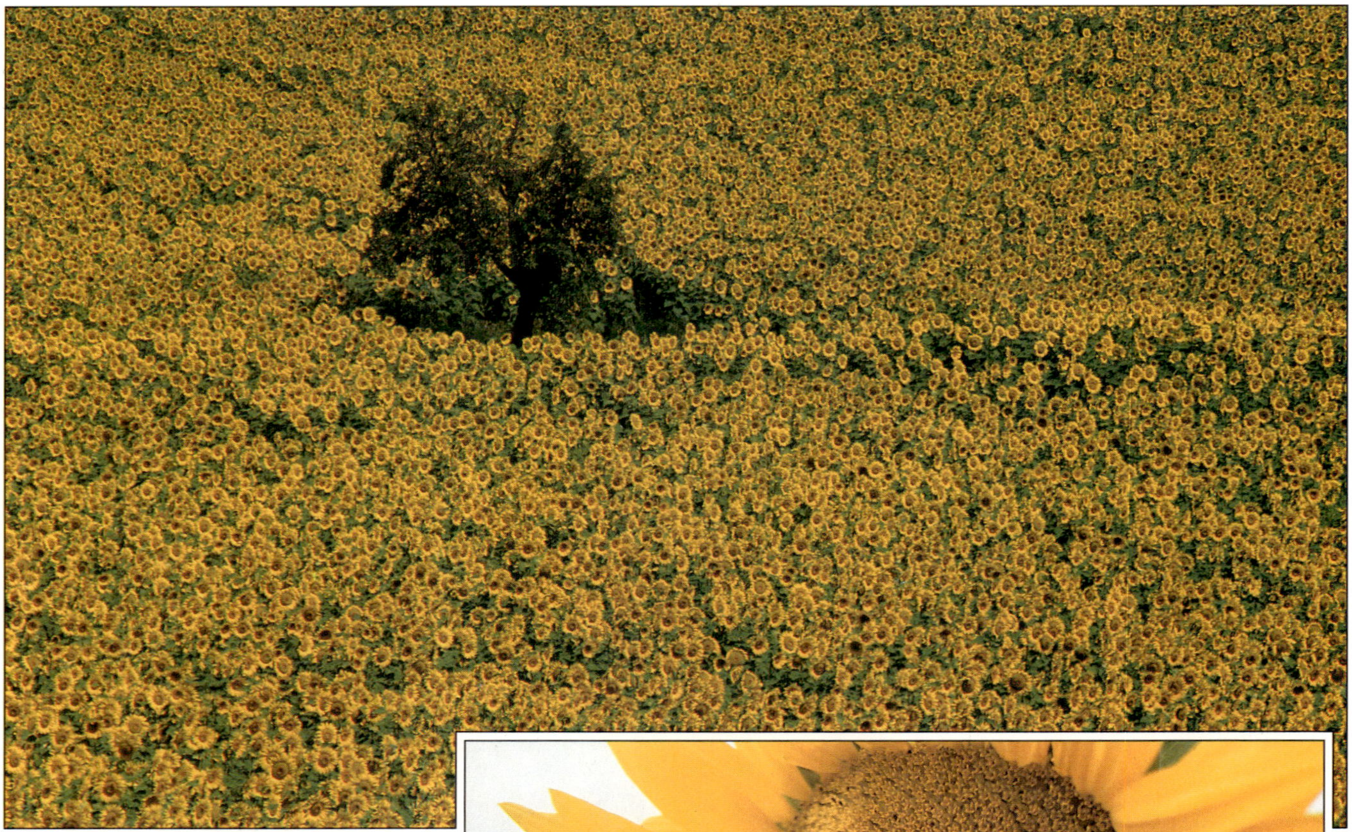

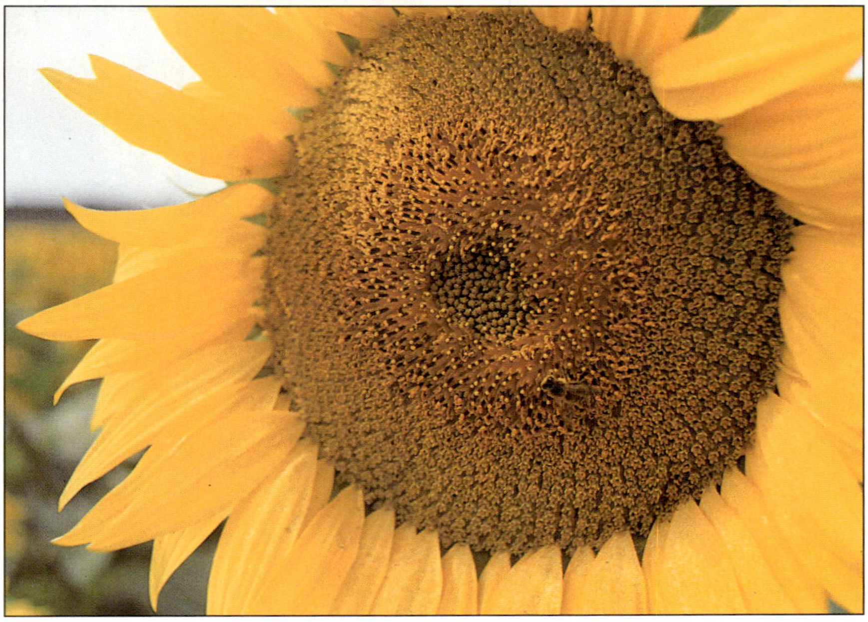

▲ **BREAKING UP THE COLOUR**
A telephoto lens turns this field of sunflowers into a riot of colour. The dark green colour provides a visual 'breathing space' from the overwhelming yellow. Instead of adding a strong focus, it gives a neutral point of interest to the shot and breaks up the brightness of the sunflowers.

▶ **FILLING THE FRAME**
Here the photographer uses a different approach to the same subject. By closing in on just one flower, the picture is filled with a stark, simple image. The bright yellow petals add a sunny frame to the darker centre.

Contrasting colours

When colours opposite each other on the wheel both appear in a photo the bold reaction between them is called colour contrast. Knowing which combinations work well together can help you achieve dramatic results.

The impact a colour has in a photo depends not just on the colour itself but also on the colours next to it.

For example, a green leaf shot against a blue sky harmonizes well with its background. This is because the colours are close to each other. But surrounding a red flower, the green is less noticeable because the red jumps out as a stronger colour. And against a white wall, green looks much richer because of the absence of a rival colour behind it.

Normal rules of composition still apply when dealing with colour contrast. Unusual combinations, such as yellow and purple, look so vibrant that, unless you control them carefully, the colours can distract from the subject of the composition.

Colours directly opposite each other on the colour wheel create the most striking photographs; however, there are several other ways you can use colours to achieve contrast:

❏ Strong colours contrast with neutral colours. For example, bright red looks good against a pale grey background.

❏ Warm colours such as reds and oranges are at one end of the colour wheel. These contrast with the cool blues opposite them.

❏ Light colours complement dark colours. A lemon yellow makes navy blue look even darker.

❏ Saturated and desaturated tones of the same colour contrast – deep red contrasts with pale pink.

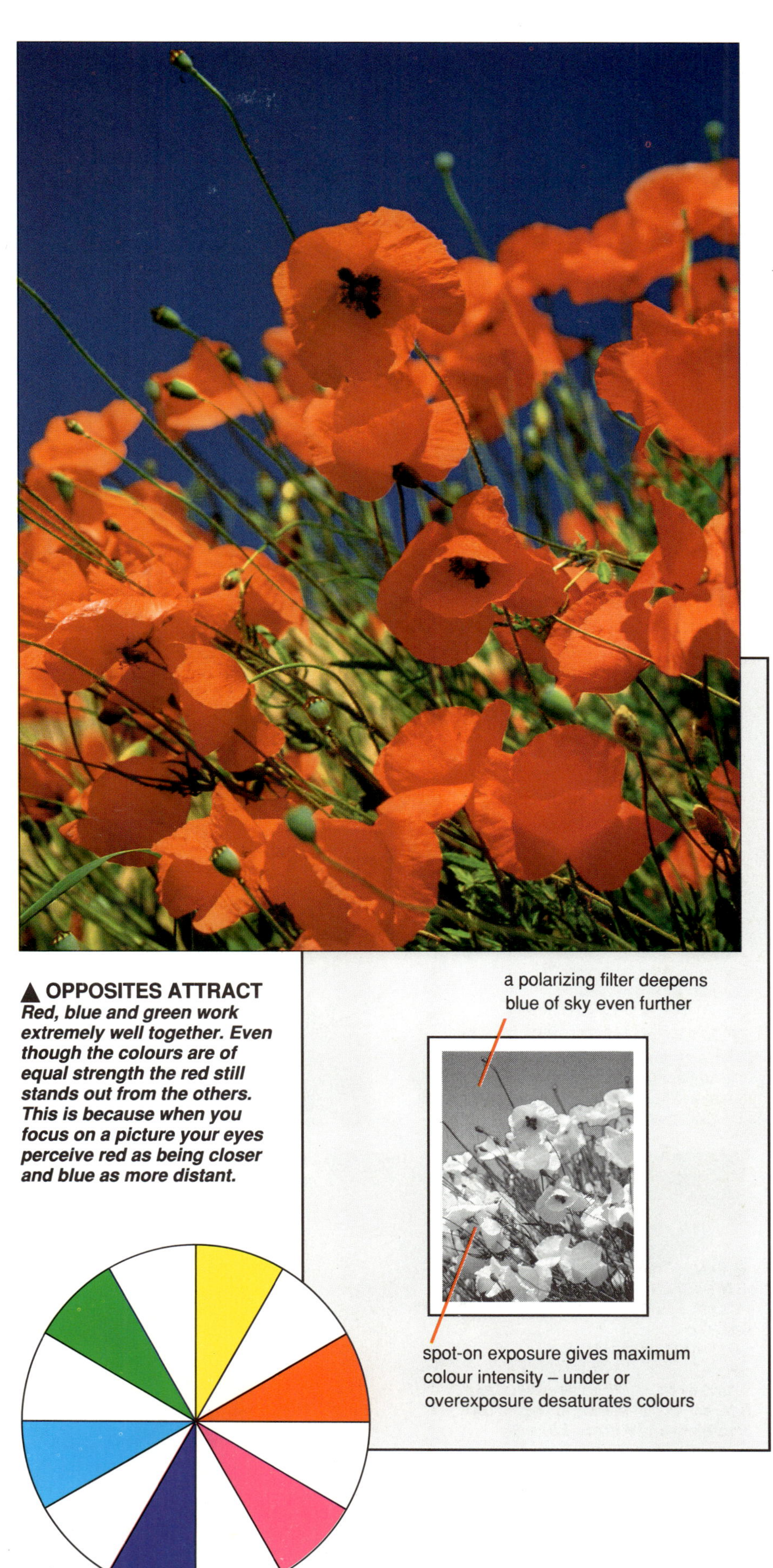

▲ **OPPOSITES ATTRACT**
Red, blue and green work extremely well together. Even though the colours are of equal strength the red still stands out from the others. This is because when you focus on a picture your eyes perceive red as being closer and blue as more distant.

▶ **WHICH COLOURS CONTRAST?**
Contrasting colours make an unusual mix and are all the more eyecatching for that. For example, pink and green create a very strong image together. However, colours don't have to be direct opposites to be effective.

Using colour contrast

You can either create contrast – as in a still life – or seek it out, as in a landscape. In a still life, try moving the objects around to see how they look against each other. Or you can create contrast between the background and the subject. Primroses set against a black background would make the yellow look paler and brighter.

If you're photographing people you may find it helpful to throw the background out of focus or go in close to ensure that the subject dominates the frame.

Towns and cities provide rich hunting grounds for strong colour contrasts. The saturated colours of plastics, paint and all things bright and artificial can look effective against muted buildings.

Nature offers examples of colour contrast, too. Vivid colours are a means of survival for many plants and creatures. For example, flowers need to stand out against their leaves to attract bees.

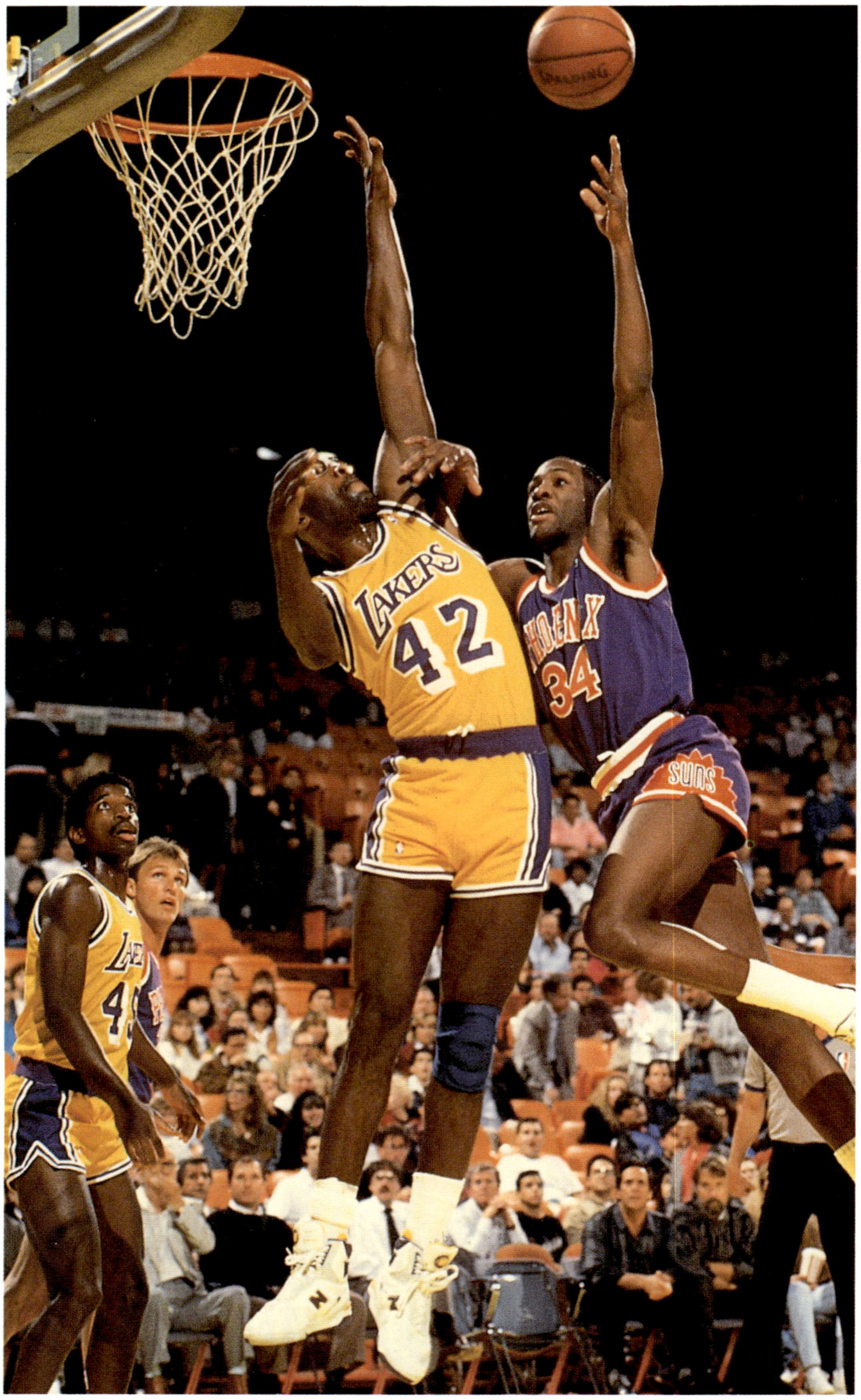

▶ **CONTRAST IN ACTION**
In the upper half of the picture the contrast between the yellow and purple is heightened by a plain, black background. The lower half is not quite so effective because the detail of the crowd is intrusive.

▼ **MAKING MACHINES WORK**
The soft shapes of the green leaves provide a pleasing contrast, both in form and colour, with the angular lines of the machine's red spokes.

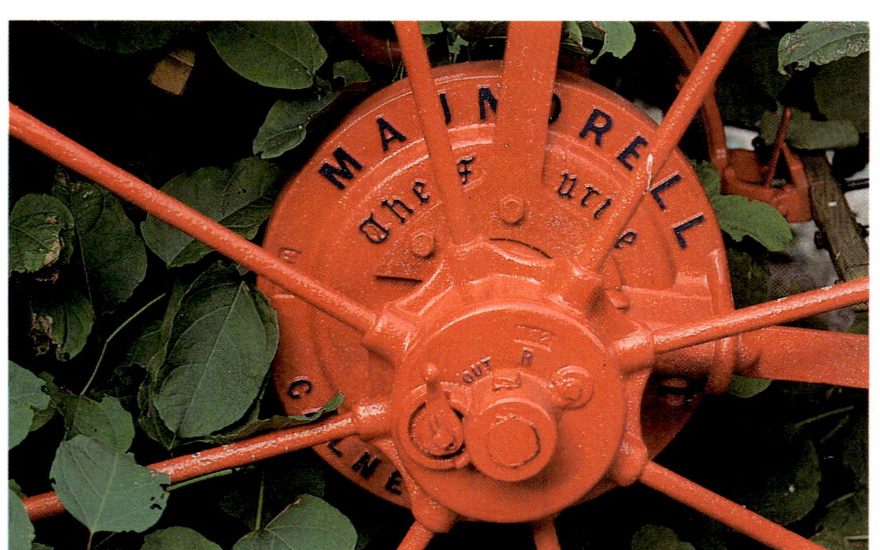

Tip **Intensifying colour contrast**

There are several tricks you can use to make contrasting colours look even more vibrant in your pictures.

❑ **Slow film** (ISO 64 or lower) gives higher contrast and makes colours appear more vibrant.

❑ **Fill-in flash** helps to lift colour when taking photos in dull or diffused light.

❑ **A polarizing filter** eliminates reflection and glare, increasing colour saturation.

Proportion – getting it right

If the areas of strong contrasting colours in your picture are of equal proportion they may detract from each other. So vary the amount of each colour used. For example, one green apple in a bowl of oranges has far more impact than a mixed bowl with equal numbers of apples and oranges.

However, you may be able to break this rule with great success. Pictures with geometrical shapes as their subject can look stunning with either two or three equal blocks of colour. Experiment and see what you think.

For landscape shots, you can't change the scenery to suit your needs, but you can alter your position to vary the proportions. A different camera angle can often help to get the balance just right. The same applies to taking close-up nature shots.

Composing and colour

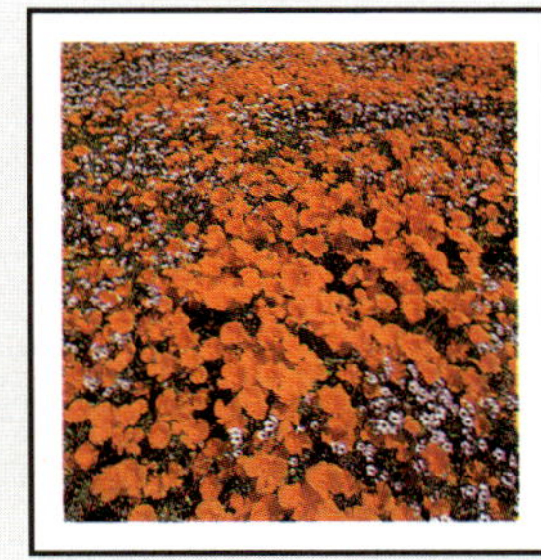

cutting out the sky shows how dull this shot would have been without it – blue and orange complement each other perfectly. Note the proportion, too. If the two colours were 50/50 the effect would be too overpowering

throwing background out of focus accentuates the orange and blue

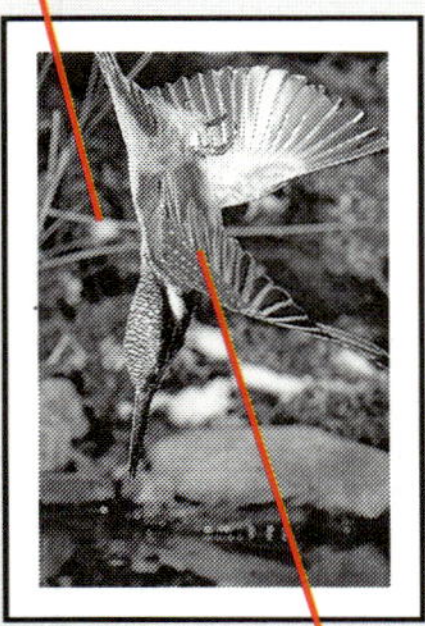

fill-in flash brings out colour contrast

▲ CLOSING IN ON NATURE
Nature provides plenty of opportunities for taking contrasting shots. Many birds have brilliant plumage to deter predators from a rather unpleasant meal. A dash of pale orange gives the kingfisher's bright blue feathers extra impact.

▶ THE NATURAL LOOK
Warm reds and oranges always stand out in contrast to sky blues because they are directly opposite each other on the colour wheel. Don't let the colours take over the picture – you still need to think about format, foreground, background and lighting.

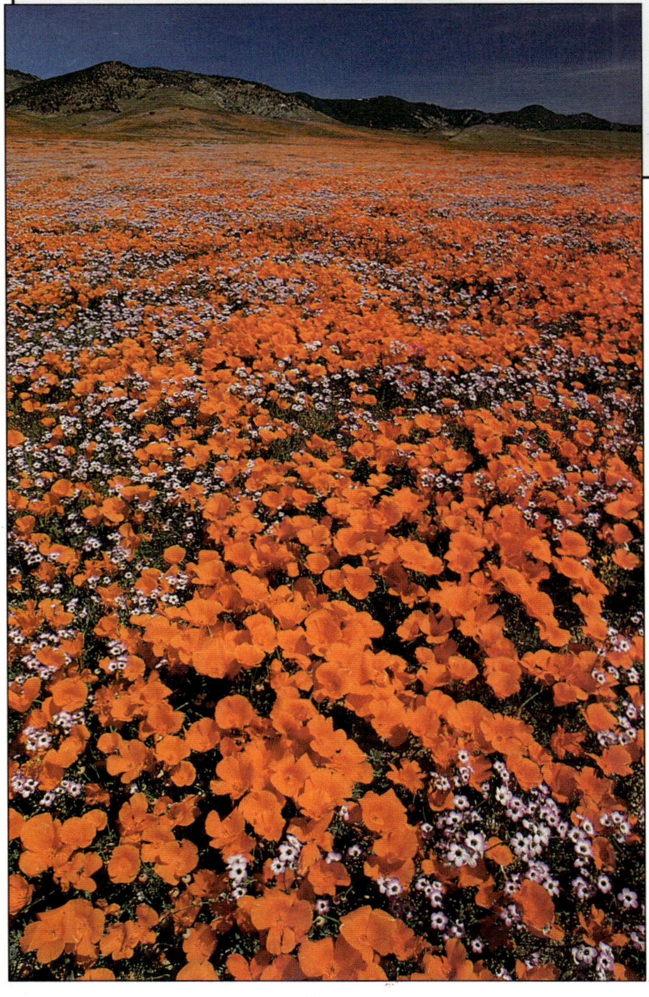

Experimenting with colour

Determining which colours contrast, harmonize or clash is largely a matter of taste. Colours don't have to be directly opposite each other on the wheel to achieve dramatic results. For example, a vase of pink and red roses can look effective, even though it includes saturated and desaturated tones of the same colour. Neutral backgrounds intensify colours, too.

Bright colours taken at close range disguise shape and form, so pictures can become quite abstract. Abstract shots should be simple to be effective. Too many details mean too many distractions for the eye. Frame the boundaries – where each colour meets the next – with care. For example, tilting the camera so the flowers in a bed form parallel lines can be effective.

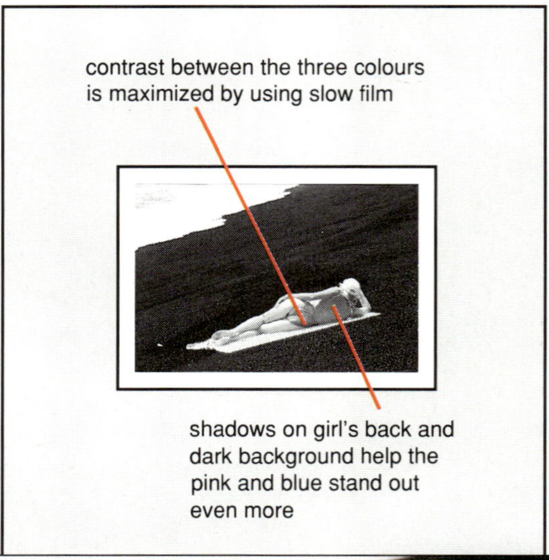

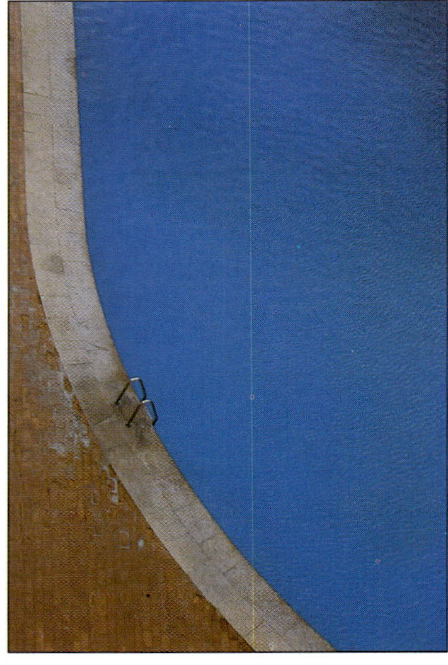

▲ **POOLSIDE SUCCESS**
By choosing a bird's eye viewpoint, the photographer has turned an ordinary scene into a clever abstract picture. The concrete line divides the bright and neutral blocks of colour.

▼ **SUBJECT VERSUS BACKGROUND**
The woman stands out in the photo because of the strong contrast between the bright pink and black background. The blue swimsuit adds interest, too.

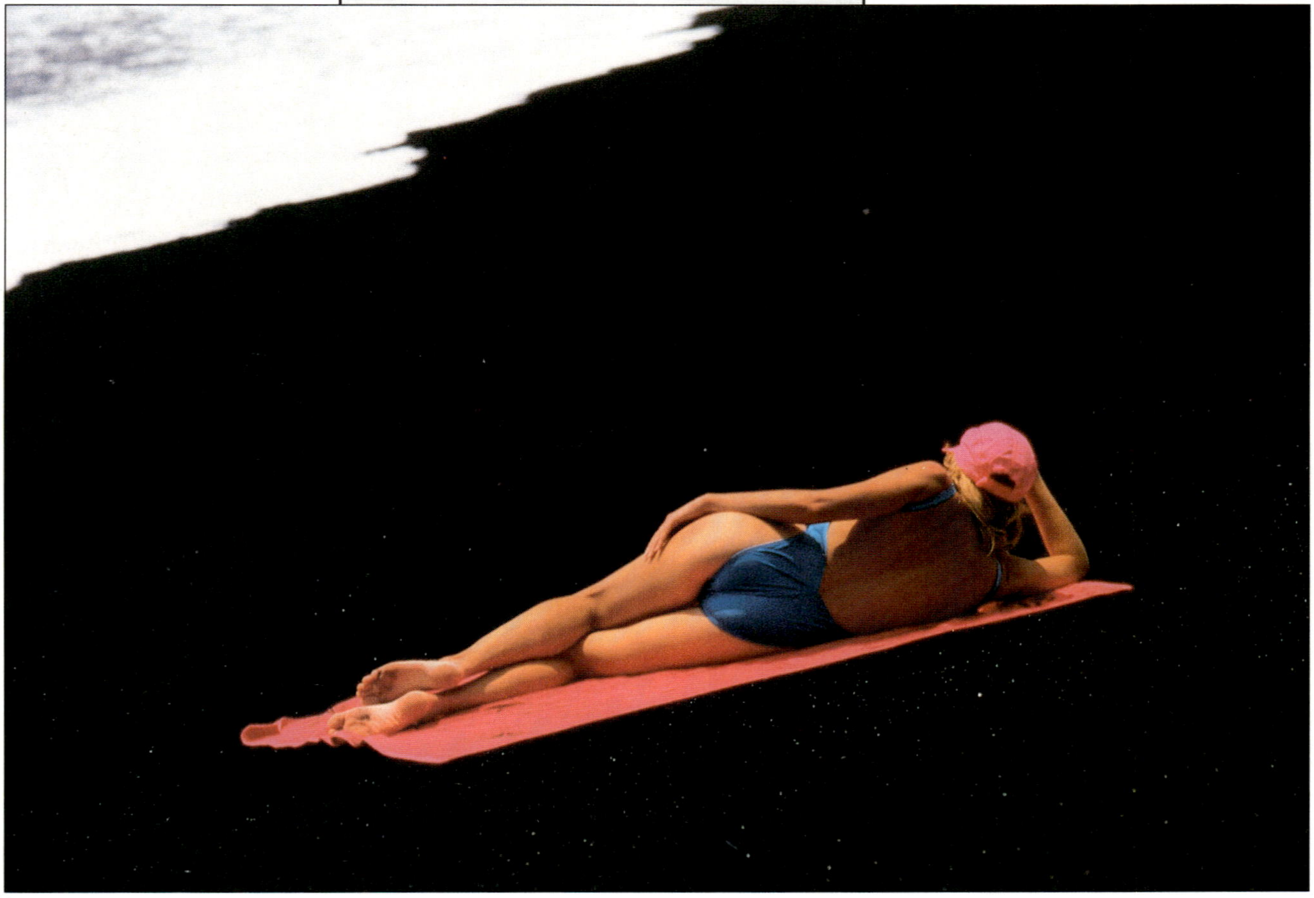

Colour contrast occurs when using:

❏ opposites

❏ strong against neutral

❏ warm against cool

❏ light against dark

❏ saturated against desaturated

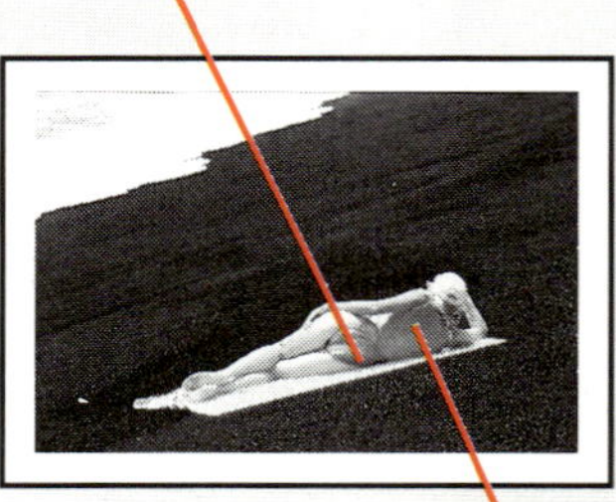

Colour harmony

When colours next to each other on the wheel are placed together, the subtle reaction between them is called colour harmony.

Harmony is probably the most evocative reaction between colours, and can help you to control the mood of a photo. You can use colour harmony to reflect the bleakness of a wintry beach scene, the warmth of a blazing sunset, the gloom of an urban landscape or the freshness of a spring morning.

If you pick two or three colours next to each other on the colour wheel you can be sure they harmonize with each other because they are closely related. Picture an autumnal scene – the yellow, orange and brown hues of the foliage look stunning, because nothing clashes or dominates the scene.

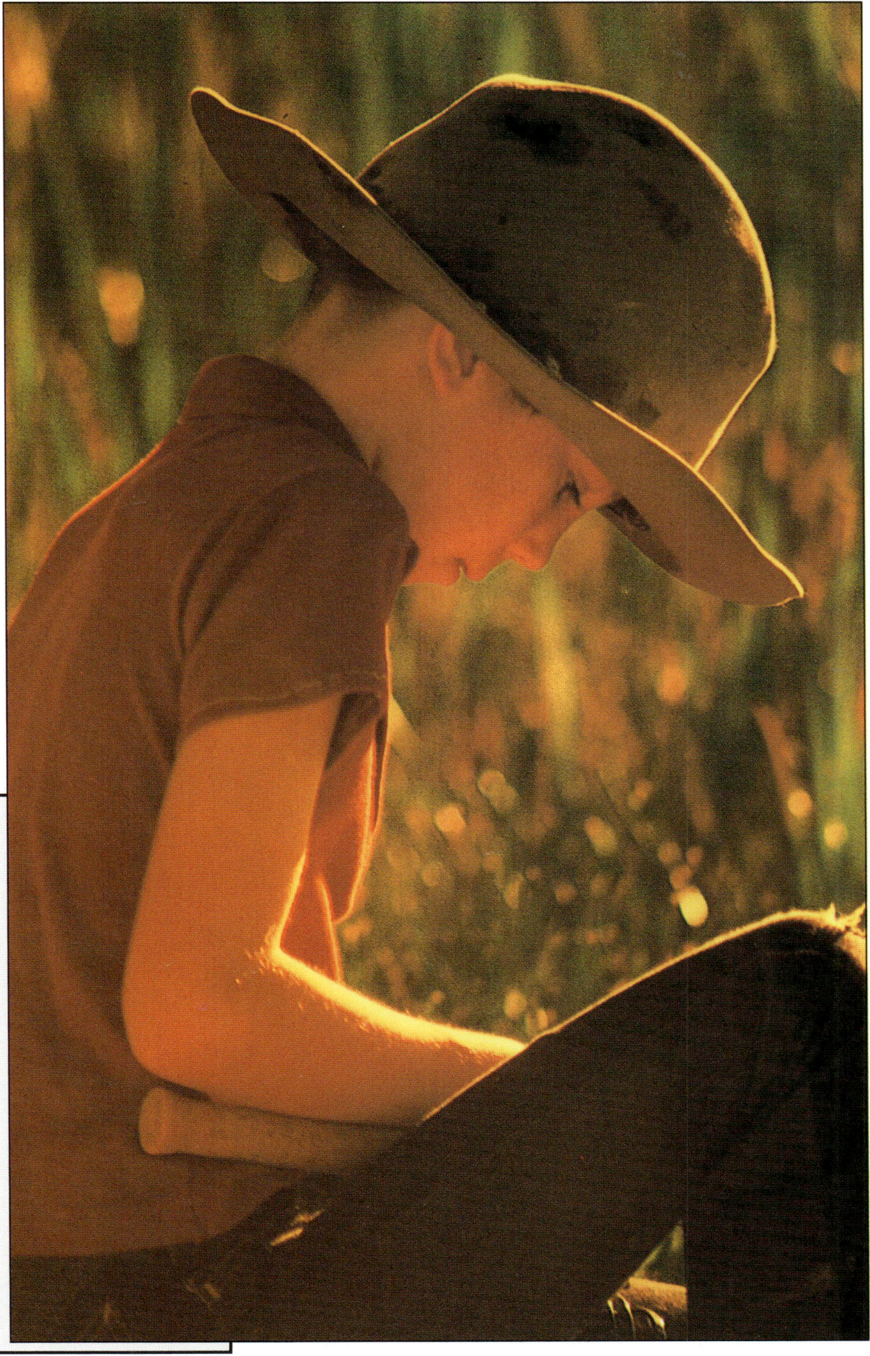

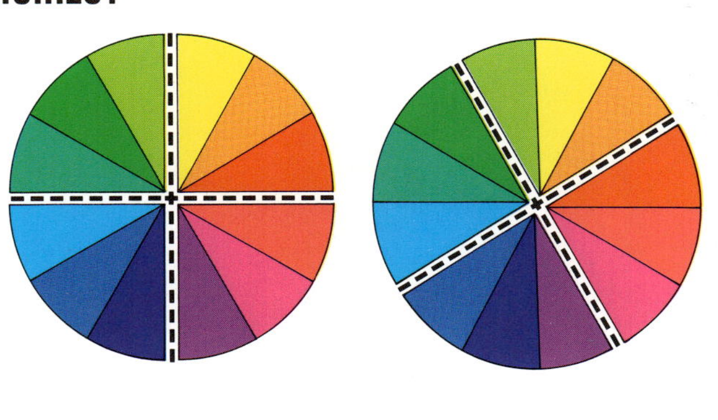

deliberate flare spreads sun's colour into shadows and backlighting rings hat with sharp, yellow line

choice of brown shirt creates harmony with surrounding colours

Which colours harmonize?

Closely related colours produce a sense of harmony. For example, look where orange is positioned on the wheel – you can either combine it with yellow and lime or with red and pink. Or you can place orange in a photo with its direct neighbours, yellow and red, to create harmony.

Using colour for harmony

The number of colour combinations you can choose from is vast, and does not necessarily have to fall into the groupings of warm and cold. But remember that fewer colours are usually more successful than a mass of unrelated ones.

One colour used in a wide variety of tones can produce harmony, too. For example, a landscape which concentrates on subtly differing tones of green evokes feelings of calm and wellbeing. Try to use varying textures to make the overall scene more interesting.

Creating harmony

As with colour contrast, you can either create harmony or it may already be present. When seeking out harmony you can't change a scene to suit your needs, but what you can do is try changing your viewpoint. Careful composition can help eliminate distracting colours from a potentially harmonious photograph.

For example, if you are photographing a field of yellow sunflowers and a blue sky is commanding too much attention, tilt your camera down to cut it out. Changing your viewpoint by moving in closer to your subject or using a telephoto lens can also help to isolate the colours you want.

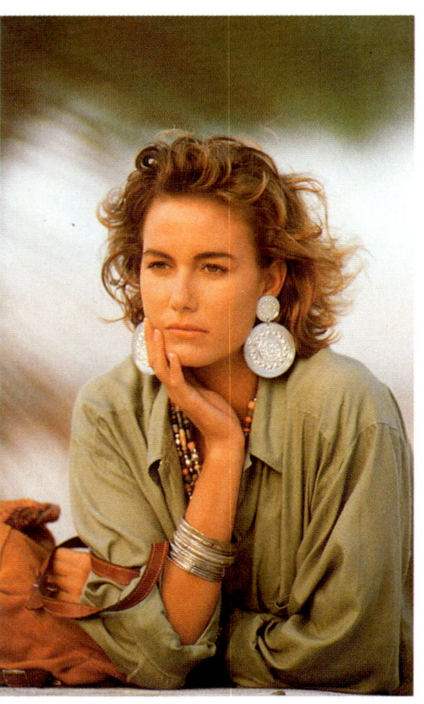

▲ **STYLISH HARMONY**
Desaturated colours together create a harmonious mood. Here, the background has been thrown out of focus to blend in further with the muted colours of the subject. Note how the shirt matches the colour of the model's eyes.

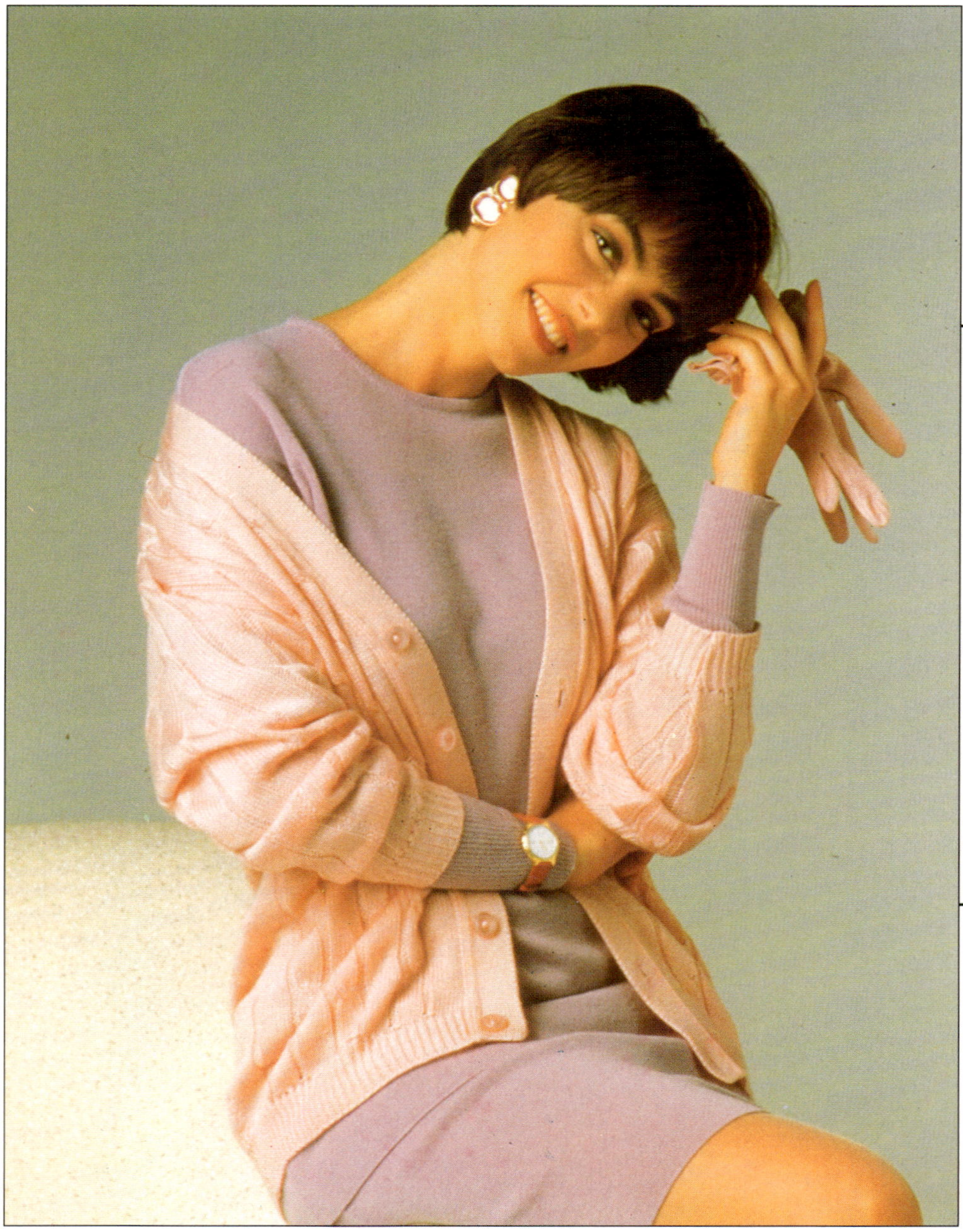

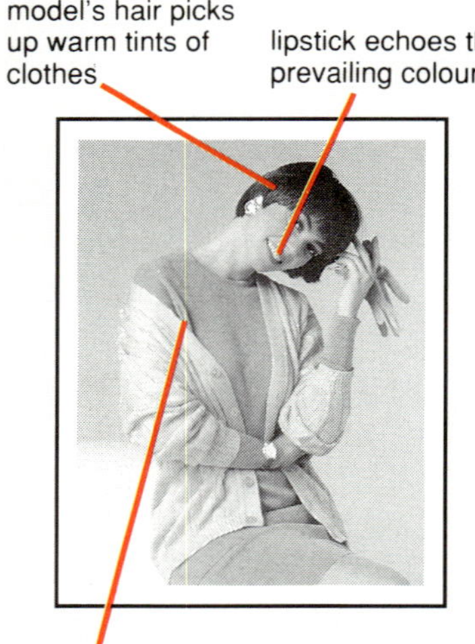

◄ **MIX 'N' MATCH**
You can create harmony by getting your model – whether she's a friend or professional – to wear co-ordinated clothes. The plain neutral coloured background focuses attention on the model and her harmonious garments.

Weakening colour

If harmony is important to your composition and changing your viewpoint doesn't bring success, you can often create harmony by weakening offending colours. You can achieve this by using natural conditions in two ways:

Shooting into the light induces flare as the light shines into the lens. This desaturates colours, making them more likely to harmonize. This happens because when light shines directly into a lens, it not only forms the image but scatters between the various glass surfaces, creating fogging and diminishing contrast.

Weather conditions can have a great effect upon colour relationships. Take advantage of hazy light, rain or mist to produce a subdued version of a subject which might otherwise have been more colourful.

You can also weaken colours in a picture by using a high speed film (such as ISO 400) and a telephoto lens. This technique blurs the colours in the background and softens the colours of your subject.

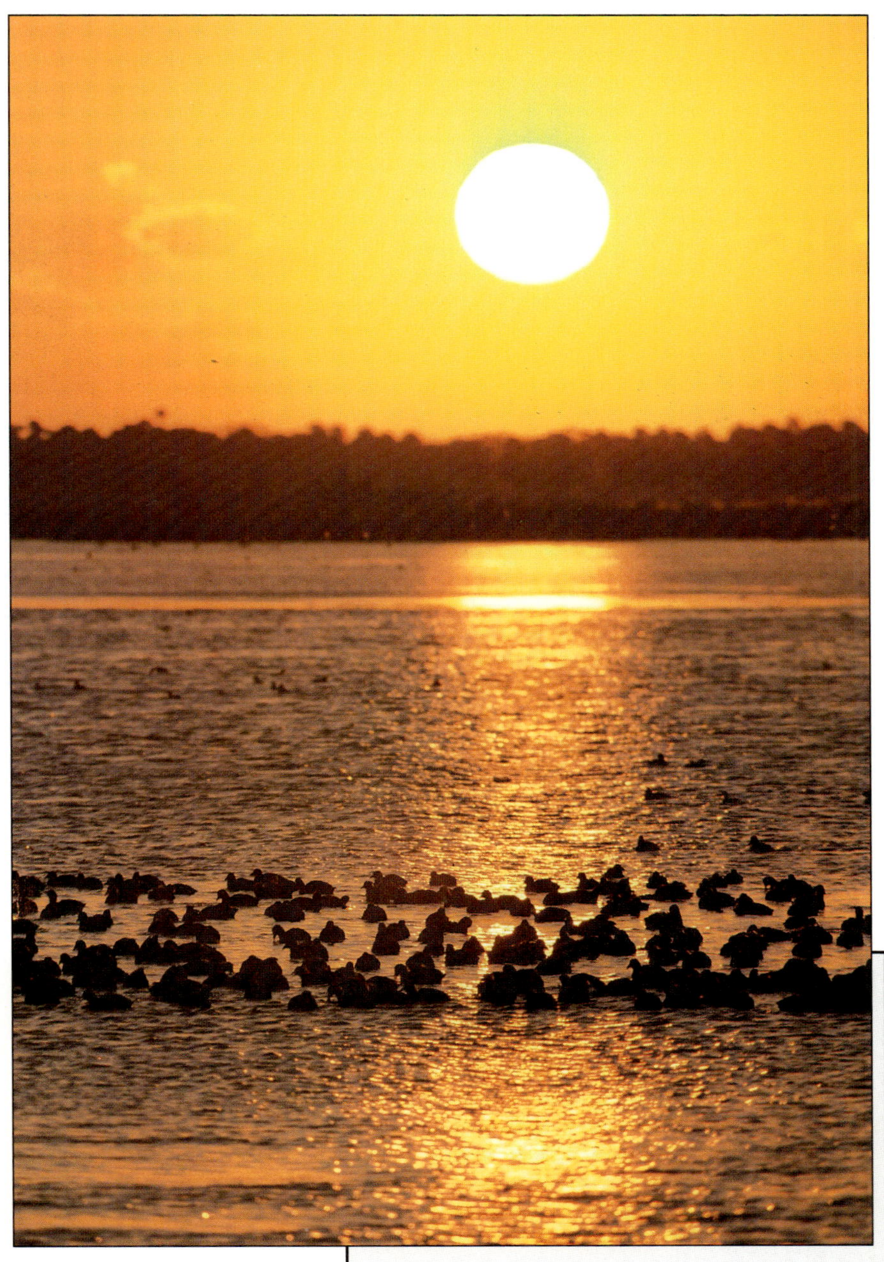

▲ THE COLOUR OF DAWN
Daylight is constantly changing, offering a range of colours for the photographer to exploit. This picture uses early morning sun to bathe the whole scene in a warm glow, enhancing the mood of the shot.

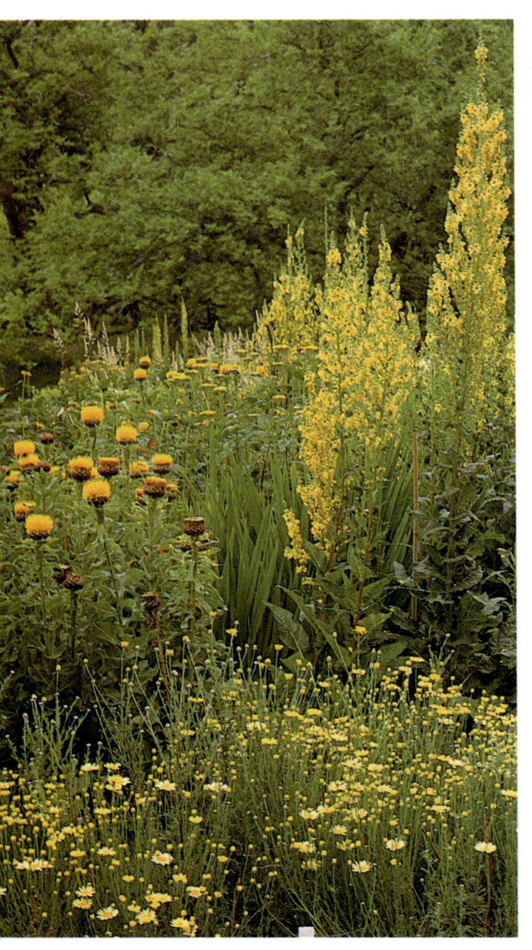

◄ HARMONY IN NATURE
Since yellow radiates light and green is the colour of growth, this combination has springlike associations. These colours harmonize well because they are next to each other on the colour wheel.

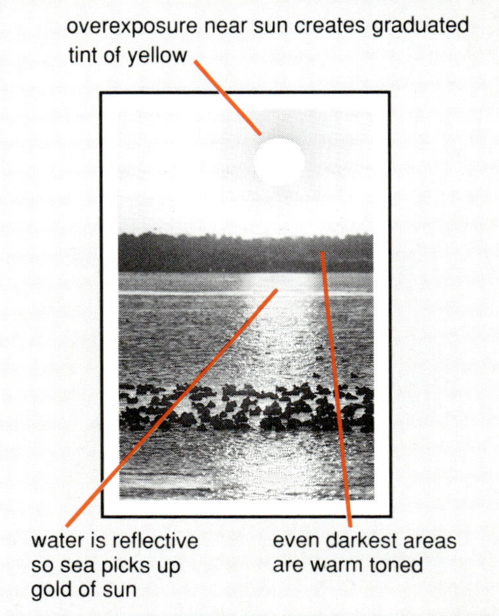

Artificial harmony

You can lessen contrast artificially to create your desired effect. Fog and soft focus filters and overexposure all soften and lighten colours – use these techniques for romantic, peaceful pictures.

Just like backlighting, under-exposure subdues and darkens colours. Try this technique to create gloomy or bleak shots – a fishing boat being tossed about on a stormy sea, for example.

You can also experiment with colour correction filters either to exaggerate a desirable colour cast or to correct an unwanted one. But make sure that the filter is not so strong as to affect the other colours in the composition unduly.

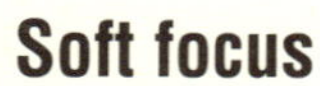

Soft focus

Fog and soft focus filters diffuse light. Use them to soften strong colours and create a more harmonious scene.

You can achieve a similar effect by smearing a thin layer of petroleum jelly on a filter, or – if you use a compact – on a sheet of plain glass and holding it up in front of the lens, or by covering the lens with transparent material, such as a stocking.

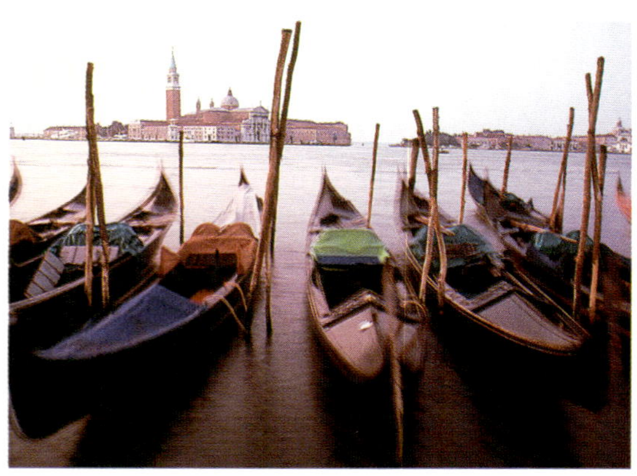

▶ ▼ **FILTERS FOR MOOD**
You can use a colour correction filter to emphasize harmony and lift the mood of a scene. Remember to use a filter of the same colour as that which dominates the picture already. In this case a purple filter was called for to enhance the romantic mood of the picture.

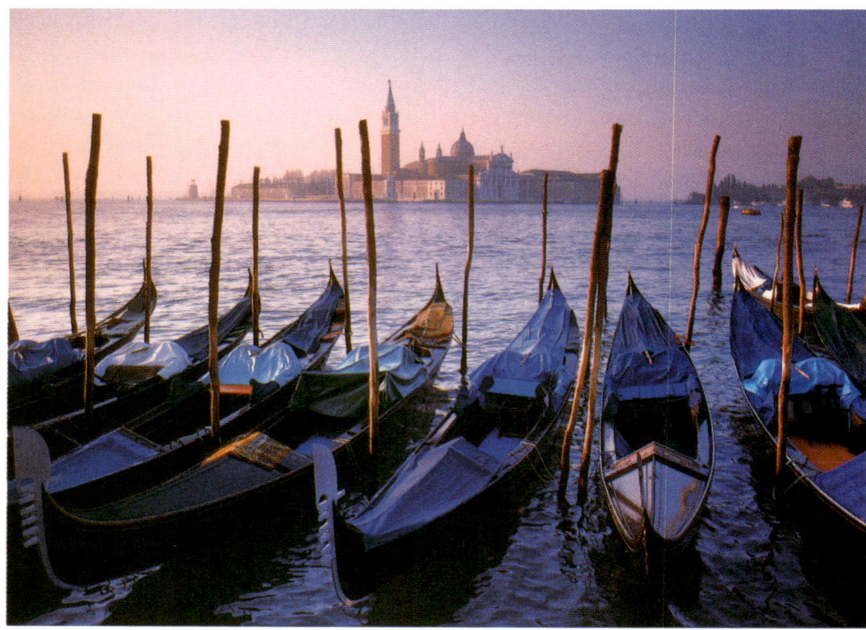

▼ **BLEAK HARMONY**
A mixture of soft, misty light, slight overexposure and use of a blue filter has combined to create a bleak, almost monochromatic, harmony.

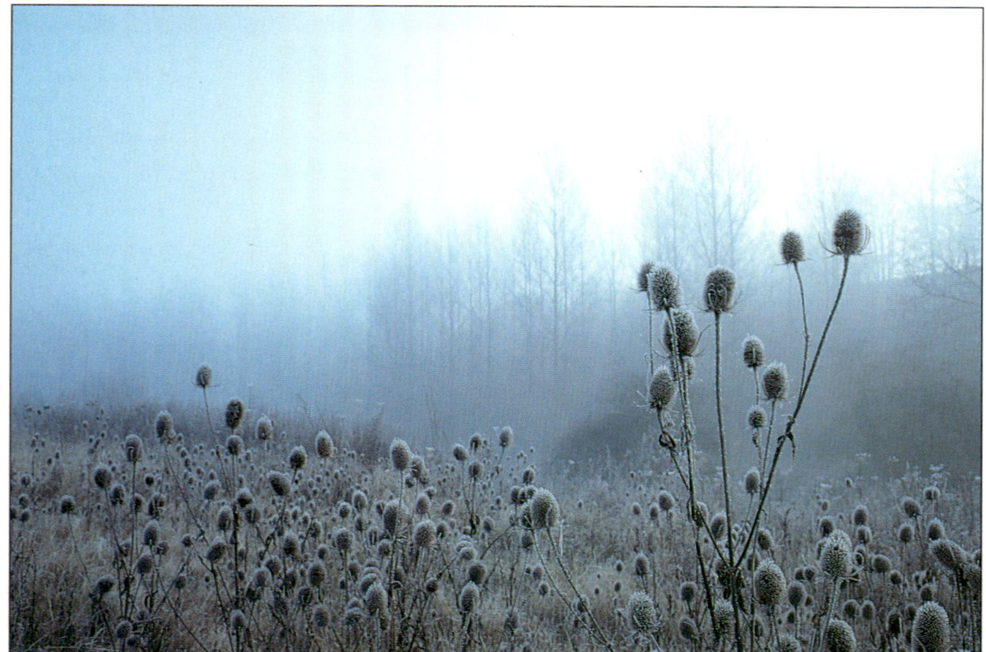

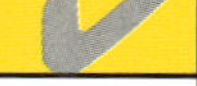

You can use colour for harmony by:

❏ using colours next to each other on the colour wheel

❏ using one colour in a variety of tones

You can lessen contrast by:

❏ shooting into the sun

❏ shooting through mist

❏ overexposing to lighten colours

❏ underexposing to darken colours

❏ using fog, soft focus or coloured filters

Using movement

You can capture the essence of an action in a single image in many ways. You can freeze movement, spread it across the frame in a sweep of colour, or record a sequence of images in one picture.

In the early days of photography, subjects had to remain still for an exposure of several minutes so that their image would appear sharp in the picture. The slightest movement would have resulted in a blur.

Today many people still automatically freeze in front of a camera because they don't expect it to be able to cope with movement. But the modern camera not only captures motion extremely well, it can emphasize and exploit it, and even give the appearance of action when none is present.

There are several techniques you can use to express movement in a photograph. You can freeze the action on film by using a fast shutter speed or electronic flash. Alternatively, multiple exposure allows you to capture a series of movements in one picture.

Or you may want to blur your subject to convey an impression of speed. In addition, there are techniques like panning and zooming which also blur an image to give an feeling of movement.

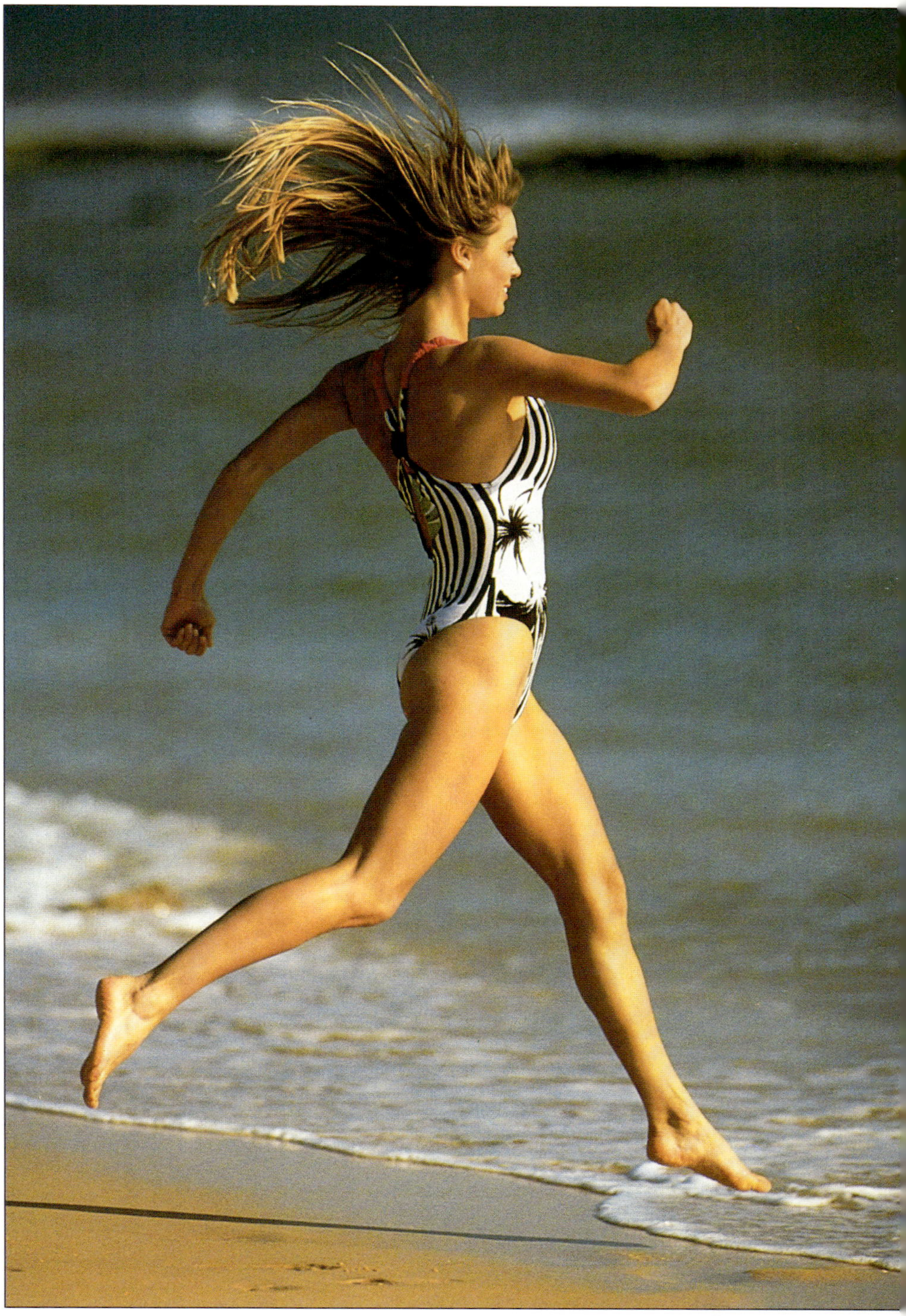

▶ **FREEZING THE ACTION**
The photographer used a fast shutter speed to record a pin sharp image of the girl. Careful timing was needed too to position her in the centre of the frame.

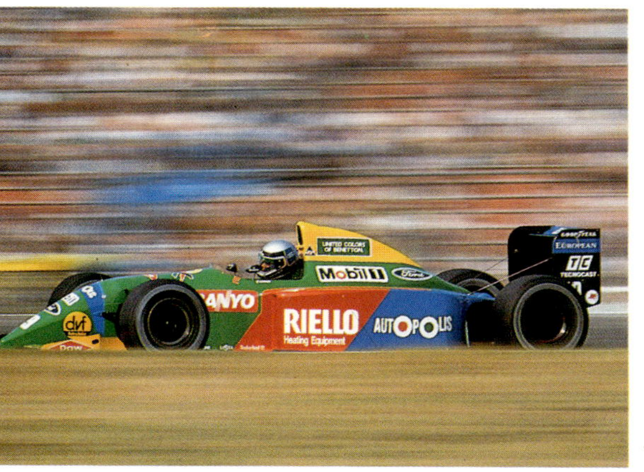

◀ **CONVEYING SPEED**
Panning (swinging the camera to follow a moving object) was used here to keep the car sharp and the background streaked, giving a strong impression of speed.

▶ **CREATING MOVEMENT**
Changing the focal length of a zoom lens during exposure creates a tunnel of lines converging on the footballers. It introduces action into an otherwise static scene.

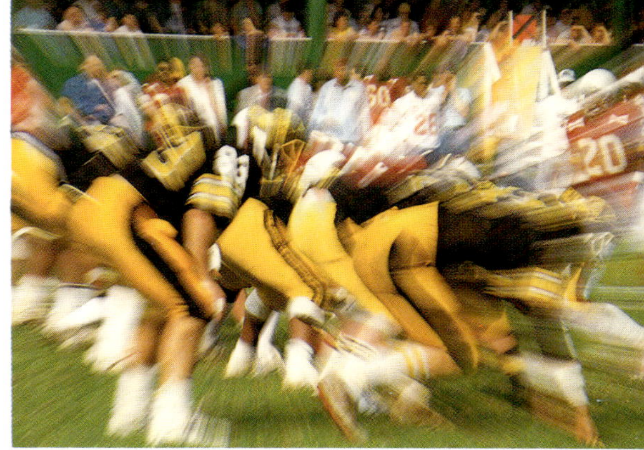

Freezing the action

A dramatic way of conveying movement, while keeping every detail sharp, is to freeze the action. There are several ways of capturing the exact moment you want on film.

Fast shutter speed

The commonest technique for bringing movement to a standstill is to use a fast shutter speed; and the quicker the motion the faster your shutter speed needs to be in order to arrest it.

For example, fairly slow moving subjects, such as people walking, can be frozen with a shutter speed of 1/125th sec; footballers in action would need a shutter speed of at least 1/500th sec; while fast racing cars need a minimum of 1/1000th sec.

Most SLR cameras can capture rapid action since they have a maximum shutter speed between 1/1000th and 1/4000th sec; while compacts can manage speeds up to 1/500th sec.

Thinking about viewpoint

Not only does a subject's pace affect your choice of shutter speed, the distance between you and your subject needs to be taken into account.

For example, a cyclist speeding past you only a few metres away moves through the frame quickly – so you need a fast shutter speed to record it sharply. But, it takes a lot longer for a cyclist who is 50 metres away to move through the frame, so a slow shutter speed is sufficient.

Similarly, you need to consider the direction your subject is moving in. A woman running towards, or away, from the camera, doesn't move far within the frame, so a shutter speed of about 1/60th sec records a sharp image. If she runs across the frame, you need to use a speed of 1/500th sec to capture the increased amount of activity.

A pause in the action

Not all fast moving subjects need a particularly quick shutter speed to freeze them on film. You can stop movement with a relatively slow one by catching the action at its peak.

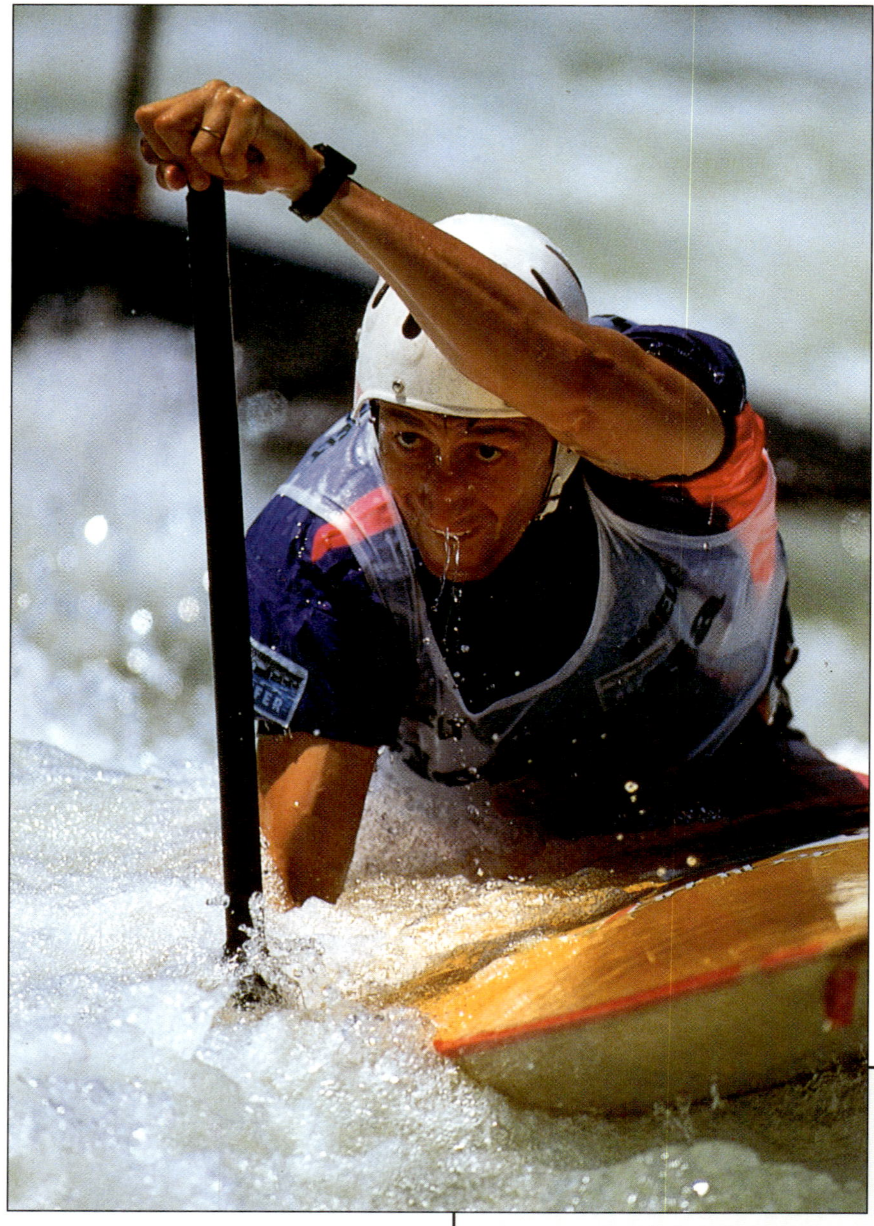

▲ **CLEAR WATERS**
Using a fast shutter speed to freeze the action can help you to capture some dramatic shots. Here, the photographer used a shutter speed of 1/1000th sec to keep both the canoeist and water crystal clear.

This is the point at which your subject seems to be in motion, but is actually still for a moment – think of a dancer being lifted into the air or a child on a swing when it reaches its highest point.

Knowing how a certain tennis player moves, say, or getting your subject to repeat an action several times before you shoot, helps you to anticipate the moment of rest.

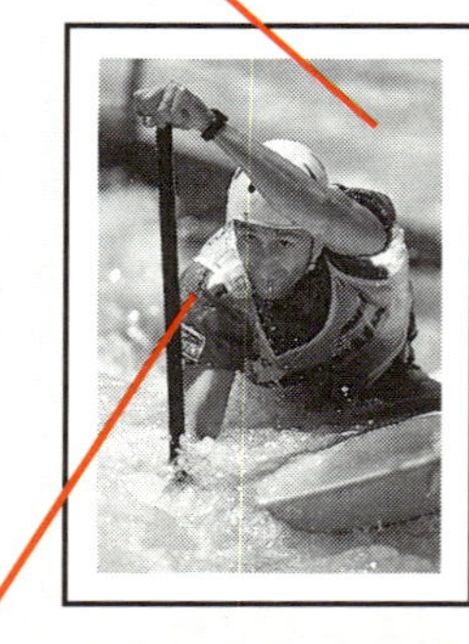

fast shutter speed forced photographer to use wide aperture, so depth of field is shallow

brilliant sunlight meant fast shutter speed was possible even with slow film

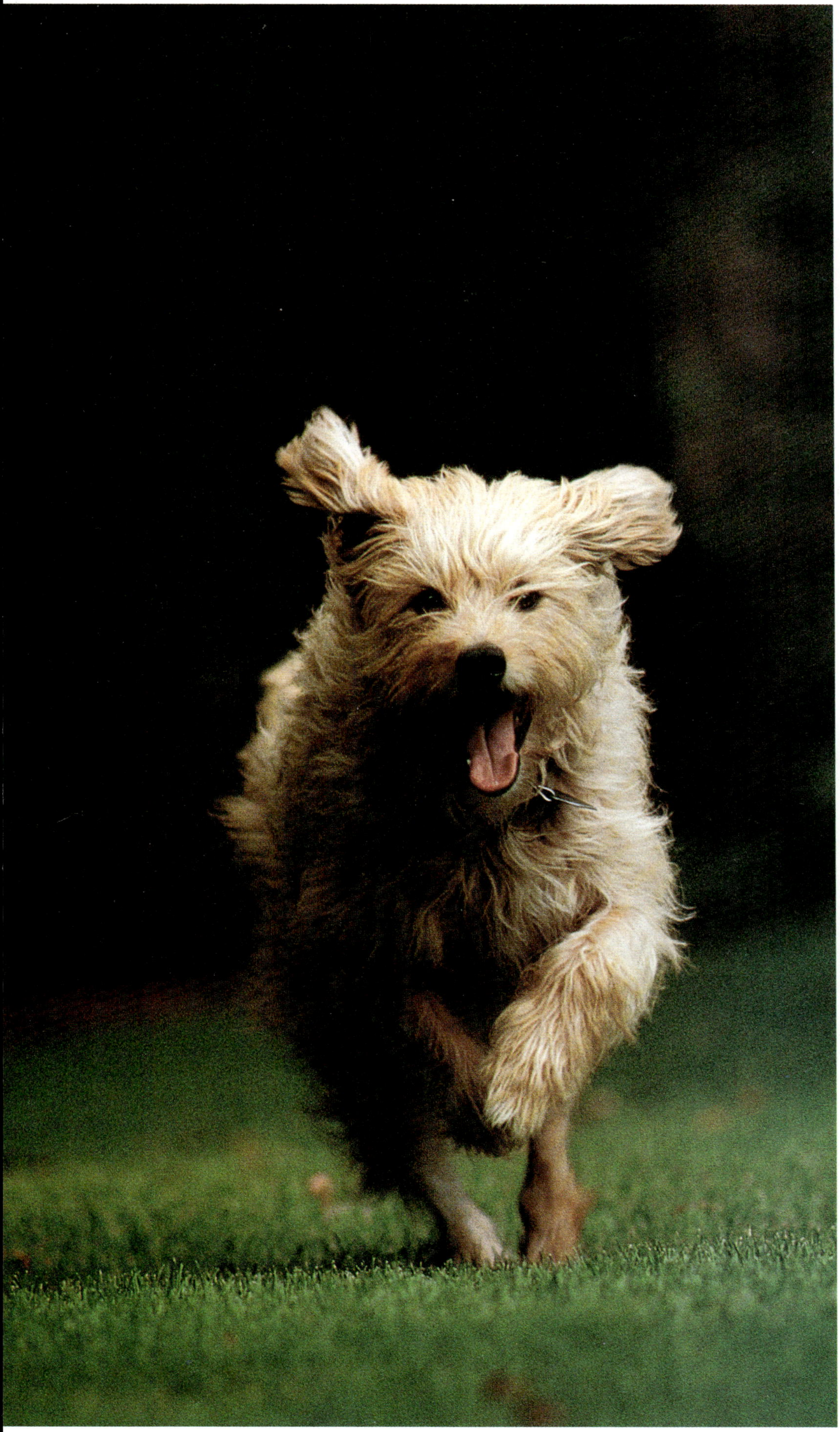

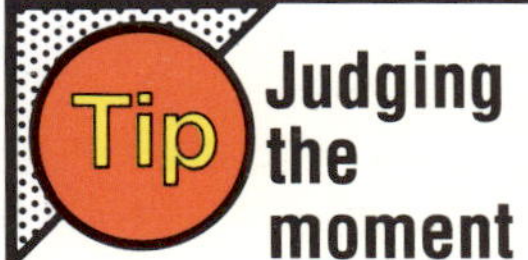

◀ MAKING ADVANCES

Because the dog is running towards the camera and not across its field of view, the photographer was able to use a slower shutter speed of 1/60th sec to keep the dog sharp.

Judging the moment

Whichever technique you use to freeze the action in the frame, remember to press the shutter release just before the subject reaches the sharpest point of focus. This allows for the short delay between you pressing the release and the shutter opening, and ensures you capture that one-off shot.

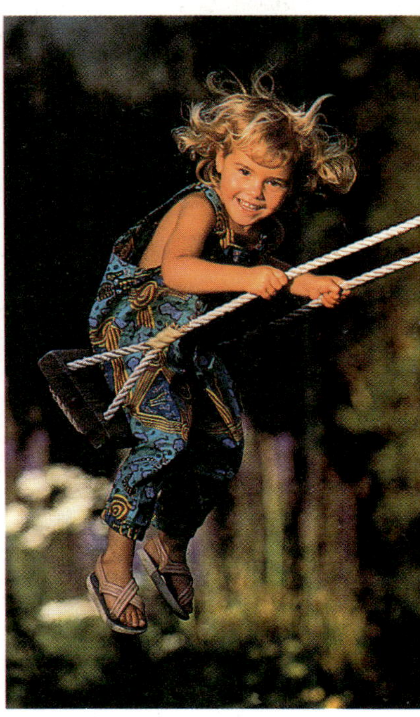

▲ A NATURAL PAUSE

By anticipating the exact moment when the girl would reach the highest point of the arc, the photographer was able to use a fairly slow shutter speed to capture a sharp image of the girl on the swing.

In a flash

In poor lighting and at night when a slow shutter speed is unavoidable, you can still record a pin sharp image by using flash.

Most electronic flash units can fire a beam of light at a speed of between 1/500th and 1/30,000th sec, depending on type; and, since only that instant registers on film, even the fastest moving subject can be recorded clearly.

Beware, however, of relying on flash to freeze action in this way in good light. If you use a slow shutter speed you'll end up with a second, blurred image recorded by the ambient light.

You should be prepared to take a series of pictures when taking any type of movement shots, because an element of luck is always involved. The more frames you take, the greater your chances of getting the exact effect you want.

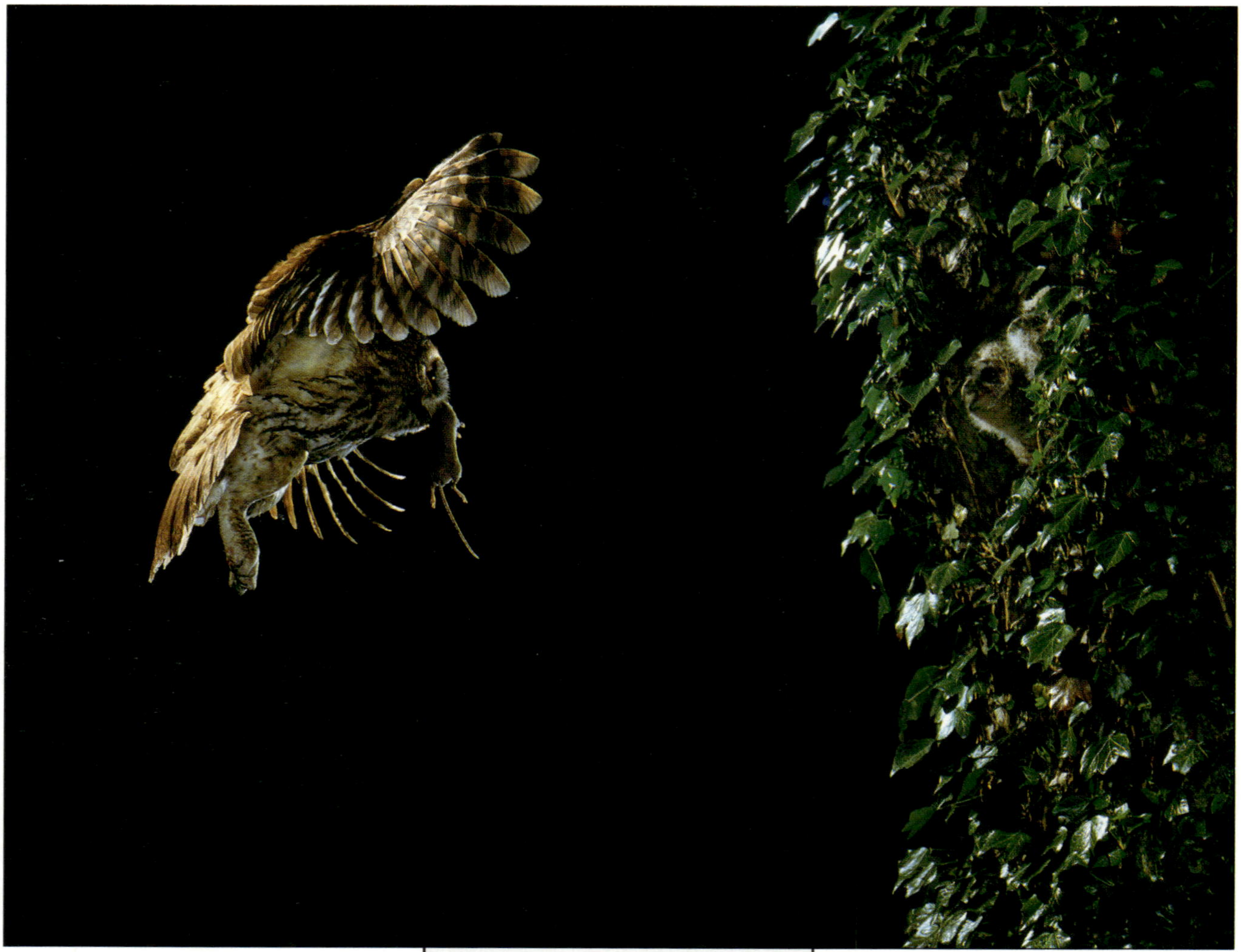

owl took its own picture by breaking an invisible beam which triggered the camera

unattended camera was set up in hide and moved slowly closer to avoid disturbing the owl

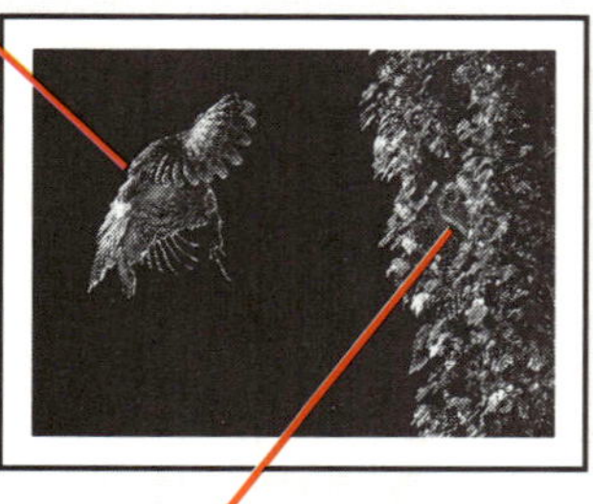

high powered flash allowed photographer to set small aperture for maximum sharpness

▲ **IN FLIGHT ACTION**
Flash is particularly useful for fast moving animals or birds. The photographer needed a lot of patience and a rapid flash of 1/20,000th sec to record this stunning image.

Blur and pan

Suggesting action in a still image may seem an impossible task, but by using the techniques of blurring and panning you will find it easier to convey a strong impression of movement.

While freezing the action gives a well defined view of a subject and can produce some dramatic results, such images lack the actual sensation of movement. For example, a picture where a pole vaulter has been frozen in mid air emphasizes the position of his body, but gives no impression of speed.

You can indicate movement in a photo by deliberately blurring either your subject or the background of a scene – or both. Even though you normally see the rapid movement of a spinning aeroplane propeller, for instance, as a blur, slower moving subjects can often benefit from being blurred in a picture too.

Blur is caused by the subject moving across the frame while the shutter is open. For example, a slow shutter speed of 1 sec enables you to record running water as silky smooth.

You can also blur movement by swinging your camera to follow a passing subject. This technique is known as panning and you can use it to blur the background elements of a scene, while keeping the moving subject sharp.

Or you may choose to blur the whole scene by panning with a very slow shutter speed – there are plenty of combinations for you to choose from.

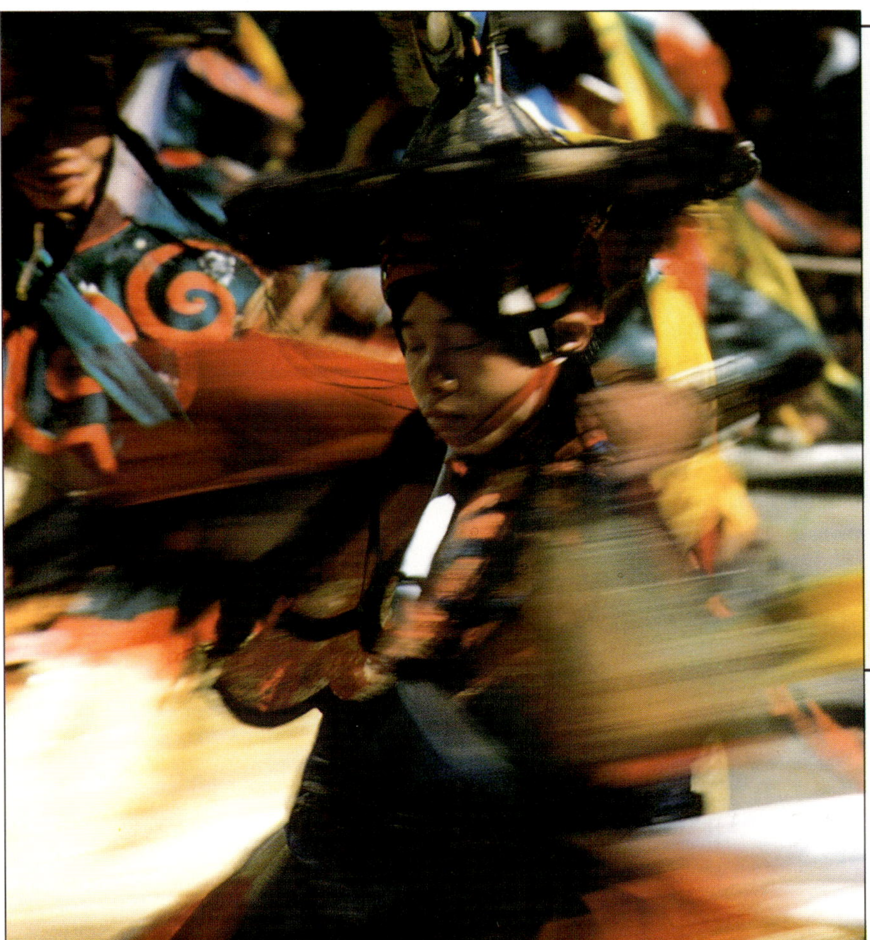

▼ **SPIRIT OF THE DANCE**
The photographer used a slow shutter speed to blur the flow and sway of the dancer's skirt, giving the image a strong sense of movement.

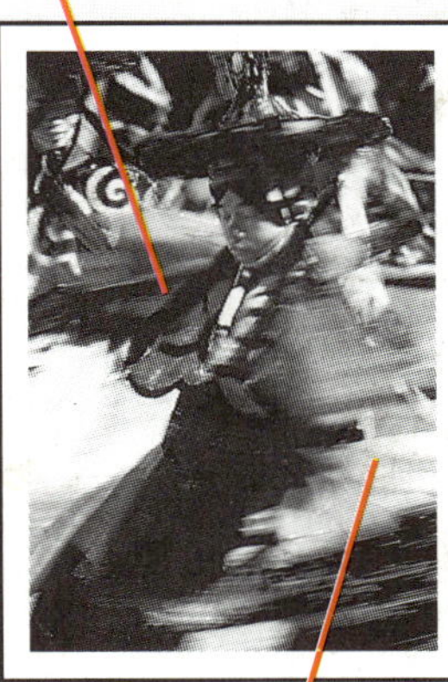

Tip

Supporting role

If you want one sharp element in the picture when you are using slow shutter speeds you must keep your camera very steady during exposure. For the best results use a tripod for still shots, or a monopod for panning.

If you don't have one available, try pressing your elbows into your waist, or resting the camera on your knee, the ground or a table, or lean against a wall for extra support.

Impressions of speed

When photographing action there are several factors you need to consider – the speed of your subject, your choice of shutter speed, the subject's angle to the camera and the distance involved.

Slow shutter speeds

Whether keeping the camera still or panning, the slower the shutter speed the greater the blur created by the subject's movement. Smooth moving objects, such as trains or cars, may only tolerate a little blurring before becoming unrecognizable. On the other hand, swirling dancers produce a variety of curves, and can look striking with a comparatively long exposure.

Try to include a still element in a scene to provide a sharp contrast to the blurred action – it helps to further emphasize the movement.

Sporting scenes are obvious subjects, but you can use this technique on anything that moves. Fairground rides, for example, record well on film using a slow shutter speed, especially in low light. A long exposure will record the lights as continuous circles.

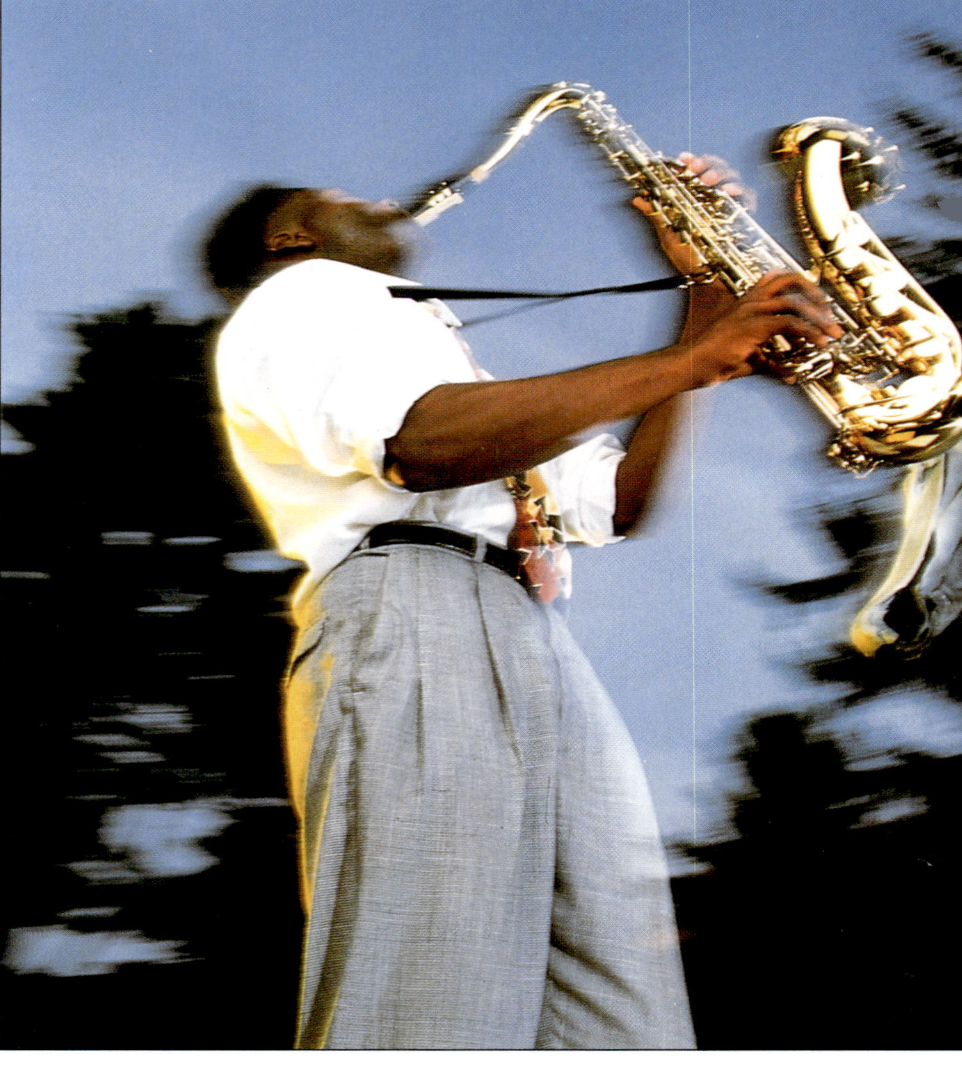

▼ **ALL A BLUR**
Using panning and a shutter speed of 1/8th sec together, nothing in this image is sharp. Notice how the runners' legs are only just visible.

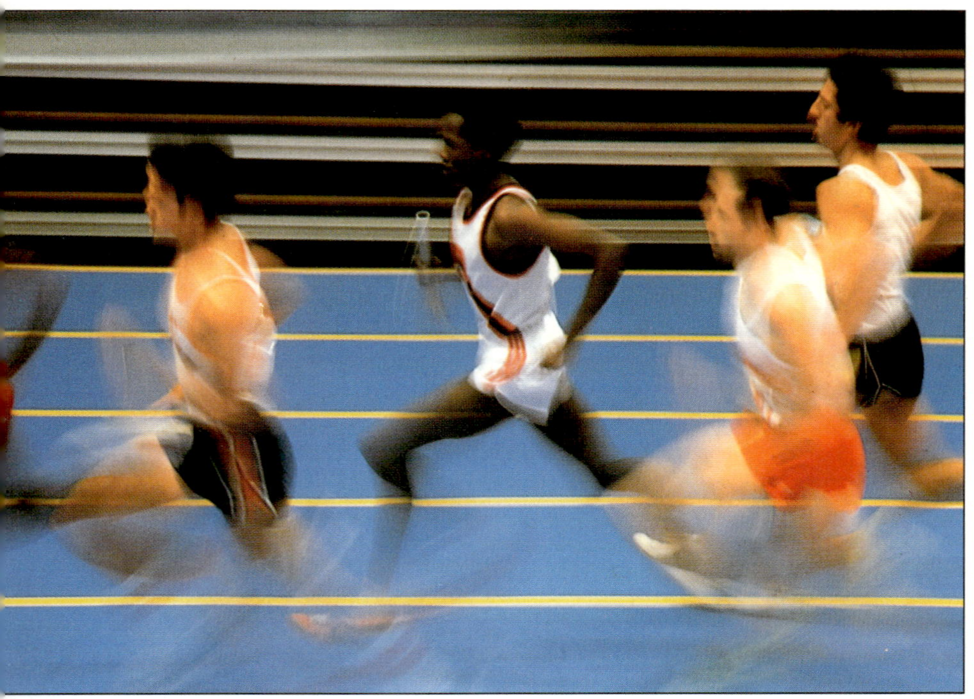

Overexposure

Letting in too much light can be a problem when you use a long exposure, but there are several steps you can take to avoid this happening:

❑ Use slow film so that more light is needed to form an image, allowing a longer exposure.

❑ Use a lens that stops down to at least f16 because the smaller the aperture the less light is let in.

❑ Use a neutral density filter, especially in bright light, to reduce the amount of light entering the lens, effectively slowing down the film.

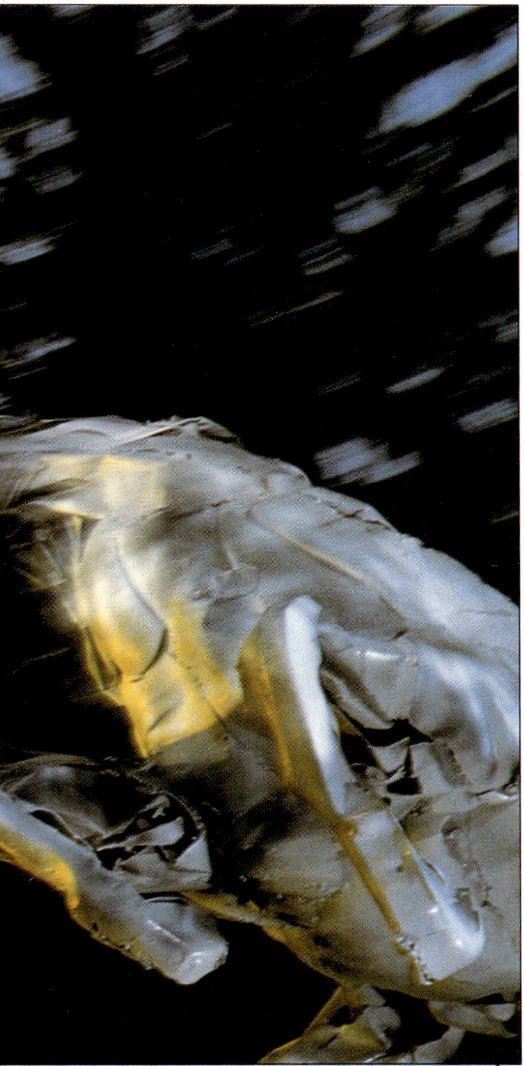

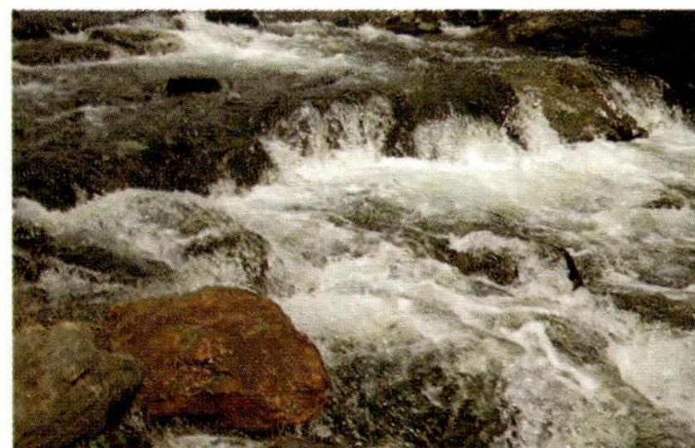
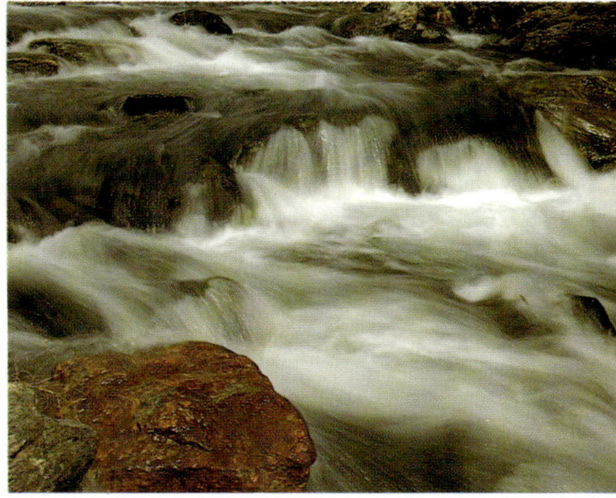

▲ ▶ TO BLUR OR NOT TO BLUR?
A shutter speed of 1/500th sec recorded the water sharply. With a speed of 1/8th sec the blur produced intensifies the feeling of rushing water.

Flash with daylight

If you use a slow shutter speed with flash you can combine sharpness and blur in the same image to produce an impression of speed. Set an exposure between 1 sec and 1/15th sec. Set the camera's film speed dial to give 1 stop underexposure and use flash. You can then let the shutter stay open while the subject moves, to add an element of blur to the sharp flash exposure. Use print film, which has greater exposure latitude.

Ghostly images

You can use a very slow shutter speed to make your subject almost disappear from view. For example, if you photograph a man walking past you, using a shutter speed of 1/60th sec, only his hands and feet are blurred. At 1/15th sec his whole body is blurred, but recognizable. At 1/4 sec only a vague impression of the man remains, producing a ghostly effect. An even slower speed will make him vanish completely.

As with freezing the action you need to think about your subject's angle to the camera. Movement towards or away from it will produce less blur than movement across the picture plane. Diagonal motion, on the other hand, has an intermediate effect.

Distance, too, affects blur; the closer a subject is to the camera the quicker it will cross the camera's field of view, and therefore the greater the blur will be on film.

image formed by ambient light overlaps that formed by flash, softening the edges

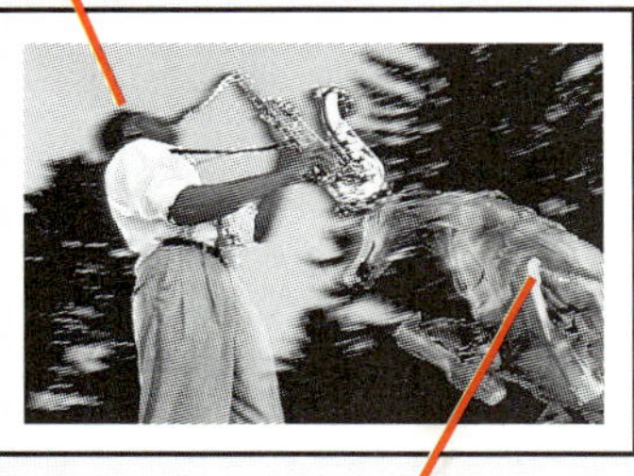

leaping horse sculpture adds further sense of motion

▲ JAZZING IT UP
The photographer combined flash, a long exposure and panning the camera to create this unusual effect.

▶ MAKING A SCENE
The speed and purposefulness of the blurred, moving figures is contrasted with the stationary people.

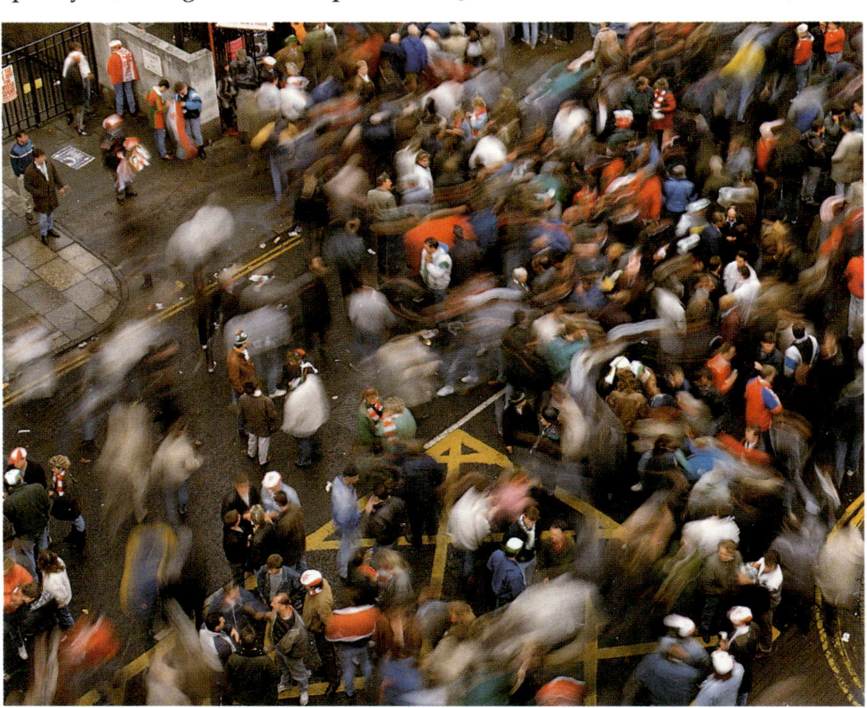

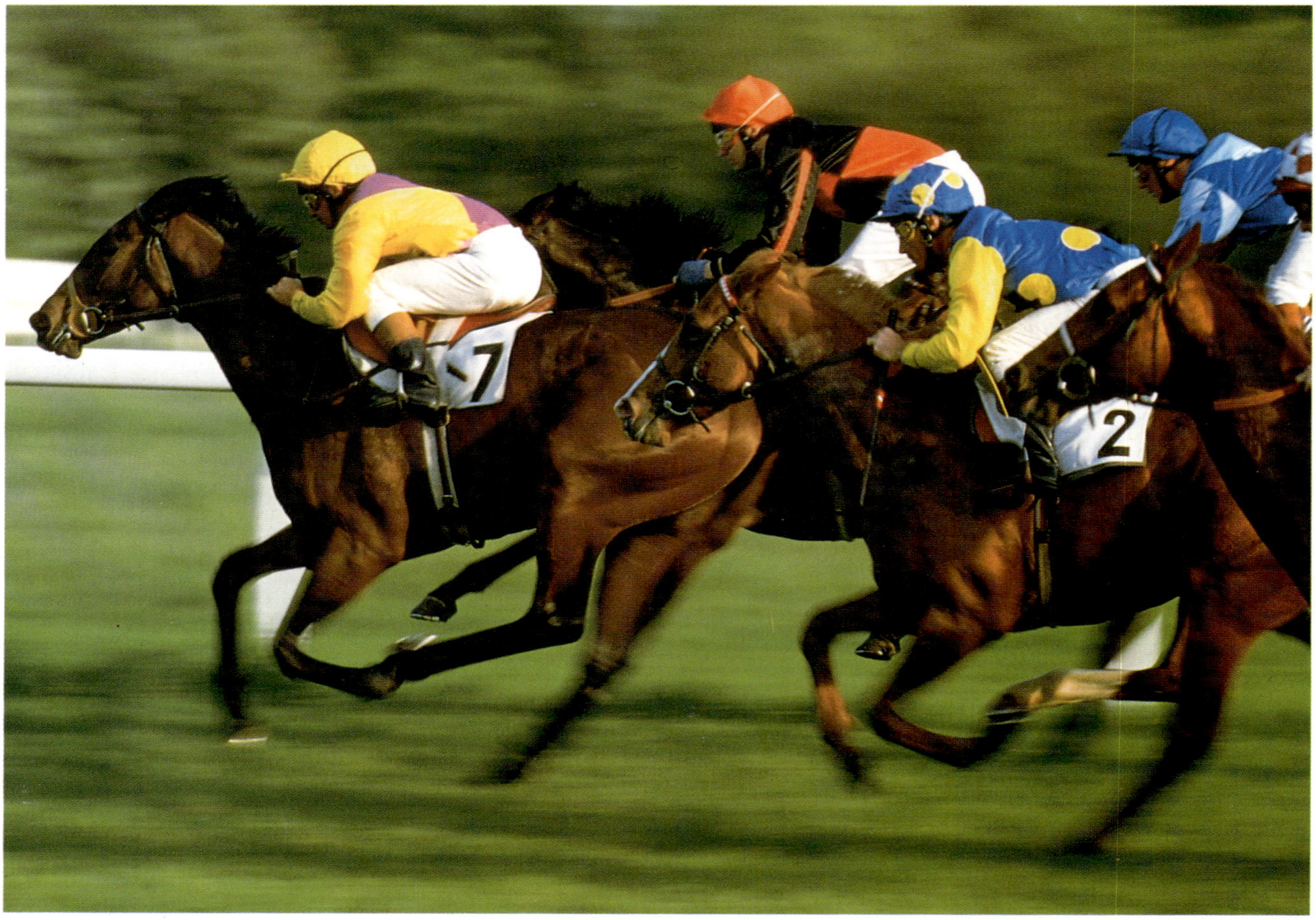

▲ **PERFECT PANNING**
A pan of 1/125th sec leaves only the tiniest amount of movement in the horses' hooves, while the streaked background emphasizes their speed and direction. Always track the subject before and after releasing the shutter to get the best results.

Panning with the action

For a crisp image of a speeding subject against a streaked background use the technique of panning. This is when you move the camera in the same direction and at the same speed as the subject while the shutter is open.

First choose a position where the subject will pass across your field of view and prefocus on the spot where the subject will be when you want to press the shutter. As soon as the subject comes into view keep it in the viewfinder and follow its motion with the camera.

Press the shutter release just before the subject gets to the point of focus. Don't stop moving the camera – keep panning both during and after the exposure so that you end up swinging the camera smoothly through a wide arc. About a third of a circle should do it.

The tricky part is to keep the subject in the same position in the viewfinder throughout the pan. This takes quite a bit of practice, and an element of luck, so don't worry if you have to take several shots to get the picture you want.

How to pan

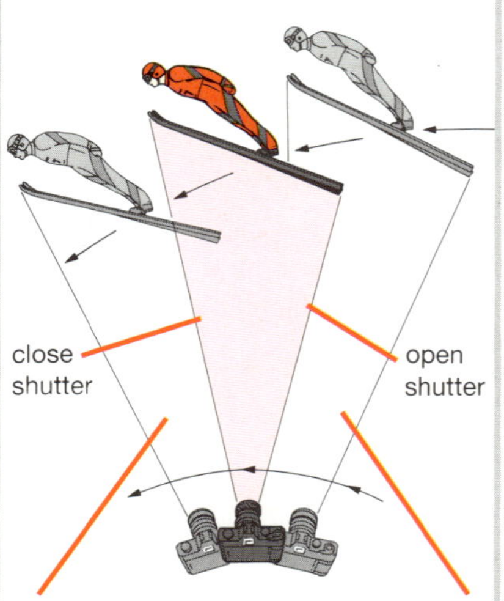

CHECK IT!

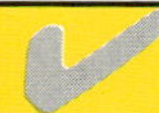

You can create an impression of speed in an image by:

❑ using a slow shutter speed to blur the action across the frame, keeping the background sharp

❑ panning with the action to keep the subject sharp and the background blurred

❑ panning combined with a long exposure so that both the subject and background are blurred

❑ choosing a close, side on viewpoint so that the subject moves across the frame more rapidly

❑ using flash in daylight with a slow shutter speed to get a mixture of sharpness and blur

◀ **PANNING EXPLAINED**
Following the action using a slow shutter speed will keep the subject sharp, while blurring the background.

Unusual picture shapes

Everyone's familiar with the standard 35mm format – but why not be different? We explore the use of panoramic and square frames, and show you how to improve existing compositions by cropping them into unusual shapes.

The shape of a photograph has a strong influence on the success of the image contained within it, so choosing the right format for your subject is very important.

The type of camera you use determines the shape of your pictures initially. Most people use a 35mm frame which produces rectangular prints with a long to short side ratio of 3:2.

This does not mean, however, that every subject is suited to this familiar shape, or that if you own a 35mm camera you are limited to this format. For example, sweeping mountain views look stunning in panoramic format, and patterns are often improved when cropped to a square.

Or why not experiment with a fisheye lens to produce distorted, circular images? Choose your subject carefully, though, because while buildings and bridges may look effective wrapped around a circle, your friends may not find the effect quite so flattering!

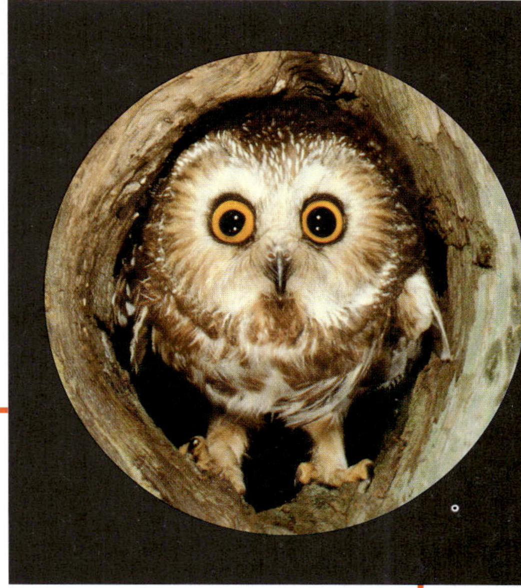

▲ ROUND ABOUT
Masks can look very effective on portraits, especially if their shape matches that of the subject. Here the photographer enhanced an existing picture of an owl by printing it through a circular mask cut in a piece of card. He rested the mask on the printing paper during the exposure.

Making circles

If you don't have a fisheye lens or converter, you can make a circular image by photographing the subject reflected in a shiny convex surface, such as a silver Christmas ball. Use the largest you can find, making sure it's glass, not plastic, for best quality. Your own reflection will be least conspicuous if you use a long lens and stand in a shadow.

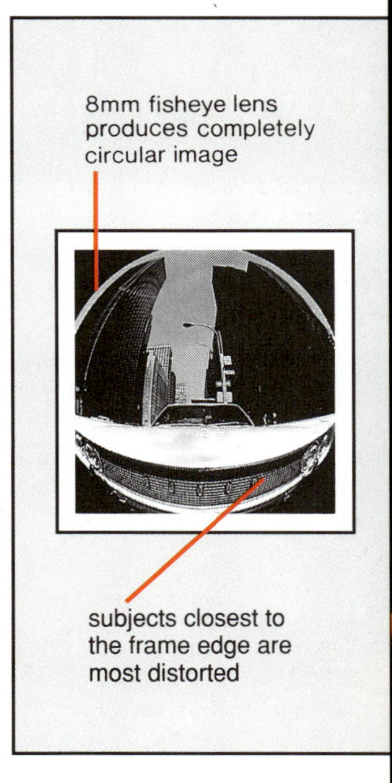

▶ SMILES ALL ROUND
A fisheye lens is great for creating whacky photos, since any straight lines in the scene become distorted. Careful alignment was needed in this New York scene to ensure that the taxi's bumper followed the edge of the circle exactly.

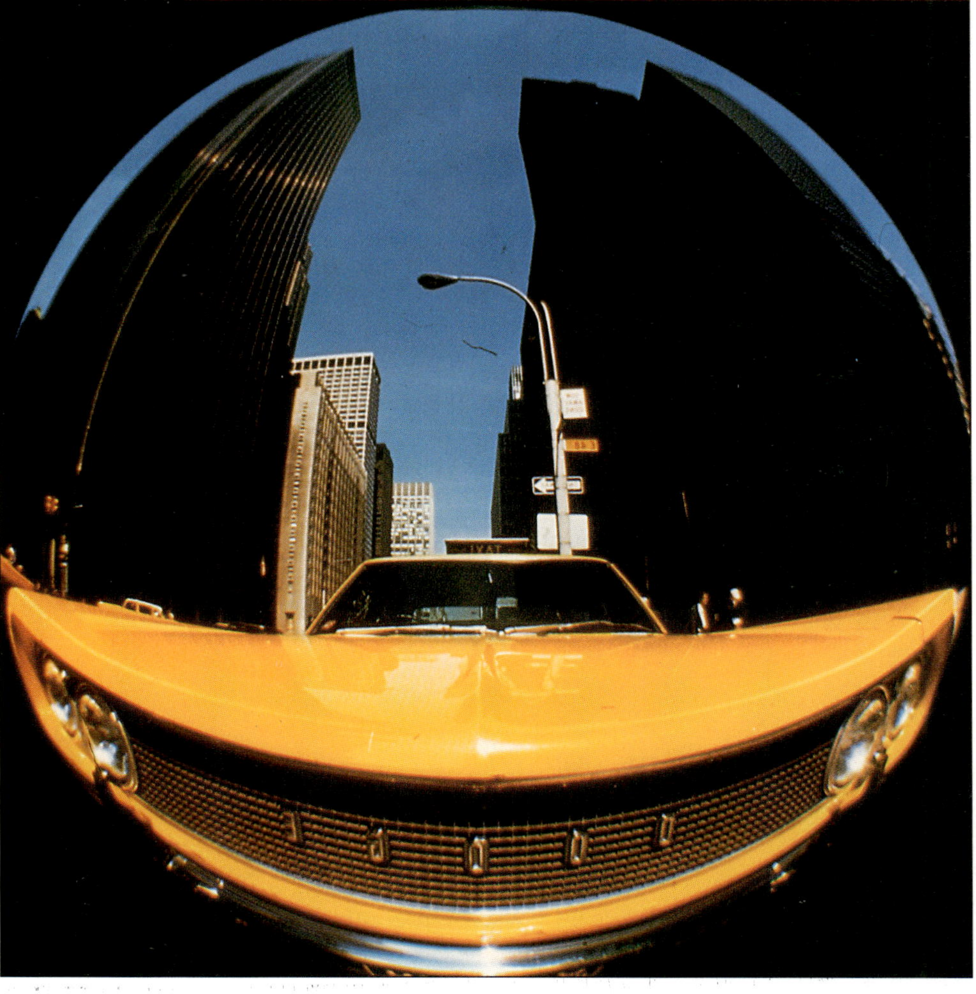

Square pictures

The easiest way to take square pictures is to use a camera designed specifically for this purpose. These are usually medium format cameras such as SLR Hasselblads and Bronicas, which can be hired from some retailers, or twin lens reflex cameras, which are often second-hand bargains.

The secret of using a square format successfully is to know the kinds of subjects that lend themselves to it. The most important thing to remember is that since all the sides are of equal length (6 x 6cm), square pictures tend to look static, and the eye is drawn straight towards the centre of the frame.

Therefore, a square format tends to be most effective for subjects organized around a central point, and for abstract designs and patterns, which spread out equally in all directions.

Head and shoulders portraits also look good in square format because a large area of the frame is filled. Portraits of children, too, don't look quite so lost in a square format.

For inspiration, take a look at the photographs on record or CD covers, and note the numerous ways of posing a person, or a group, to produce an interesting design.

Square frames also give scope for the use of symmetry (see **Through the viewfinder** Diagonals). They often make the directional lines of a subject much stronger, too, because the angle of the lines to the frame's sides is more acute.

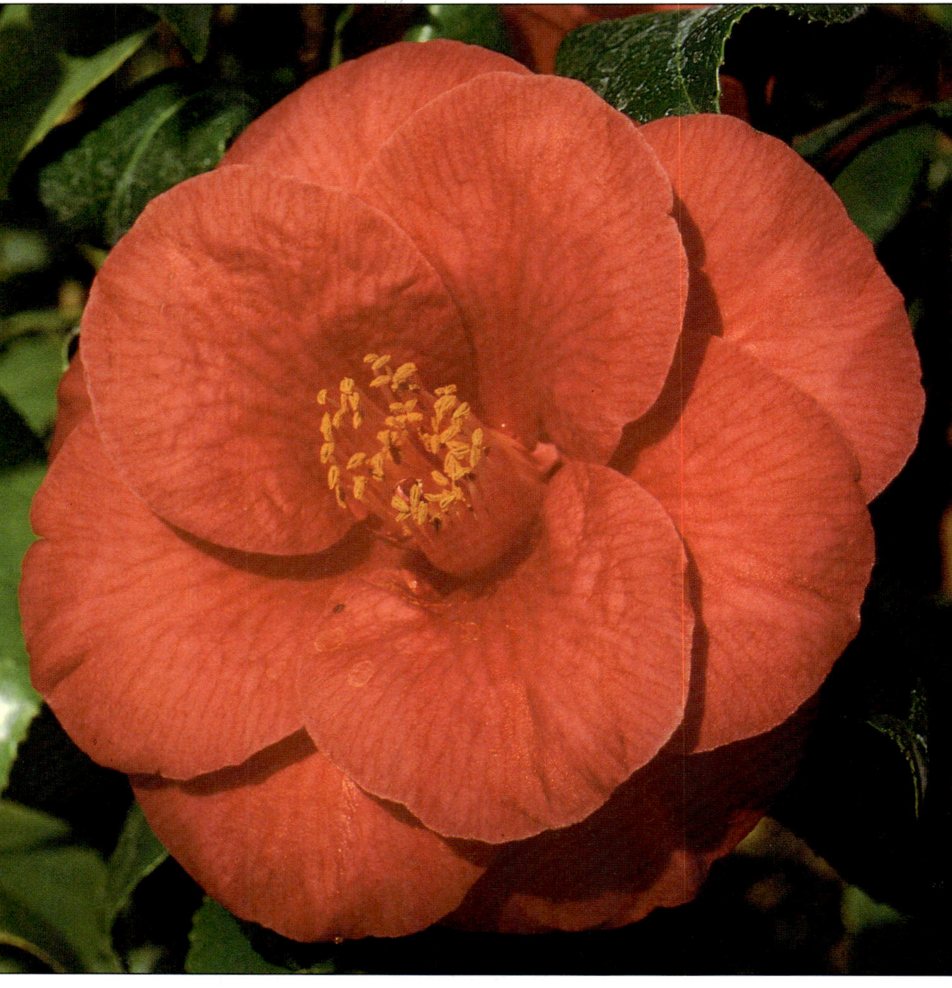

▲ CLOSE QUARTERS
Near circular subjects, such as this camellia, often look good in a square frame. The two shapes contrast well against each other, and give the subject much more impact than would result with a rectangular frame.

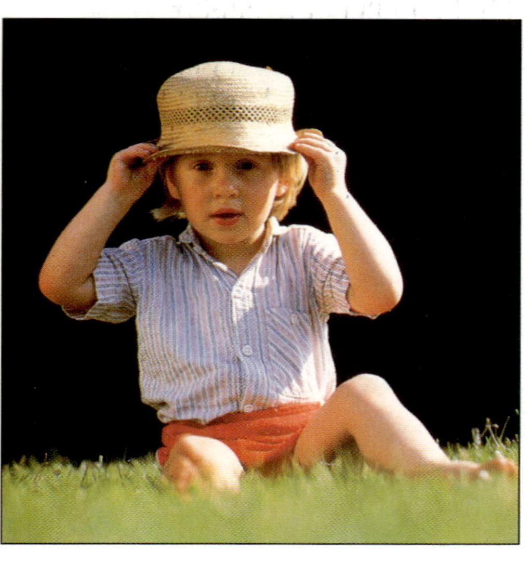

◄ A FITTING SUBJECT
This portrait of a child suits a square format because a large amount of the frame is filled. It meant that the photographer could move in closer to the child and capture more detail than if she had used a 35mm frame.

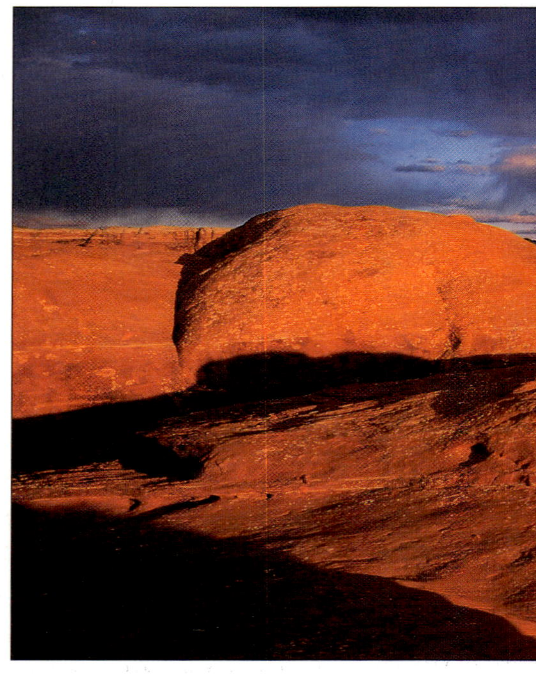

Tip

Squaring up

When shooting square pictures on 35mm film make sure you compose the shot very carefully. This is because when you crop the scene later you will lose a minimum of a third of the negative area – so it's important that you know precisely what you want in the picture at the start.

Panoramic views

Although its proportions sound extreme, the panoramic camera has a versatile format. At least twice as long as it is high (6 x 12cm or longer), this frame has an angle of view of more than 90°, producing a wide and informative presentation of a scene.

As its name suggests, the panoramic format is ideal for shooting landscapes and rows of objects, because we scan the length of such photographs as we would a real life scene. A long, low picture lends a feeling of vastness to a land-scape, and is particularly effective for views in which there is a strong horizontal element.

Don't forget you can always turn a panoramic camera on its side too, to capture tall structures, such as a church spire or a mountain peak, in their entirety. The long, thin dimen-sions of the format also exaggerates the height of tall subjects.

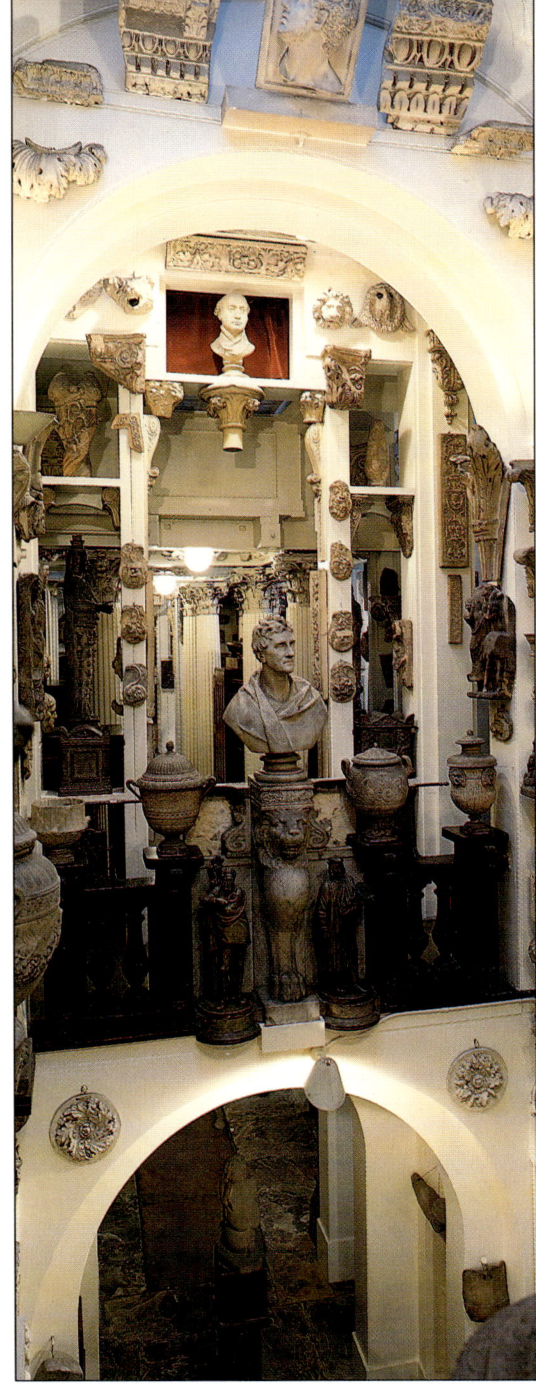

▶ VERTICAL VISTA
The panoramic format needn't be confined to the horizontal. Here, the photographer turned his camera on its side in order to capture as many of the impressive artefacts adorning the museum walls as possible.

▼ AS FAR AS THE EYE CAN SEE
Such a huge, sweeping landscape as the Grand Canyon in the USA, certainly benefits from being shot with a panoramic camera, because it helps to convey the vastness of the scene.

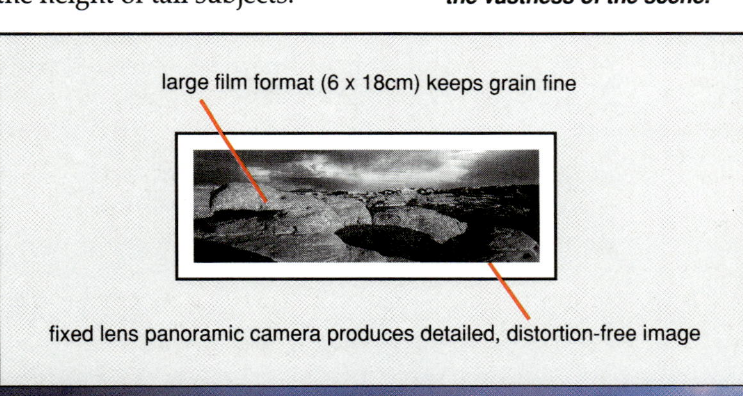

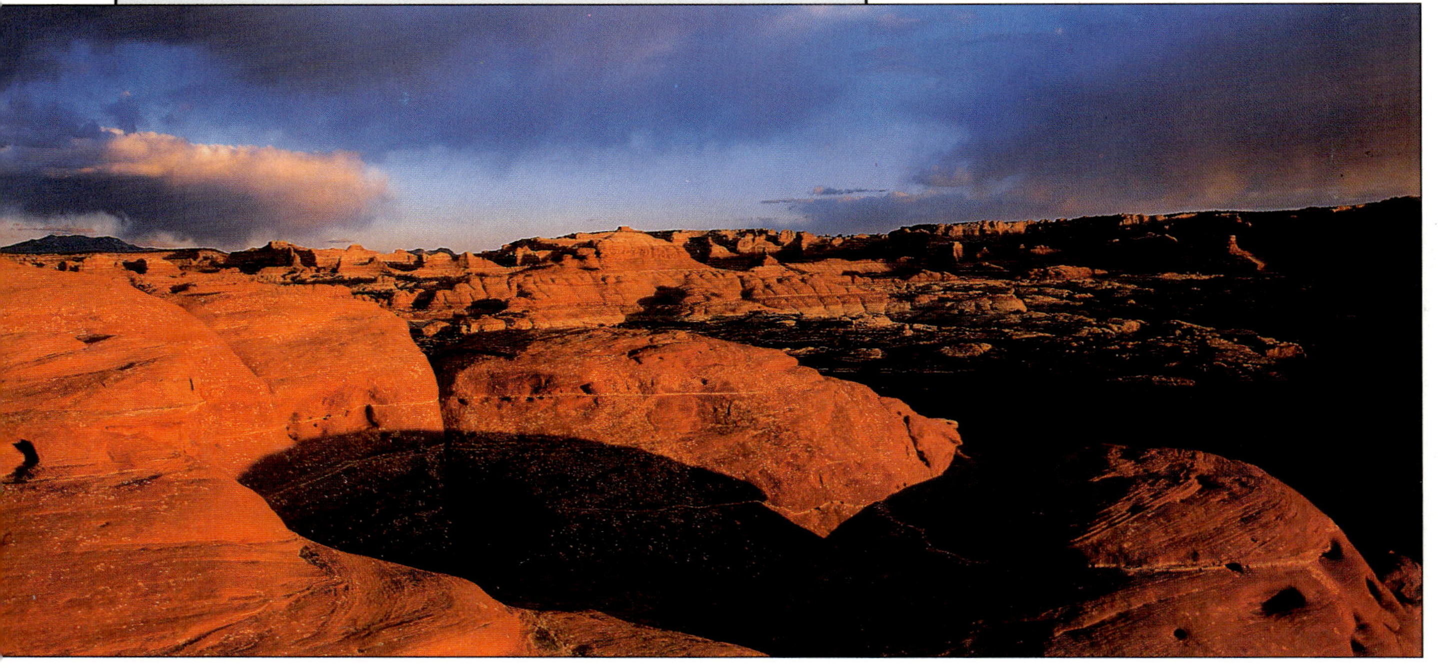

Creative cropping

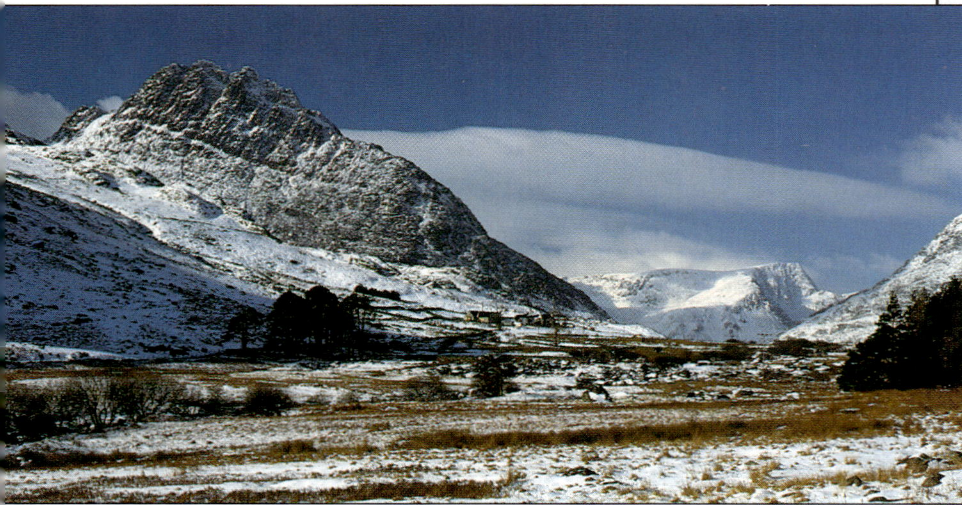

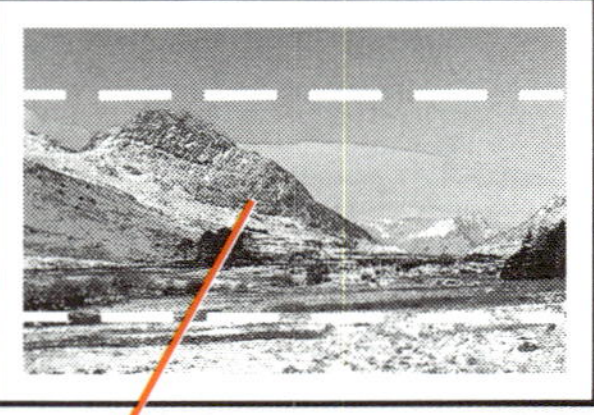

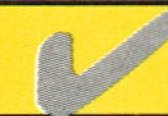

cropping directs attention to important elements of scene

Don't despair if you only have use of a 35mm camera – there are plenty of possibilities for making unusual picture shapes once your film has been developed. You could mask part of the negative before making the print, hide a section of the slide when mounting it or you can crop the finished print.

Cropping helps to tighten up and add impact to some compositions. For example, a picture of a skyscraper or a waterfall may be improved if cropped to panoramic proportions, since their height is enhanced. Or you could make a square picture by cutting out any irrelevant space in a portrait. Faces can sometimes look good when cut into a circle, too.

Remember, however, to only crop a picture if it will actually improve a composition. Check what the resulting scene will look like before cutting, by placing a paper mask over the image to reveal your intended shape.

▲ WASTE LAND
With 35mm proportions (above right) this picture is fairly pleasant. But crop out the plain expanse of sky and some of the large foreground (above) and this wintry scene gains far more impact, because your attention is directed to the important elements.

▼ THE EYES HAVE IT
By cutting out some of the blurred background, which is irrelevant to the subject, to create a square frame, this portrait of a fox is improved. This is because your attention is directed to the most revealing feature of any face – the eyes.

To make the most of unusual picture formats:

❏ use a panoramic format horizontally to capture sweeping vistas and rows of objects

❏ use a panoramic format vertically to exaggerate the height of your subject

❏ use a square or circular format to echo or contrast with the shape of your subject

❏ crop 35mm format prints to give existing scenes more impact

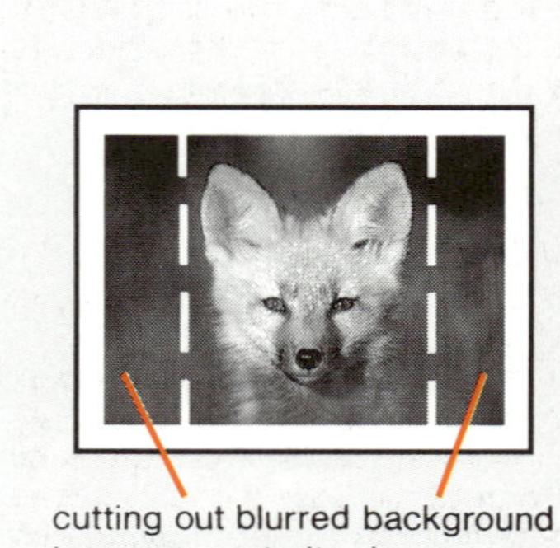

cutting out blurred background improves portrait's impact

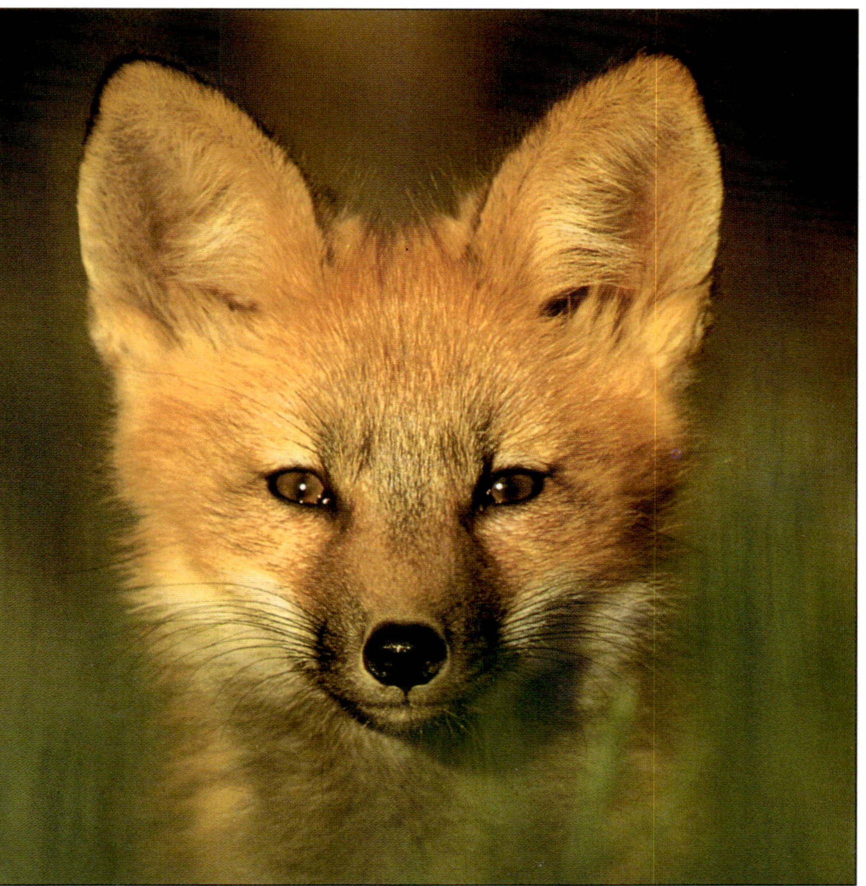

Smile please!

And finally, never neglect the power of humour. Amusing situations are usually unpredictable – so always have your camera at the ready to capture the lighter side of life.

Catching a rib-ticklingly funny snap is easier said than done. Many comic situations lose their humour when the action's frozen; often the viewer needs to know the build-up in order to appreciate the joke.

However, certain situations lend themselves to humour: children's parties and animal antics spring to mind. As in all comedy, timing is crucial: it's no good having the perfect lighting and angle if you miss the moment.

Humour is very subjective: not everyone finds the same things funny. Some situations may appear offensive or even tragic to your subject. Discretion and sensitivity should be your watchwords.

Be careful when taking pictures of people who look amusing – they may not find their strange physique or peculiar dress at all funny. Be sensitive when photographing animals, too. Don't dress them up or make them perform tricks.

Be sure to have lots of film with you. You'll probably have to take plenty of shots – and perhaps have a little luck – before you get the one that really makes people laugh!

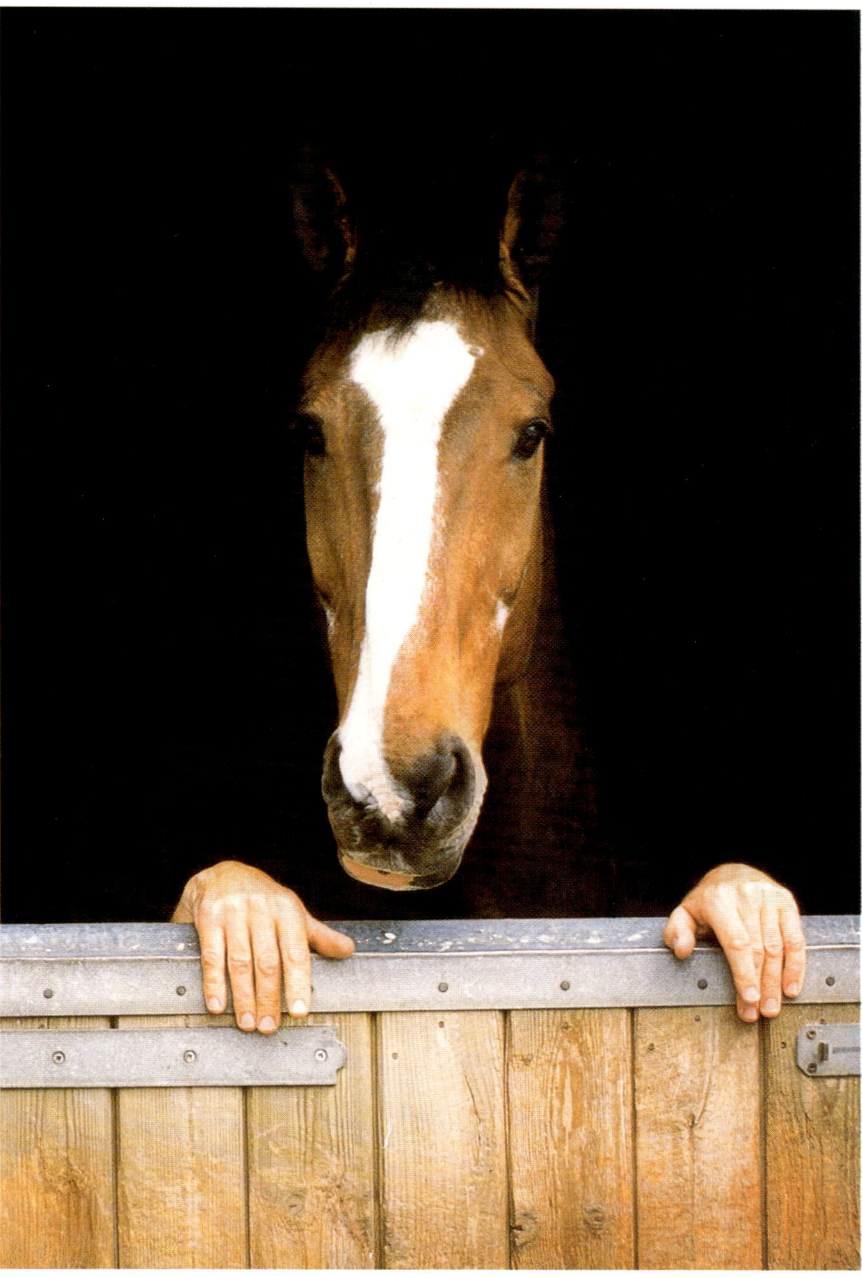

▲ HORSE AND HANDS
The photographer cropped tightly to make the stable door a neat frame for the horse, and excluded all elements that might spoil the illusion. The shot wouldn't work if the top of the figure's head was visible. Even at the smallest aperture, there wasn't enough depth of field to keep the horse sharp from nose to tail, so the stable light was switched off to darken the interior.

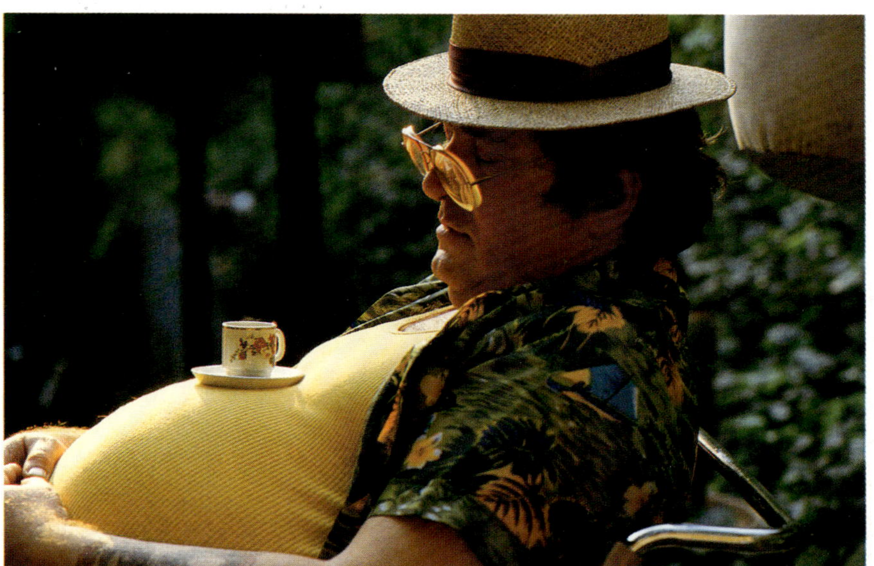

◀ SIESTA
There's nothing wrong with setting up a picture, provided the joke is not too laboured. Here, the subject's slumbering pose makes the shot look realistically candid. Out of scale props are a good source of visual gags. For this photo, the photographer chose a particularly small cup and saucer to emphasize the size of the man's vast stomach.

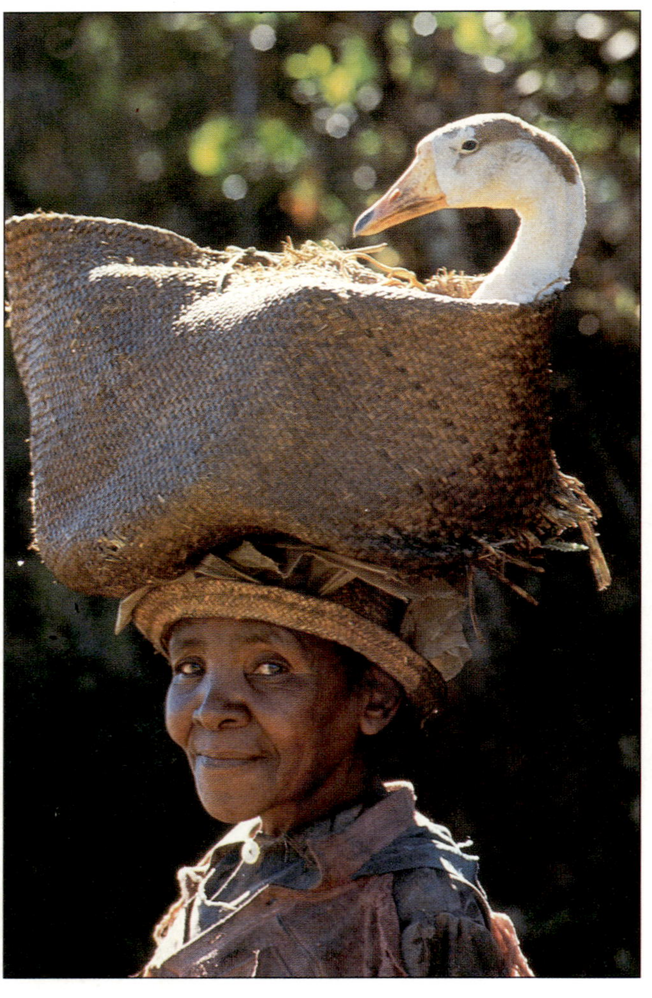

◄ TAKING A GANDER
When the scene has quiet charm, as this one does, even the simplest camera will get a great picture. Don't be tempted to overdo the technical wizardry. A straight snap on a standard lens will be no less funny than a picture taken with lots of sophisticated equipment.

▼ HOLY SMOKE
This is a monochromatic scene, so it works well in black and white. Because it was shot from some distance away a short telephoto lens was used, which threw the background out of focus. The photographer has cleverly caught a moment of humour simply by standing far off, to avoid intruding on the scene.

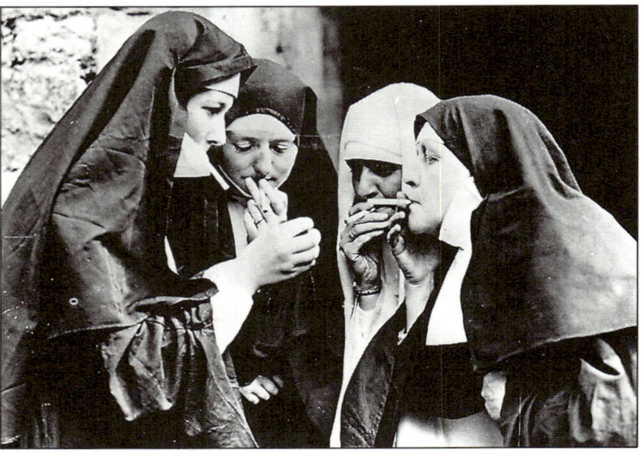

▼ HUMPS IN ROAD
Incongruous subjects shouldn't prove difficult to capture if you keep your eyes open and your camera at the ready. This picture was taken with a moderate wide angle lens, which has a wider depth of field than a standard lens. This keeps the whole scene reasonably sharp.

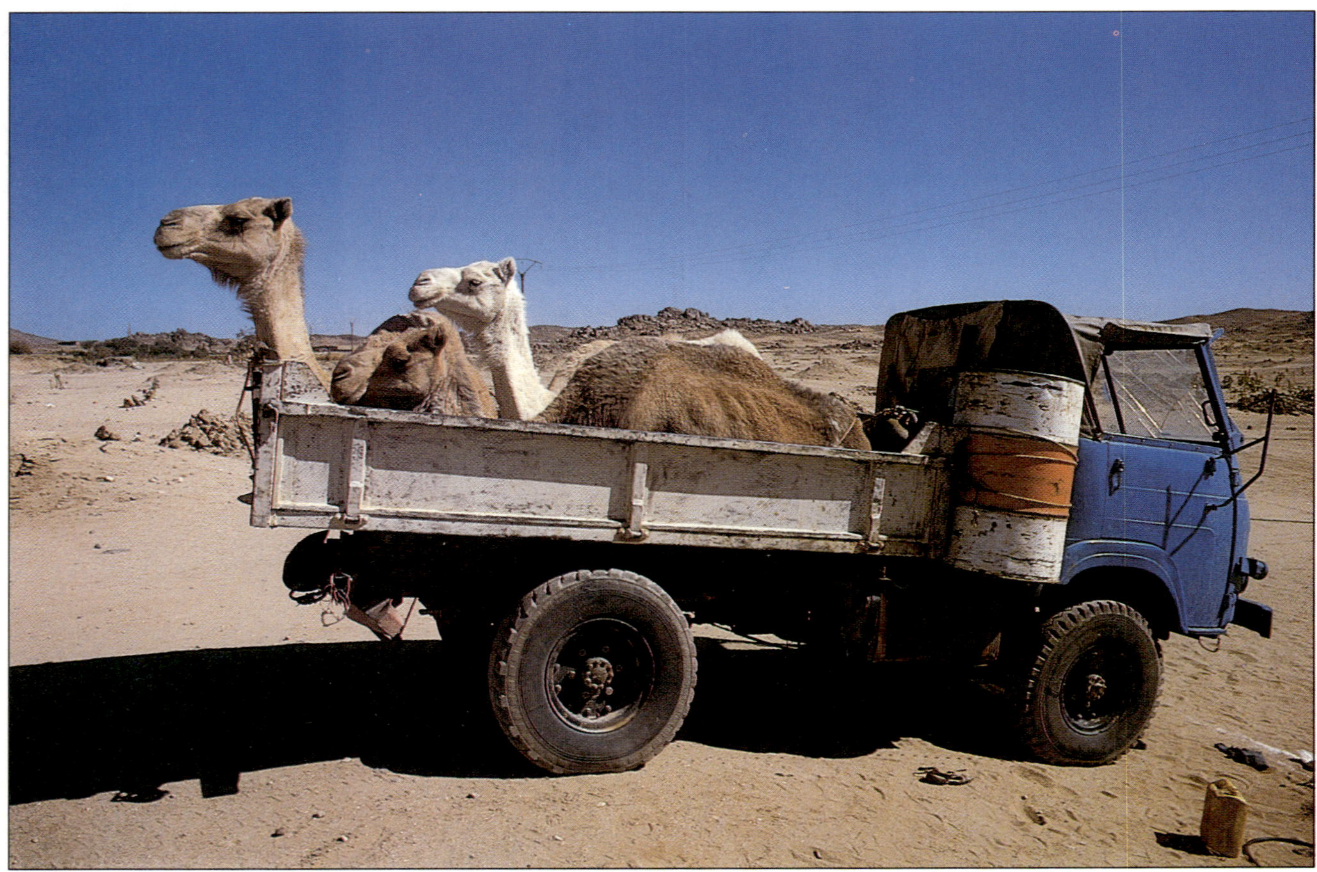